Communication
in the Organization
An Applied Approach

Communication in the Organization

An Applied Approach

Thomas R. Tortoriello

Director of Executive Training and
Organizational Development
F. & R. Lazarus

Stephen J. Blatt

Assistant Professor of Communications
University of Dayton

Sue DeWine

Assistant Professor of Communications
Ohio University

McGraw-Hill Book Company

New York   St. Louis   San Francisco   Auckland   Bogotá   Düsseldorf
Johannesburg   London   Madrid   Mexico   Montreal   New Delhi   Panama
Paris   São Paulo   Singapore   Sydney   Tokyo   Toronto

DEDICATED TO

Joanne   Beth

Patty   Stephanie   Erin

Mike

Library of Congress Cataloging in Publication Data

Tortoriello, Thomas R.
    Communication in the organization.

    Includes index.
    1. Communication in organizations. I. Blatt,
Stephen J., joint author. II. DeWine, Sue, 1944–
joint author. III. Title.
HD30.3.T67   658.4'5   77-25451
ISBN 0-07-064989-8

COMMUNICATION IN THE ORGANIZATION: An Applied Approach

1 2 3 4 5 6 7 8 9 0 FGRFGR 7 8 3 2 1 0 9 8 7

This book was set in Press Roman by Allen Wayne Technical Corp.
The editor was Donald W. Burden
and the production supervisor was Milton J. Heiberg.
Fairfield Graphics was printer and binder.

Contents

v

Preface

As the title suggests, *Communication in the Organization: An Applied Approach* is a book that applies major theoretical and conceptual issues to organizational communication. In today's society all daily interactions occur within some type of organizational framework. Therefore, the people who read this book will soon be looking for or have already begun careers in organizations. Our purpose is to assist them in two ways. First, we want to help them to understand better the importance of communicating in an organization and to develop a more accurate map of the organizational territory—interpersonal communication, group communication, the interaction of human and structural variables, and the managerial function. Second, we want to help them see how this knowledge can contribute to their effectiveness as managers and as organizational persons.

Accordingly, the text is designed to provide the undergraduate student with a unique approach that integrates organizational communication theory and practical applications in real situations. As the student moves through the text he or she is constantly reminded of how these concepts and theories actually operate in today's organizations. The text is an activity-oriented book designed to provide a comprehensive collection of experience-based exercises. As a result, the student is continually provided with an opportunity to evaluate some of his or her own behaviors in terms of organizational theories in operation, leadership, self-concept, interpersonal relationships, nonverbal communication, interviewing skills, group communication, and public speaking. A series of case studies allows the student an opportunity to identify and analyze communication breakdowns. For a more detailed discussion of the content of the text, see Chapter 1, "Communication and the Organization: An Overview."

We wish to express our appreciation to Professor Vince DiSalvo of the University of Nebraska, Alice Chalip, Professor Jo-Ann C. Graham of City University of New York, Jon Huegli, University of Eastern Michigan, Robert Kelley, Miami (Ohio) University, Dr. John Muchmore of William Rainey Harper College, Dr. Robert E. Peffers of Willamette University, Dr. James Phipps of Cedarville College, C. D. Porterfield, University of Texas, Robert Pruett, Wright State University, Dr. Vito N. Silvestri of Emerson College, Robert Smith, Wichita State University, Professor Gary Owen Turner of Miami University, Dr. Rudy Verderber of the University of Cincinnati, and Dr. Robert Vogel of Miami (Ohio) University for their helpful prepublication reviews. We appreciate the conscientious job that Joanne Tortoriello did in preparing the index. We wish to thank our spouses, Joanne, Patty, and Mike, for their patience, support, and gentle encouragement during the endless hours we worked on the manuscript.

Finally, a personal word of thanks to Charles Y. Lazarus, Chairman of the Board, and Tom Brown, Executive Vice President, of Lazarus, who were instrumental in helping the authors gain insight into the dynamics of a complex business organization. And a special thanks to Beth Tortoriello who not only provided inspiration but also provided an occasional welcomed diversion for her grateful father.

Thomas R. Tortoriello
Stephen J. Blatt
Sue DeWine

Part One

Introduction

This section is a basic introduction to organizational communication. It is designed to start you thinking about you, the communicator, in a career environment. Chapter 1 will provide you with a general introduction to the book. It will also examine the general concept of communication and provide a working definition of organizational communication.

When the reader has completed this section, he or she should be able to:

1 Describe the communication process, and define its most essential dimensions
2 Discuss a working definition of organizational communication
3 Define formal and informal channels of communication

Chapter 1

Communication and the Organization: An Overview

The work of the world gets done because people actively cooperate with one another. We are all almost completely dependent upon what other people do for us. Our world is not a jungle of competition as we have so often been told, but rather it is a place of cooperation. The cooperation that makes human society possible is manifested most visibly within the organization and it is almost entirely dependent upon the skill with which we communicate. If we do not understand the needs of others, then we cannot meet them. Beyond that, if we do not understand our own needs, then we cannot fulfill them.

WELCOME TO THE ORGANIZATION

If ever a word was synonymous with Western civilization it is the word "organization," a certain no-nonsense system of consciously coordinating activities. This system has evolved in response to an extremely complex society. Have you ever analyzed how many organizations have dominated your life? Today most of us live, play, and work as members of well-organized groups of people. Visible signs of organized activity are all around us—in schools, in business and industry, in the military, in government, in church, even in crime. These signs simply reflect society's attempts to adapt itself to the ever-increasing pace of technological change. Technological advancement has come

Figure 1-1 "An organization is a social grouping that establishes task and/or interpersonal patterns of relationships for the attainment of specific objectives."

to be synonymous with an abundant life, and society has organized and reorganized in order to produce and consume on a grander scale. We all want to share in the "good life" and to enjoy the fruits of affluence and leisure, which are so often the by-products of technological advancement. In order to receive our fair share we must work, and, according to Harry Levinson, "90 percent of those who work do so in organizations."[1]

Alvin Toffler, in *Future Shock*, suggests that our involvement with organizations, especially our occupational organizations, is like that of a transient—we move from one to another.[2] What further proof do we need than the realization that the average worker under 35 years of age looks for a new job every 18 months. In addition, experts estimate that the average worker will change careers three to five times in his or her lifetime. Occupational organizations will obviously play an important part in your life. Your ability to deal with and to function within them will, in large part, determine both the character and quality of your life. It is the occupational organization we want to focus upon.

For most of you this will take the form of a business-oriented organization; for others, it may be a governmental, educational, or religious organization. No matter which occupational organization you are involved with, at the time it will most likely dominate your life. While you may only put in a minimum of 8 hours a day, your personal satisfaction during those 8 hours, the financial rewards you receive, and the people you work with may influence directly or indirectly the other 16 hours. On the other hand, an argument with your girlfriend or boyfriend, an increase in your rent, a

---

[1]Harry Levinson, "Asinine Attitudes Toward Motivation," *Harvard Business Review*, **51**(1): 70–76, January 1973.

[2]Alvin Toffler, *Future Shock*, Bantam, New York, 1971, pp. 149–151.

flat tire on the way to work, or a death in the family may influence your job performance and satisfaction. You may be concerned with the President's decision to raise or not raise taxes but the effect of this decision is minimal compared to your employer's decision to transfer you to another city, to hire someone you disdain but must work closely with, or to close down a business you have been associated with for 25 years. The concept of the "organization man" may have changed since William H. Whyte, Jr., coined the phrase in 1956, but the basic idea still remains—our lives are dominated by our occupational organizations.[3]

As early as 1938 Chester Barnard observed that "in an exhaustive theory of organization, communication would occupy a central phase, because the structure, extensiveness, and scope of the organization are almost entirely determined by communication techniques."[4] If this is the case, it is apparent that central to the study of organization is communication. It is the one aspect that allows an organization to be an organization. Think about it. If we removed all forms of communication from the organization, would there be an organization? For example, how many of your daily activities within the organization involve communicating with other people either orally or in writing? Studies indicate that depending upon your position within the organization it can range from 50 percent to 95 percent of your working day. Can there be any doubt that "organization man" depends upon communication.[5]

The rationale for this book should be obvious. You may possess all the book knowledge in the world and hold a straight "A" average, but (1) if you do not understand how your organization communicates, and (2) if you are not able to communicate your ideas to others within and outside the organization, then as Yossarian said in the novel *Catch 22*, "The whole world is crazy but me."

Put more pragmatically, a reason for improving your communication behavior is vocational success. Employers are placing increasing emphasis upon their employees' communicative abilities, because they recognize the close relationship between successful communication and job proficiency. In addition to being costly, poor communication can cause tensions, anxieties, and frustrations that can have a dramatic effect upon the general atmosphere surrounding the worker. In turn, a poor atmosphere and low morale can encourage decreased productivity and lagging profit structures. To a businessman functioning in the business world, it is obvious that many highly skilled and competent people have lost their jobs because they simply did not know how to communicate in an occupational setting. In this book we are concerned with concentrating on the individual communicating in an organizational setting. In this chapter, we want to present a preview of the book, examine the concept of communication from a general perspective, and provide a working definition of organizational communication.

Preview of the Book: Where Are We Going?

Before we talk about where we are going, perhaps it would be a good idea to answer the question, Where do we begin? The most obvious answer to this question is that we

[3]William H. Whyte, Jr., *The Organization Man,* Simon and Schuster, New York, 1956, p. 4.
[4]Chester Barnard, *The Functions of the Executive,* Harvard, Cambridge, Mass., 1938, p. 4.
[5]Gerald M. Goldhaber, *Organizational Communication,* Brown, Dubuque, Iowa, 1974, p. 7.

Figure 1-2 "I want a job!"

begin with you. Since the purpose of this text is to examine communication from the perspective of the communicator in a career environment, we intend to move you from outside the organization through the various communication experiences that you may be exposed to as a member of an occupational organization (see Figure 1-3).

Figure 1-3 The road to success.

Chapter 1 will provide you with a general introduction to the book that will familiarize you with both the purpose and the organizational pattern of this text. Chapter 1 will also examine the general concept of communication and provide a working definition of organizational communication.

Next we will examine the different organizational environments in which you may be working. These environments are referred to by some scholars as the principal schools of thought governing how organizations are structured. Chapter 2 then provides the underpinning for and a natural transition to the consideration of message flow and impact. In Chapter 3 the emphasis will be on message purpose (what kinds of messages are sent in organizations), networks (where the messages originate, where they go, and how they get there), and message receivers (whether either inside or outside the organization). This chapter represents the development of some of the basic concepts we introduced in the previous chapter.

One of the most important interpersonal interactions you will have in the organization will be with your subordinates. Chapter 4 will attempt to provide answers to general questions about superior-subordinate interactions while examining how knowledge of leadership characteristics can facilitate better communication.

While on the job you will constantly be sending messages to and processing information from acquaintances, customers, fellow workers, supervisors, and so on. In other words, you will be assessing the roles of both the sender and receiver of messages, a function that involves constant adaptation and spontaneous adjustment to the other person. This "face-to-face interaction between people who are constantly aware of each other,"[6] will be discussed in Chapter 5, a chapter about interpersonal communication.

Chapter 6 will examine the importance of nonverbal communication and its place in influencing the flow and impact of messages within the organization. This is a fascinating subject since in our everyday activities we pay little attention to the influences that such things as space utilization, dress, movement, and gesture can have on our communication behavior.

The interview is the first and perhaps the most important interpersonal setting that you will experience within the organization. We will examine the interviewing process with specific emphasis on the employment interview. The thrust of Chapter 7, therefore, will be on helping you seek and acquire the position that best enhances your career objectives. After all, if you can't get your foot in the door, learning all about communicating in the organization won't mean much.

Chapters 8 and 9 examine specific speech communication functions you will often be asked to perform within the organization. At the interpersonal level we will examine the task-oriented discussion, and at the group level, public speaking functions are examined with particular emphasis on the informative and persuasive presentations.

To conclude the book we will present actual case studies that will demonstrate the application of select principles, concepts, and ideas with respect to communication breakdowns. Perhaps we will find that when communication fails, it is not necessarily the source or receiver who is at fault, but that part of the process has broken down.

[6] Bobby Patton and Kim Giffin, *Interpersonal Communication,* Harper & Row, New York, 1974, p. 12.

Our Three Examples If there is one thing your authors have gained from their own teaching experience, it is that you want to be in touch with the real world. Too often the student becomes disenchanted with artificial examples and ideal-type illustrations. For this reason we will be using examples drawn from three real organizations. We have selected a small, a medium, and a large organization, each representing a different organizational purpose. The first organization represents what many would think of as the traditional bureaucratic establishment—it is the Oakwood Police Department. Oakwood is a small suburban community located in northeastern New England. The department has thirty-two sworn officers serving a population of 10,000. The second, WDTN (television station), is located in Dayton, Ohio. It is a larger organization employing approximately 120 people. The third organization is Richdales. Richdales is a department store in Southern California. It consists of twelve stores and employs over 8,500 people.

A Qualifying Note Just as no two people are exactly alike, no two organizations are exactly alike. One of the dangers of the ivory tower is that many times the student leaves with solutions in search of problems. We are providing you only with the cognitive tools that *you must adapt* to each organizational situation. Remember, life is not like a textbook. You may have mastered certain principles, but then you must apply those principles appropriately.

COMMUNICATION: A GENERAL PERSPECTIVE

Have you ever been involved in a situation in which you did not really understand what someone said or they did not understand what you really meant? The results of this kind of situation can be many and varied. Perhaps

Figure 1-4 "Fellow voters, the problem with our world is one of communication and if you elect me, I will straighten out everything."

- You ended up doing the wrong homework assignment.
- You waited in the rain on the corner of First and Main for your roommate to pick you up, only to learn later that she was on the corner of Fifth and Main looking for you.
- You addressed a letter to the wrong person or place.
- You improperly filled a customer's order.
- And at home—you're in total agreement with the person who said "There are only three races—men, women, and children. And none of them speak the same language."

The aggravating part of all this is that you may feel that you are a pretty good communicator. After all, you've been talking all your life, and with all that experience at something, shouldn't you be an expert by now? And besides, everyone knows that once we learn the language, we are able to understand each other fairly well. Undoubtedly, most of us view the general complexities involved with the concept of communication as a rather simple and natural process. And therein lies the problem. Perhaps it would be worthwhile for us to reexamine the process by which we communicate.

Let's begin with a general working definition of communication. *Communication is an interactional process in which meaning is stimulated through the sending and receiving of verbal and nonverbal messages.*

Communication: . . . an interactional process . . . The key to the definition is *process*. More than 2000 years ago Heraclitus provided a basic insight into the concept of process when he stated that "a man can never step in the same river twice" (the very act changes the man and the river; that is, they both have been affected by the passage of time). *Communication is a process.* And when we accept this concept of process, we view events and relationships as dynamic, ongoing, ever-changing, continuous. Communication, therefore, is not static for it cannot be properly understood as fixed elements in time and space. Perhaps all communication should begin and end with the word "and." It would help remind us that no experience ever begins—there is always something that precedes it. What really began for us was our awareness of something going on. By closing our conversation with the word "and," we would also remind ourselves that no communication ever really ends—something more will happen—it is only the event that is ending.

You might say that *communication is an irreversible and unrepeatable process.* Have you ever found yourself in a situation when you've said something unthinking to a friend (or more germane to this book—your boss) and realized from his look that he didn't take it the way you meant it? Your next line was probably, "But what I meant was. . . ." You have already said what you have said, and nothing can erase that fact; therefore, communication is irreversible. There are many times when you wish instant replay could be applied to your communication experiences, and this may be one of them. But would it really help? Let's think about this question in terms of our current example. Even if you could repeat your original message exactly the same way as you said it the first time, would it be the same message? No, because both you and your friend have changed attitudinally as a result of your first message. The repeated message has, therefore, taken on new meaning for both of you; therefore, communication is unrepeatable.

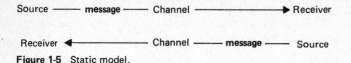

Figure 1-5 Static model.

Confusion in communication sometimes results because, to understand any process, we must freeze that process and study each of the components separately. This enables us to better understand each component, but in so doing, we lose sight of the ongoing, dynamic nature of the event. A good example of this would be looking at individual snapshots of a boxing match as opposed to watching a motion picture of the fight. As a result, we are left with a static picture of the complex happening. This is an important point to remember as we continue our discussion.

The word "interactional" means that communication is reciprocal. Both parties continually affect each other as they send and receive messages. You may be the person speaking, but the person on the receiving end is simultaneously sending his or her own messages by means of facial expressions, eye contact, gestures, movement, and so on. In summary, you may not be consciously attending to the other individual's nonverbal cues, but reciprocal communication is taking place. A classic illustration of the simultaneous effects of communication was the psychology professor who, in explaining the principles of reinforcement, had the tables turned on him. The class secretly conspired to nod their heads every time the professor mentioned the word "reinforcement." The result was the professor increased his use of the word "reinforcement" to the point where he was using it in some context ten to twelve times a class period. The professor had not realized that he had increased his use of the word nor was he consciously aware of the effects the students were having on his subsequent communication behavior.

The tendency at first in explaining this interactional process is to display a static model as in Figure 1-5. A source transmits a message over a channel to another person. This person, upon receiving the message, then becomes the source and transmits a message back over a channel to the original source who now becomes a receiver.

Figure 1-6 represents the reciprocal feeling of communication by changing the communication to one of mutual affect with closed arrows at either end. The point is communication is so reciprocal and ongoing between the two parties that it is impossible to isolate who is the source and receiver. It is the continual process of sending and receiving feedback that makes this mutual effect possible. Feedback is that part of the communication process that allows the source to monitor the effects of his message (to evaluate the success of his attempt to derive a desired response) so he can know what to do or say next. There is a constant mutual feedback between the communicators. Notice that we now use the term *communicators* for both parties; each is a sender and receiver at the same time.

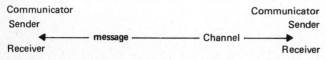

Figure 1-6 Interacting model.

Communication: . . . in which meaning is stimulated . . . Meaning is what communication is all about. When we communicate with someone we are attempting to symbolize either verbally or nonverbally through facial expression, pitch or rate change, etc., a meaning we have in our head. If all goes well, we select symbols (words) that stimulate a meaning similar to ours in the head of the other person; that is, the receiver understands the message. Keep in mind (no pun intended) that the function of the symbols we use is to help make meaning appear in peoples' minds. Meanings are in people, not in symbols (words), and meanings are rather personal. We change them, color them, and add to them. When you stop to think about it, the word "dog" really doesn't resemble a dog at all. Yet, if we were to ask a group of English-speaking people what the word "dog" meant to them, each person could assign a denotative (dictionary) definition to the word; that is, the symbol "dog" *represents* the real thing. Denotative meaning is concerned with physical reality. This is only one kind of meaning, however, for at the same time, the person will assign a connotative response to the word. For example, you may have had a pleasant encounter with a dog or have been bitten by one. The experience will very much affect your response to the word, for you now have a favorable or unfavorable attitude toward dogs. Connotative meaning is meaning that is being responded to on an emotional level; therefore, it is concerned with personal reality. As a result, "people can only have similar meanings to the extent they have similar experiences."[7]

When we communicate with other people, it might be helpful to remember that our common words may not stimulate the same image in someone else's mind as they do in our own mind (see Figure 1-7).

Communication: . . . through the sending and receiving of messages The key to understanding this part of the definition is *transmission.* These are the forms and channels by which you transmit the message to be sent and/or received. There are *two forms* by which people transmit messages, verbal and nonverbal. By *verbal* messages we mean those messages that are spoken as well as those paralinguistic factors that are included in speech. *Nonverbal* messages refer to nonspoken meanings, things like body language (facial expressions, gestures, and posture), objects (clothing), and voice (volume, tone, and rate).[8] Notice that verbal and nonverbal forms of communication are used together. This is intentional for whenever we communicate verbally, we are also simultaneously communicating nonverbally. The reverse is not true; we often can communicate nonverbally without employing a verbal form of the message.

The channel is the means employed to transport the symbols. Air waves deliver words from one person to another, while gestures and facial expressions are delivered by light waves. Sound and light are the channels used most often in human communication. Although a tender feeling can be conveyed by a delicate touch and a mood created by a whiff of seductive perfume, touch and smell commonly function as secondary channels. By increasing the number of channels used to carry the message, we substantially increase the likelihood of successful communication.

---

[7]Gail E. Myers and Michele T. Myers, *The Dynamics of Human Communication*, McGraw-Hill, New York, 1973, p. 58.

[8]Mark Knapp, *Non-Verbal Communication in Human Interaction*, Holt, Rinehart and Winston, New York, 1972, p. 102.

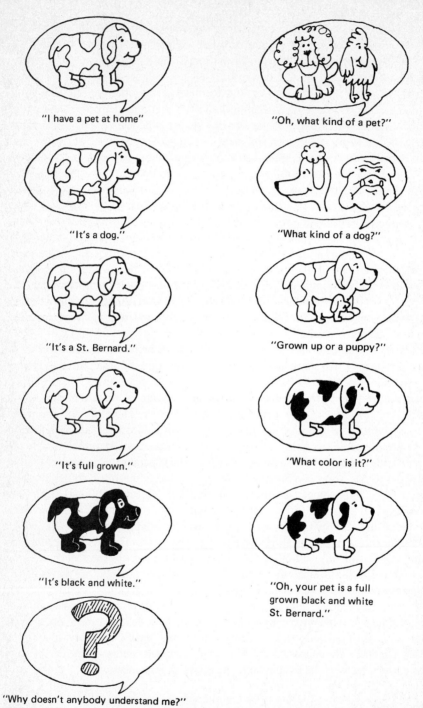

Figure 1-7 Communication as a cumulative—and partial—process. (*From* Don Fabun, *Communications: The Transfer of Meaning*, Glencoe Publishing, Encino, Calif., © 1968, Kaiser Aluminum & Chemical Corp.)

Communication: Three Principles

We might summarize the general perspective of communication under three principles; meaning is in people, not in words; communication is imperfect; and communication is an irreversible process.[9] No matter what communication experience you are involved with, these three principles will always be present. These three principles will be developed throughout the book.

   1 Meaning Is in People, Not in Words[10] A word is only a word by virtue of the meaning people give to that word. As illustrated in the cartoon (Figure 1-8) we forget that a word is but a symbol, and we tend to think of the word as reality itself. For example, the word "gun" may denote a piece of ordnance usually with high muzzle velocity and comparatively flat trajectory that propels a projectile. The same word, "gun," may connote for one person something good that helps to feed the family and brings prosperity. For another person "gun" may connote something bad that brings to the world pain, suffering, and death.

   2 Communication Is Imperfect[11] This principle is very much intertwined with the first principle. You can program a computer to send and receive the messages exactly the way you intended but this is not the case with human beings. Communication scholars use the word "noise" to refer to all those things that interfere with and/or cause distraction from communication, thus creating an imperfect process.

   Noise is perhaps most easily understood as anything that causes distraction from

---

[9]It is important to stress that some scholars would disagree with our choice of three principles. Others might list five or six; for example, see C. David Mortensen, *Communication: The Study of Human Interaction*, McGraw-Hill, New York, 1972, p. 18.

[10]Raymond V. Leskar, *Business Communication Theory and Application*, Irwin, Homewood, Ill., 1964, p. 30.

[11]Ibid., p. 31.

Figure 1-8 "Sticks and stones may break my bones but names will kill me."

the communication process. Noise can be separated into two basic categories, internal and external. Internal noise refers to the uniqueness of human beings that causes them to bring different perceptions to a message. These internal noises have become an entire field of study called *semantics*, the study of meaning, of language, and its effect on man. In addition, internal noise is also caused by an abnormal psychological or physiological state. If, while you were reading this paragraph your stomach signaled strong and hard that dinner was needed, you would be experiencing, at the point your hunger distracted your attention from the paragraph, internal physiological noise.

External noise refers to those environmental qualities that interfere with communication effectiveness, for example, temperature, light, room size, acoustics, etc. You can never achieve perfect communication. However, through the content and exercises in this book we perhaps can help you to maximize your communication effectiveness.

3 Communication Is an Irreversible and Unrepeatable Process Mortensen states, "Communication does not necessarily stop simply because people stop talking and listening."[12] The following incident illustrates this principle. A customer had ordered carpeting from Richdales. It was the normal policy of the carpeting department at Richdales to go out to the customer's home within 72 hours of the order to measure the room. Business, however, had been so brisk that the department manager was unable to send anyone out for 2 weeks. Sales had extended far beyond the installation service capability of the department. By that time, the warehouse supply of the carpeting that the customer ordered had been depleted. The customer subsequently lodged a formal complaint with the department store's management and cancelled the order. The management, embarrassed over the situation, tried to correct what they said was "a breakdown in communication." On the contrary, communication had not broken down. The carpeting manager's principal job was to sell carpet. That's what contributed to the growth of the store but also to the growth of the department manager's salary. The customer received this message loud and clear despite the excuses rendered by the carpeting department. The department store management would have liked to have backed up the communication process, but the damage was done despite all the efforts to correct the communication situation. Management in this case offered to provide free carpeting until the order could be filled and apologies were personally given by the chairman of the board. The customer accepted this offer that, I might add, cost the company handsomely; yet the situation had occurred, and the customer would always remember Richdales as the store that goofed up the carpet sale. Fortunately, due to the intervention of the chairman of the board, the customer would also remember Richdales as the store that cared enough to make things right, regardless of cost.

LEVELS OF COMMUNICATION:
A MULTIDIMENSIONAL APPROACH

Mortensen indicates that communication may be received "from within a multidimensional framework of differing yet closely interrelated levels of activity."[13] The concept

---

[12]C. David Mortensen, *Communication: The Study of Human Interaction*, McGraw-Hill, New York, 1972, p. 11.
[13]Ibid., p. 23.

of level is concerned with both the range or inclusiveness of the events under observation and the size of the unit. For example, an interior decorator will be concerned with every piece of furniture and all the trappings in a room as well as with all the rooms in the apartment or house.

Two researchers, Ruesch and Bateson, asked a relevant question, "What level of communication are you talking about?" Isn't there a difference between mass communication (television, newspapers, radio, etc.) and communication on a one-to-one basis? In short, any discussion of communication must be specific to the level you are describing. Employing the Ruesch and Bateson framework, the above definition of communication can be viewed on four levels: intrapersonal, interpersonal, group, and cultural.[14]

Intrapersonal communication is an interactional process in which meaning is stimulated through the sending and receiving of messages within the person. Intrapersonal communication focuses on the development of the individual's self-concept and the relation this has to communication behavior with others around him or her.

Interpersonal communication is an interactional process in which meaning is stimulated through the sending and receiving of messages between two people. This is a more inclusive range and is the level most often referred to when we use the term communication (i.e., the conversation). A still more inclusive range is the group level. *Group* communication is an interactional process in which meaning is stimulated through the sending and receiving of messages from one to many and many to one. The study of group dynamics falls in this level. Public speaking is also appropriately studied on this level, although this form of group communication can be approached from other levels. What we often think of as mass communication is also studied at this level.

The last level is the cultural level. It is the most inclusive range. *Cultural* communication is an interactional process in which meaning is stimulated through the sending and receiving of messages from many to many. Of all the levels of communication, this is the most abstract and often the most difficult to visualize. We might think of cultural communication as representing a cumulative design for living. It consists of the common shared way of perceiving and relating around us, in both material and nonmaterial ways, e.g., language, religion, and government. An individual born into a culture takes that culture for granted as if it were part of a natural order. Within any culture are subcultures, groups that are part of the overall culture but that have distinctive lifestyles and values, e.g., commune, monastery, street gang, and the artists' colony.

While we may focus on any one level of communication, it should be emphasized that each level can be studied from the perspective of each of the different levels. In short, all the levels are interacting.

HOW DO WE APPROACH THE STUDY OF COMMUNICATION WITHIN THE ORGANIZATION?

Imagine yourself as the chairman of the board. Your task is to think of the total operation. While others are hired to run their specific departments and divisions, your

---

[14]Jurgen Ruesch and Gregory Bateson, *Communication: The Social Matrix of Psychiatry*, Norton, New York, 1951.

job is to bring some direction and integration to the organization. Much like the workings of a machine, each part of the organization is dependent upon and affected by the other parts. We may examine one part separately as we did in explaining our interpersonal communication definition, but we must constantly stand back and see the organization from a total perspective.

Let's use an actual organization, WDTN television station, Dayton, Ohio, for this discussion (see Figure 1-9). Even though it is a relatively small organization, employing approximately 120 people, the principles that apply here are just as applicable in approaching the study of communication in an organization employing over 8,000 people.

Organizational Communication: A Working Definition

Let's go back to our original working definition of communication: *Communication is an interactional process in which meaning is stimulated through the sending and receiving of verbal and nonverbal messages.* Now, let's repeat the definition of an organization we presented earlier (see Figure 1-1). *An organization is a social grouping that establishes task and/or interpersonal patterns of relationships for the attainment of specific objectives.* In order to study communication within any organization, it will have to be analyzed as it relates to the stated objectives of the organization. One of the principal objectives of the television station is to make money. To accomplish this objective, other objectives have to be satisfied, e.g., the selling of advertising and the production and selection of programming. To build in the dynamic, ongoing process of communication, let us substitute the word "flow" for "send" and "impact" for "receive." Thus, our working definition of organizational communication will be *the study of the flow and impact of messages within a network of interactional relationships.*

Studying the flow of messages within any organization is a complex process; the flow can go in many different directions. Within the organization, this is most often referred to as the analysis of the horizontal and vertical flow of messages. Using our television station as an example (see Figure 1-10), the stated objective of the sales division is to maximize profits by selling the maximum advertising time at the maximum profit. If we studied the flow and impact of messages in relation to this objective, we would find the sales manager transmitting a message "sell more advertising" (or something to that effect) to the salespersons (downward communication). Subsequently, messages would be going outside the organization (externally) to the client and back within the station (internally). Here the message of the sale is transmitted to the sales manager from the salesperson (upward communication) who then horizontally sends the message to the systems department for processing. Within the systems department the traffic department makes sure that the commercial will be slotted in the right time period to be shown. The continuity department provides the right film to be shown by the engineer in the control room. Impact in this case means whether the message is being received properly; that is, does traffic get the ad slotted in the right time period, and does continuity provide the right film?

The Four Levels While you must have the ability to study the organization from a total perspective, you must also be able to study the organization from different

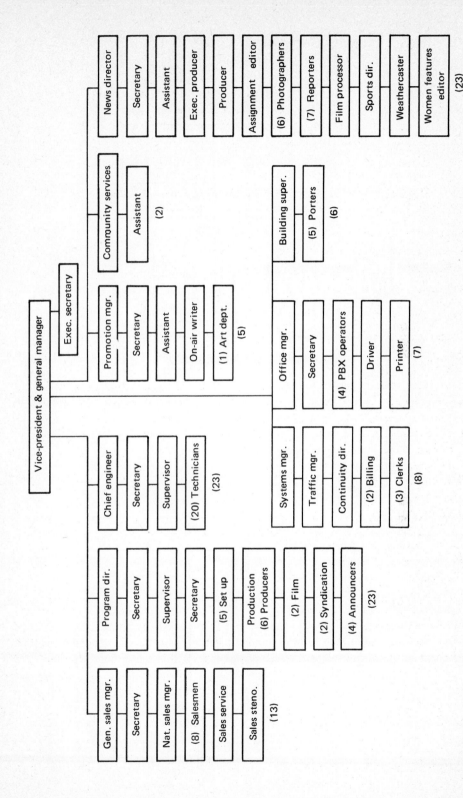

Figure 1-9 WDTN, Dayton.

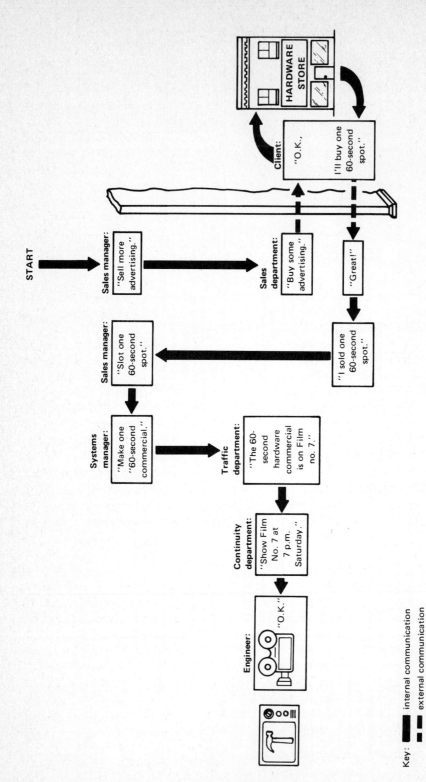

START

Sales manager: "Sell more advertising."

Sales department: "Buy some advertising."

Client: "O.K., I'll buy one 60-second spot."

HARDWARE STORE

"Great!"

"I sold one 60-second spot."

Sales manager: "Slot one 60-second spot."

Systems manager: "Make one 60-second commercial."

Traffic department: "The 60-second hardware commercial is on Film no. 7."

Continuity department: "Show Film No. 7 at 7 p.m. Saturday."

Engineer: "O.K."

Key: ▬▬ internal communication

▬ ▬ external communication

Figure 1-10 Message flowchart.

18

perspectives. This is a most difficult task and one that can become so complex that organization communication consultants are sometimes brought in when higher management is unable to bring this perspective to the study of their organization.

The study of the flow and impact of messages associated with the selling of advertising, for example, could be approached from four different perspectives: cultural, group, interpersonal, and intrapersonal. The *cultural* level might give us an insight into (1) how that station functions within its social environment. This might include an understanding of the station's coverage area, i.e., the competition, the people who watch their programming, ratings, attitudes, values, etc. (2) The overall managerial philosophy of the station. The importance of this is well stated by Professor Redding: "A member of any organization is, in large measure, the kind of communicator that the organization compels him to be. In other words, the very fact of holding a position in an organization determines many of the ways in which a person speaks, listens, writes, and reads."[15]

The *group* level brings the systems idea into play. Here you can study how the flow and impact of messages look from a total perspective or from the perspective of various individual subsystems, i.e., the separate departments with their specific goals. In studying the messages involved with the selling of advertising, the group level analysis would reveal the interdependent of other parts of the organization. For example, the program director will be involved, for it is that division that produces the commercial to be aired. The chief engineer schedules the technicians who will support the efforts of the program director and the systems manager schedules the advertisement for the desired time. To better understand the sales division, we would most likely want to spend time studying how each department operates separately and in so doing each department would be treated as a subsystem; for example, to understand the systems department involves a carefully orchestrated plan of coordination between traffic, continuity, and billing.

It is at the *interpersonal* level of communication where we are best able to see the flow and impact of messages taking place. Following our advertising example, we could observe the message flow and impact between salesperson and client, talent and director, salesperson and systems manager, salesperson, systems manager, and sales manager. The list could go on and on as we follow the flow and impact of messages from the interpersonal perspective.

The *intrapersonal* level of communication could give us an insight into the personalities of several key people within the organization. In any organization, if you are to understand the managerial philosophy, it is vital that you have an understanding of the personality of top management. It is also just as important to understand the personalities of the employees. For example, when an ad is sold for television, it is sent through the systems manager to the continuity department where a clerk will identify the commercial to be shown for the engineer who must run the ad at the designated time. In one particular instance, one of the continuity clerks was excited over planning for her upcoming marriage. As a result of her excitement she identified the wrong film for airing and subsequently the station lost several thousand dollars.

[15] W. Charles Redding, "The Organizational Communicator," in W. Charles Redding and George A. Sanborn (eds.), *Business and Industrial Communication: A Source Book*, Harper & Row, New York, 1964, p. 29.

Formal and Informal Communication

Most of your time studying the organization's communication flow will be from the perspective of the group and interpersonal levels, for it is these levels that are the most observable. When studying organizational communication on these two levels, you will want to also consider the flow of messages from a formal and an informal perspective. *Formal* communication refers to the sanctioned pattern of communication that the organization prescribes for the accomplishment of its objectives. The organizational chart of an organization usually represents the formal communication patterns as in the case of WDTN-TV (see Figure 1-9).

   Informal communication represents those patterns that arise from the spontaneous interaction of personalities and groups within the organization.[16] Nowhere on the WDTN organizational chart does it indicate that the salesperson communicates with the production supervisor before promising a certain commercial for his or her client. The reason that this is important is that the production supervisor coordinates the facilities for the production of commercials and if you have a good working relationship he or she may find time to produce your commercial, even when the facilities are fully booked. In summary, we view organizational communication by studying the flow and impact of messages from the perspective of four levels with a focus on the formal/informal message flow on the group and interpersonal levels.

SUMMARY

In this chapter we first presented a preview of the book, emphasizing that the organizational pattern started with you and moved on into the organizational environment. Next we examined the organization from a general perspective, stressing the importance of communication to any organization. Communication was then examined as a multilevel phenomenon that can be viewed from the intrapersonal, interpersonal, group, and cultural levels. We examined the communication process emphasizing three principles—meaning is in people, communication is imperfect, and communication is an irreversible and unrepeatable process.

   Employing the same multileveled approach, we briefly discussed how to approach the study of communication in the organization. While we may concentrate on one level, all the other levels are involved.

   We concluded with a discussion of the importance of formal and informal communication networks.

---

[16] Ibid., p. 46.

Part Two

Organizational Theories and Communication

Underpinning the study of organizational communication is a body of literature about organizations, their structure and behavior. To our way of thinking, it is difficult to discuss organizational communication without having some appreciation for, and understanding of, organization theory.

One of the problems immediately confronted by the beginner when studying organizations is that there is not one but several schools of thought on the subject. These differences are often noted by proponents of one school or the other with the implication and/or direct assertion that the other school(s) are in error. Jointly the opposing schools of thought contain elements that would fit together into a concept larger and more inclusive than any single school of thought.

Chapter 2 is concerned with what happens in an organization; how organization activities are allocated, what makes coordination difficult, and how integration is obtained. Chapter 3 translates the organization structure, as presented in Chapter 2, into an elaborate system for gathering, evaluating, recombining, and disseminating information. In this way, we are better able to identify, anticipate, monitor, and/or control the flow of messages within the organization. Chapter 4 provides theoretical insight and practical suggestions for effective leadership. After reading this section, the reader should be able to:

1 Describe four different perspectives for analyzing organizations
2 List and define the most important structural elements of organizations

3 Take any structural element and identify its impact on the communication process

4 Describe the communication process and how it is effected by the individual schools

5 Discuss important concepts of network analysis

6 Identify common network problems in organizations and design strategies to overcome them

7 Discuss those variables that affect leadership style

Chapter 2

Organizational Theory

One of the interesting things about organizations is the fact that we all interact with them on a daily basis. For the most part, we are unaware that we are involved in organizational communication. Because of the organizational setting surrounding our communication, the flow and impact of our messages are being affected in special ways. Yet, we treat organizational communication situations much the same way we do any other communication situations.

Why does this happen? One reason is that we have been brought up in an environment that accepts "the organization" as a way of life. We take organizations for granted because they are there, much the same way we once took nature for granted or our parents or those precious, less-complicated days in the lower grades when our biggest problem was what kind of a sandwich we could swap for a peanut butter and jelly. Less-complicated times, our parents, and nature all took on new meaning for us as we matured in our understanding of them. In a similar manner, a better understanding of those concepts and principles basic to organizational theory will help develop a more sophisticated concept of "the organization."

You have been introduced to our department store so let's use it as an example and look at a relatively common situation, one I'm sure we've all experienced. Remember the last time you returned an unwanted gift to a department store? The situation probably went something like this. The clerk asked if you had a receipt. "Of course not, it was a gift." Well, under those circumstances it was a store policy to issue a credit memo that could be used like cash toward a purchase anywhere in the store. "But I don't need anything, and I prefer the money." "Well, then, you'll have to take the credit memo to the credit department on the fourth floor and they will help you." Remember thinking on your way up to the fourth floor, "This is so much bureaucratic B.S."? It may have been, but let's take a look at this example from an organizational perspective. To Richdales, the credit memo represents one of two organizational messages, each with its own distinct channel. If used for an in-store purchase, that message (credit memo) would have been traded for merchandise and channeled to the proper receiver like cash; that is, the message would have used a standard channel.

You wanted cash (which represents to the store the output of energy resources—money) not a merchandise exchange (a trade of one energy resource for another). This second message is important to the department store; therefore, a special channel has been established in order for the store to inform itself immediately of this potentially dangerous change in its normal environment (the output of unplanned energy resources). In short, you became the channel and had to carry the message (credit memo) from the source (sales clerk) located on the first floor to the receiver (credit department) located on the fourth floor.

You are made a part of this communication system for several reasons. Department stores have learned, from past experience, that (1) ordinary channels do not always report the refund quickly enough. As a result, it is not posted with that day's transactions. This causes the creation of additional work in the form of the generation of from four to seven messages to correct both the daily and weekly financial report. (2) The high degree of personal involvement on the part of the customer insures that the message will be moved from the source to the receiver quickly. (3) Due to the inconvenience of this particular system many customers will accept a credit memo (a trade of one energy resource for another) rather than go through the bother necessitated in obtaining a cash refund.

When you have a problem, you expect help and understanding from those organizations with which you interact, but how much do you do to understand the uniqueness of organizations and the reasons behind their actions?

In Chapter 1 we defined an organization as a social grouping that establishes task and/or interpersonal patterns of relationship for the attainment of a specific objective.[1] This definition implies that every organization contains a structure, people, and not only creates, but also interacts environmentally. Thus, we can distinguish four main lines or schools of development in organizational theory. The first school is generally referred to as the *classical* school and is concerned with how jobs are divided up, with specialization of job function, with how fast the job can be done, and with the concepts of control and authority. The *human relations* school deals with the attitude and morale of the workers, with the informal groups in the organization, with the social-psychological needs of the employees, and with the role and status relationships that are assigned or evolve. The third school, the *social system* school, focuses upon

---

[1] See Chester J. Barnard, *The Functions of the Executive*, Harvard, Cambridge, Mass., 1938, pp. 3-7, 65-81; Peter M. Blau and W. Richard Scott, *Formal Organizations,* Chandler Publishing Company, San Francisco, Calif., 1962, pp. 2-8; and Anthony Downs, *Inside Bureaucracy,* Little, Brown, Boston, Mass., 1967, pp. 24-31.

the internal and external interactional characteristics of the organization. The *industrial humanism* school is concerned with how the concepts of change and motivation affect organizations.

THE CLASSICAL SCHOOL

The classical theory of organization deals almost exclusively with the "anatomy of formal organization."[2] As such, its principal concern is the structure of formal organizations. Historically, classical theory was a product of the industrial revolution. It emerged during the late 1880s as a separate discipline when Frederick W. Taylor started what is often referred to as the *scientific management movement*. The scientific management approach was more concerned than other classical models with specifically how tasks should be organized. "Taylor and his associates studied primarily the use of men as adjuncts to machines in the performance of routine production tasks."[3] Time and motion studies were its basic tools. For example, what we presently know as the all-important coffee break was an outgrowth of time and motion studies designed to analyze the frequency and the length of rest periods needed during the working day to provide optimum recovery from physiological fatigue. Of prime importance to Taylor and his associates were the topics of human capacity (production rate), speed, durability (fatigue), and cost. Wages and incentive pay were seen as the principal way to motivate the worker to perform at peak efficiency.[4] Taylor, Frank and Lillian Gilbreth, and Henry Gantt were the original "industrial engineers." *Taylorism*, as the scientific management movement came to be known, developed scientific management principles that dealt almost exclusively with the production structure of the organization.

Henry Fayol and Max Weber were instrumental in the development of the classical school. It was Henry Fayol who extended Taylor's management principles beyond the field of production. Fayol, who was particularly interested in top management, developed a general theory of administration that he embodied in the following fourteen principles:

1   Division of work (specialization)
2   Authority and responsibility (power)
3   Discipline (obedience)
4   Unity of command (one boss)
5   Unity of direction (one plan)
6   Subordination of individual interests to general interests (concern for the organization first)
7   Remuneration of personnel (fair pay)
8   Centralization (consolidation)
9   Scalar chain (chain of command)
10   Order (everyone has a unique position); i.e., everyone and everything has a place

[2] Joseph A. Littener, *Organizations: Structure and Behavior*, Wiley, New York, 1963, p. 14.
[3] James G. Marsh and Herbert A. Simon, *Organizations*, Wiley, New York, 1958, p. 13.
[4] S M. Lowry, H. B. Maynard, and G. J. Slegemerten, *Time and Motion Study*, McGraw-Hill, New York, 1940, p. 6.

11 Equity (firm but fair)
12 Stability of tenure of personnel (low turnover)
13 Initiative (thinking out a plan)
14 Esprit de corps (high morale)[5]

The degree and extent of Fayol's influence has been profound, and is still being felt today.

Weber was of the opinion that the average worker did more to hinder the smooth operation of the organization than he or she did to advance it. He believed that if people were to achieve the most efficient type of organization it would be through the bureaucratic model. In response to this concern, he formulated his ideal-type bureaucracy.

Weber, recognizing the importance of Karl Marx's premise of class conflict (the struggle for power) and its organizational application, began his discussion of bureaucracy by dealing with the concepts of power and authority. Weber defined power as the ability to impose one's will upon others, while authority (domination) was legitimized power—the right of the ruler to exercise his power, and the obligation of the ruled to obey his command.[6] Weber identified three basic methods for legitimizing domination, each with a separate administrative apparatus.

1 *Charismatic domination*—associated with a loose and unstable administrative apparatus. The charismatic leader is obeyed because of extraordinary personal qualities that inspire people to follow. When the charismatic leader dies, or steps aside, orderly transition of power is difficult. The quality of the leader's managerial capacities is uncontrollable.

2 *Traditional domination*—associated with an apparatus of sanctions by custom. The traditional leader is obeyed because the right to govern has been passed on to him. When the traditional leader dies or steps aside, transition of power is generally smooth. The quality of the leader's managerial capacities is uncontrollable.

3 *Bureaucratic domination*—associated with a legal/rational apparatus. The bureaucratic leader is obeyed because he has been selected by compliance with established rules and regulations that are designed to produce the most effective leaders. Because its structure and procedures can be modified to rapidly respond to its environmental needs, a smoother transition of power and a higher quality of managerial capacities are insured.

Thus bureaucracy is an administrative apparatus that structurally impacts on the individual in such a way as to impose extreme limitations on personal freedom. In addition, it is a structure through which legitimized power is directed toward the accomplishment of the organization's goals.

In writing about the technical advantages of the bureaucratic model, Weber said: "The decisive reason for the advance of bureaucratic organization has always been its

[5] Edgar Huse and James Bowditch, *Behavior in Organizations*, Addison-Wesley, Reading, Mass., 1973, pp. 42–43.
[6] Max Weber, *The Theory of Social and Economic Organization*, trans. A. Henderson and Talcott Parsons, Oxford, New York, 1947, pp. 139–140.

purely technical superiority over any other form of organization. The fully developed bureaucratic mechanism compares with other organizations exactly as does the machine with the nonmechanical modes of production."[7] Among its superior features, Taylor noted precision, speed, unambiguity, continuity, discretion, unity, and strict subordination. He considered reduction of friction, material and personal cost by-products of these features.

You are probably thinking, "This isn't an accurate picture of any organization I know." Too often we think of bureaucracies as large, unwieldy governmental agencies or businesses that are unresponsive to the needs of the individual. Remember, this is what the ideal bureaucratic model is and, according to Weber, can be. After all, Xerox, IBM, and NASA are bureaucratic units, and in terms of meeting their organization goals, they do a good job.

Basic to Weber's theory of bureaucracy was the concept of the universality of the bureaucratic model. Weber believed that this form of organization would provide optimum efficiency for a wide variety of organizational units ranging from a small retail store with a few employees to a giant manufacturing company with tens of thousands of employees. It would encompass all business, military, governmental, and social service organizations. It was Weber's belief that because people were too often emotional and not always rational or predictable that they would interfere with the efficient operation of the organization; therefore, he established a depersonalized organizational structure intended to minimize the effects of the individual.

The classical principles of organization are based upon the assumptions that people behave as individuals, that all the organizational activities are impersonal, that all relationships are ideal, and that ideal lines of communication can be created and maintained. "Classical organization theory rests upon four key pillars. They are the division of labor, the scalar and functional processes, structure, and span of control."[8]

Division of Labor

One of the basic principles of classical theory is that *division of labor* refers to the process of dividing all of the work to be done by the number of people available to do it. According to Littener, there are several conditions that can signify the need for such a division. For example, the simple size of the task may require breaking the work into its component parts. A second consideration is that by breaking down the overall job a more efficient operation may result. Rather than worrying about planning, setting up, and performing the actual work in addition to obtaining the raw materials and selling the product, the worker can concentrate on one phase of the total operation. This leads to increased job specialization. Another consideration is that the job may be so complex that it would be difficult to find a sufficient number of workers with the necessary knowledge to complete the job. Thus, division of labor is often determined by the nature of the job to be performed, i.e., a functional division of labor, or by the amount of authority each person assumes, i.e., a scalar division of labor.

[7]H. H. Gerth and C. W. Mills, *From Max Weber: Essays in Sociology*, Oxford, New York, 1946, p. 214.
[8]Littener, op. cit.

Increased division of labor has principally resulted in greater productivity, output, efficiency, and profits for the organization, and often boredom and dissatisfaction for the worker.

Scalar and Functional Processes

The scalar and functional processes deal with the vertical and horizontal growth of the organization, respectively. *Scalar* refers to the chain of command and the delegation of authority. In the classical view, one of the fundamental principles of organization is authority, and without the establishment of authority, organization has no meaning. The concept of an official hierarchy of authority in an organization is universal as witnessed by the importance given to the organizational chart of the company. In the formal organization, authority is pictured as a pyramid with the board of directors at the top and with the mass of workers at the base. Delegated authority and instructions flow down through the president, the group vice presidents, general managers, supervisors, and foremen, and information about the lower activities flows upward along the same neat lines. Figure 2-1 illustrates the scalar process. The division of the organization into specialized parts and the grouping and regrouping of those parts (sections) into compatible units (departments) are matters relating to the horizontal evolution of the line and staff in the formal organization. Thus, the work assignment of each worker by job and the grouping of jobs is the *functional process*. An example of functional specialization within Digital Equipment (they make and sell computers) might be the division of the organization into specialized units such as purchasing, engineering, finance, personnel, manufacturing, and sales. Figure 2-2 illustrates the functional process.

Structure

The network of relationships that exist throughout the organization is referred to as *structure*. Implicit in this definition are the concepts of system and pattern. Classical

Figure 2-1   Scalar process.

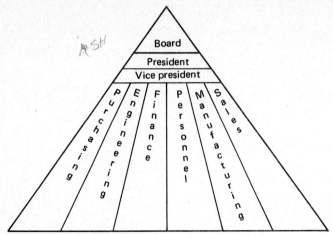

Figure 2-2 Functional process.

theory is generally concerned with two structures, the line and the staff. *Line functions* are those that have direct responsibility for accomplishing the objectives of the organization. In an organization whose principal objective is to manufacture and sell a product to consumers, the production and sales departments would be viewed as providing line functions. Organizationally, the line is the chain of command, i.e., the channels along which authority is passed down through the organization. Referring to the earlier example of Digital Equipment, the board of directors delegates responsibility to the chief executive (president) for managing the business so it will meet the objectives established by the board. He or she delegates most of this work to subordinates who, in turn, redelegate it to successively lower levels. This process continues until the primary objective of the organization is accomplished, in this case, the sale of computers. Figure 2-3 further illustrates this concept. Remember, the line of direct delegation and redelegation is the chain of command and the relationship of one level in the chain to another level is a line relationship.

Line authority is the relationship between superior and subordinate. A superior exerts direct command over his or her subordinates. Each member of the line knows the superior from whom he receives orders and to whom he is accountable.

When a line manager's job expands beyond a certain size, he or she needs help to continue to perform adequately. *Staff* refers to those elements of the organizational structure that provide advice and/or service to the line. It is perhaps best to think of staff in terms of a relationship. When one position exists primarily to provide advice and service to another, a staff relationship exists. In addition, if the work of a department is primarily that of advice and service to another department (or departments) it is classified as a staff department.

A staff manager has no authority over line personnel. In addition, the line manager decides whether to act on the staff advice.

From this definition of line and staff there is apparently a clear distinction that exists between the two; however, in practice the distinction can break down and is often complicated by several factors. Consider, for example, the concept of a line

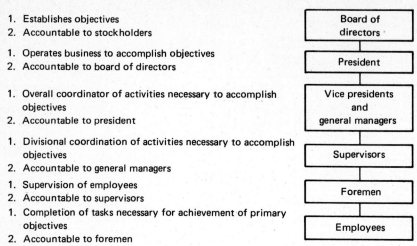

1. Establishes objectives
2. Accountable to stockholders — **Board of directors**

1. Operates business to accomplish objectives
2. Accountable to board of directors — **President**

1. Overall coordinator of activities necessary to accomplish objectives
2. Accountable to president — **Vice presidents and general managers**

1. Divisional coordination of activities necessary to accomplish objectives
2. Accountable to general managers — **Supervisors**

1. Supervision of employees
2. Accountable to supervisors — **Foremen**

1. Completion of tasks necessary for achievement of primary objectives
2. Accountable to foremen — **Employees**

Figure 2-3 The chain of command.

within staff—a line of command that runs from the top to the bottom of each staff department, just as it does within each line component. Thus, a staff manager has staff authority in relation to the entire organization, but line authority from the point of view of his or her own department. In other words, the head of a staff department has direct command over other members of the staff unit. Nor is it unusual for some positions within a staff department to exist primarily to provide advice and service to other segments within the same department. For example, in an organization whose principal objective is the manufacture and sale of computers the finance department could easily be a staff department (see Figure 2-4). Within the finance department we might find a computer programmer whose principal function is to advise and serve accounts payable.

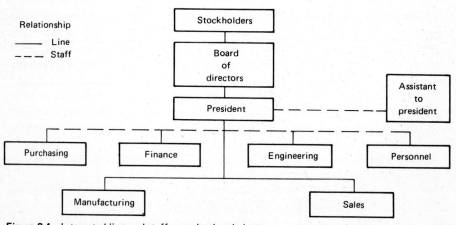

Figure 2-4 Integrated line and staff organizational chart.

Figure 2-4 is a typical example of an organizational chart. Its purpose is to demonstrate the integration of line and staff structure.

Span of Control

The concept of span of control is an ancient one. Military organizations were probably the first to implement it. General Ian Hamilton is credited with bringing public attention to the principle, while Lyndall Urwick was the first writer to apply this principle formally to organizational theory. *Span of control* refers to the number of subordinates that any one executive can effectively manage. More accurately, this concept impacts on the amount and kinds of communication with subordinates that a superior can effectively handle.[9] It relates closely to the hierarchical structure and to the concept of departmentalization. Thus, the span of control deals with the necessity for the coordination of the activities of the subordinate by the superior. The principle of span of control also implies that there are mental, physical, and time limitations on the supervisor's ability to deal with the problem of directing subordinates.

For example, if workers are involved in work of a routine nature, the supervisor will require less control (and therefore be able to deal with a greater number) than if they are performing work of a special nature. Graicunas was the first to develop a mathematical theory to explain the number of possible relationships between manager and employees.[10] His idea was basically very simple. In dealing with his employees, the manager must not only keep in mind the direct relationship between himself and each subordinate, but must also be mindful of relationships with different groupings of his subordinates and the cross-relationships among subordinates. By formula, Graicunas illustrated that a manager with four subordinates has forty-four possible cross-relationships, i.e., interrelationships. With the addition of one subordinate, which represents a 25 percent gain in the supervisor's power to delegate, the number of group and cross-relationships increases from 44 to 100. This increase represents more than a 125 percent increase in the burden of supervision and coordination. When we add a sixth and then a seventh subordinate, the figure of group and cross-relationships jumps to around 500. As the power to delegate increases arithmetically, the burden of supervision and coordination increases geometrically.

In 1935, Urwick stated that the optimal span of control was five with a maximum of six.[11] He supported this position with the idea that the individual had a limited span of attention. Contemporary research tends to indicate that typical spans of control range from between five to fifteen predicated upon the managerial skills and style, employee skills, type of organization, etc.

Span of control has a direct effect on the shape of the organization. Figure 2-5 illustrates this point. A short span will result in a tall structure because of the necessity of multiple levels. Tall structures are often referred to as *centralized organizations*

---

[9] Barnard, op. cit., p. 106.

[10] A. V. Graicunas, "Relationship in Organization," *Bulletin of the International Management Institute*, International Labor Office, Geneva, 2:112–118, February, 1933.

[11] Lt. Col. L. Urwick, "Executive Decentralization with Functional Coordination," *The Management Review*, 13:356–359, December 1935.

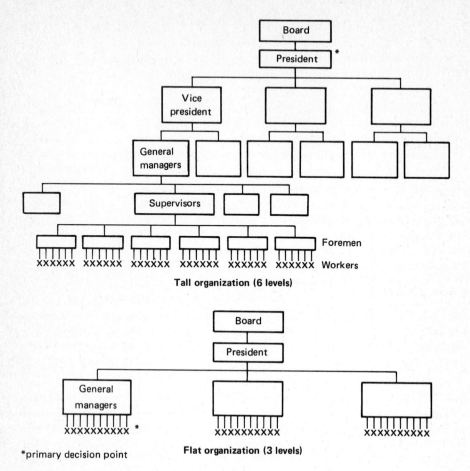

Figure 2-5 Tall vs. flat organization.

because there are so few power and decision points. Because of the centralization of authority, decisions concerning the company can be made quickly since fewer people are involved. Unfortunately, in many centralized organizations, the people at the top become isolated and often fall out of touch with the people at the bottom. One might speculate that this is what happened to one of our former presidents, Mr. Nixon.

A wide span will produce a flat structure, referred to as a *decentralized organization*, because of the reduction in the number of levels. Here there are many decision points throughout the organization and there is more face-to-face contact between management and worker. Because all of the employees have an opportunity to participate in a decentralized organization, morale may be higher, but decisions will take more time. The implications for communication of a tall vs. flat organization will be elaborated upon in Chapter 3.

In summary, those concepts that have been collectively presented under the general heading "The Classical School" can be seen in their clearest application in military and paramilitary (police and fire) organizations. They were developed principally for application to large organizations engaged in mass production. The assembly line of the automobile factory is an example of the efficiency that is sometimes attainable through the use of this approach to organizations. The concepts of scientific management have influenced thinking about all types of organizations.

THE HUMAN RELATIONS SCHOOL

Change was minimized during the scientific management era. Rules and regulations generally governed behavior and increased productivity was brought about by increased wages. The industrial revolution brought change, not only in what we produced but also in how we produced it. As technology became more and more complex, people became more dependent on each other and the problems of people working together became more important.

The industrial revolution was a human relations as well as a technological revolution. For example, two effects of advanced technology introduced by the industrial revolution were specialization of job function and increased organizational size. Both created more favorable economic results; however, from the human relations point of view, they also brought many disadvantages. Specialization often led to boredom, and a loss of a sense of individual importance. Because a single worker was no longer responsible for the total development (creation) of a product, as he had been prior to the industrial revolution, his sense of accomplishment and pride in his work were also affected. The major disadvantage of increased size was that the resulting increase in bureaucratization ultimately led to communication problems. Add to this the fact that people normally like to maintain internal and external states of balance. Change creates imbalance, therefore people normally resist change. Thus the industrial revolution was responsible for creating new and intensifying old management problems.

Productivity was not being maximized, and people were not working well together. Yet wages were continually going up. The fallacy of motivation through wage increase alone became apparent and new methods to motivate people to work together were sought. This came about because the principles of scientific management were really "guides to practical action and not theories about human behavior. They were never intended to explain human nature or the dynamics of a business organization, but merely to set out systematic procedures for the investigation of shop work as a means to improve it."[12]

The human relations, or neoclassical, school of organization evolved to compensate for deficiencies in classical theory. Basically, the human relations school accepted the structural aspects of organization as previously discussed, but modified the concept that regarded each worker as an isolated unit whose work output was primarily controlled by a profit motive. As a result, Weber's advocacy of the impersonality of relationships among organizational members was being challenged as an inhibitor to maximizing productivity. Furthermore, the human relations school was responsible for a systematic treatment of the informal organization that attempted to determine

[12]T. Lupton, *Industrial Behavior and Personnel Management*, Institute of Personnel Management, London, 1968, p. 23.

its influence on the formal organization. The discovery of the concept of informal organizations was an accidental by-product of the Hawthorne studies.

In 1927, a group of researchers from the Harvard Graduate School of Business Administration began some of the most significant experiments in the field of industrial psychology. The study, completed in 1932, was directed by Elton Mayo and took place at the Hawthorne plant of the Western Electric Company in Chicago.

In spite of the fact that the Western Electric Company was one of the most progressive companies of the day (they provided recreational facilities and pension plans), management was aware of severe dissatisfaction on the part of its 29,000 employees. Attempts by efficiency experts to increase productivity and reduce tension had failed. Mayo and his associates were called in and established an experimental program based upon the industrial psychology of Taylor. They believed that the low productivity on the part of the workers was a direct result of the wrong physical environment. Consequently, attention was principally devoted to such factors as inadequate heating, poor lighting, excessive noise, wasted motions and subsequent time loss, inadequate incentive pay, and other physical factors inherent to the worker and in his environment. As the studies progressed, the researchers made an important discovery. They found little support for the basic assumptions upon which their research rested. Unknown factors, factors they had not planned on, appeared to be interacting with the physical factors. During a study of light intensity, the researchers noticed that work output increased not only when lighting intensity was increased (an expected outcome), but also when it was decreased (an unexpected outcome). Output apparently increased no matter how they manipulated the physical conditions of the job. This was caused, of course, by psychological factors that had not been anticipated by the researchers. Indeed, until these variables were uncovered during the Hawthorne studies, they had not been applied to industrial research. This effect, known as the *Hawthorne effect*, was attributed to the fact that the researchers were simply paying attention to the workers. "These studies marked the beginning of the human relations movement in industry."[13] The Hawthorne studies were one of the first organized attempts to understand morale, status systems, communication, executive development, interaction, and the attitudes of production workers. Production could no longer be viewed as solely a function of the classical elements of the formal organization. The worker, as a unique person, could no longer be ignored.

Studies stressing people-oriented variables and their effects within and upon the organization became popular.[14] Perhaps the best known of these undertakings were the Ohio State studies. Conducted by Fleishman, Harris, and Burh, one of the five findings suggested that a philosophy of management that was principally concerned

---

[13]Gerald M. Goldhaber, *Organizational Communication*, Brown, Dubuque, Iowa, 1974, p. 35.

[14]See Melvin Dalton, "Conflicts Between Staff and Line Managerial Officers," *American Sociological Review,* 30:342–351, June 1950; J. M. Juron, "Improving the Relationship Between Line and Staff," *Personnel*, 36:515–524, May 1956; Leon Festinger, Stanley Schockter, and Kent Back, *Social Pressures in Informal Groups*, Harper, New York, 1950, pp. 153–63; Lester Cork and John R. P. French, Jr., "Overcoming Resistance to Change," in Schuyler Dean Hoslett (ed.), *Human Factors in Management*, Harper, New York, 1951, pp. 242–268; Robert Saltonstall, *Human Relations in Administration*, McGraw-Hill, New York, 1959, pp. 328–332.

with people would be more effective than a philosophy that was principally concerned with production.

One of the principal effects of the human relations approach was to increase concern for the workers. Managers trained in human relations learned to be friendlier toward their employees, to call them by their first names, and to allow them to participate in decision making. In an attempt to create an atmosphere of one big happy family, companies sponsored recreational activities and outings and increased emphasis on fringe benefits. The bottom line was, of course, that these activities would improve worker satisfaction and morale resulting in an increase in worker productivity and decreased resistance to management's authority.

Another important outgrowth of the Hawthorne experiment, specifically the Bank Wiring Room study, was the identification of the informal organization. A *formal organization* is any organization that has been established by management for a specific purpose. Within a formal organization, all lines of authority, channels of communication, and patterns of interaction occur by design. However, as the Bank Room study pointed out, a large organization tends to break down into small groups and informal channels of communication and patterns of interaction develop. These channels, often referred to as the *grapevine,* will be studied in Chapter 3. In addition, organized social structures appear, leaders emerge, codes of conduct develop, and the group evolves its own social norms.

Think for a moment about your senior year in high school. Your homeroom can be likened to a formal organization. All messages and school-related matters were coordinated by your teacher from the administration to you, the student. Generally any interaction that took place was supposed to be between the individual student and the teacher—on a one-to-one basis. When the teacher was out of the room, the student monitor he or she appointed was in charge. Now think again. Somehow important school news always found its way to you before the teacher made the formal announcement, and there was always interaction that occurred in the room that did not go through the teacher. And was the teacher's appointed monitor always in charge or was there some other classmate that you looked to for leadership? Oh, one last thought. Within your homeroom, weren't there small cliques, some more important than others? When this happens and it almost always does, we have the development of an *informal* organization. As long as the goal and objectives of the informal organization do not become more important than those of the formal organization, there are no problems. Have you ever tried to pay a parking ticket when the security office staff was huddled around the coffee pot socializing? This is clearly a conflict between informal and formal organization goals.

The following is a good example of the informal organizational structure. One police officer (Jim) working in a department with 460 other sworn personnel had the dubious distinction of being the last uniformed officer hired as a beat officer before the big hiring freeze. He worked the graveyard shift (cops don't call it that for obvious reasons) midnight to 8:00 A.M., with fifty-seven other patrolmen. Jim had no seniority and little street experience; however, he achieved recognition on his shift because he had instinctive street sense and quickly developed a network of reliable informants. As a result, he became respected throughout the department and steadily gained influence. When decisions regarding street assignment, patrol techniques, and timing a bust were made, the shift commander often asked Jim for advice. The shift commander realized that the informal power that Jim had (his ability to influence his fellow workers) could be used to make his own job easier or more difficult.

The strength of the human relations school and its fundamental tenets of concern for employee morale and attitudes were to be the vehicle for its ineffectiveness. As the concept of more frequent and less impersonal communication flourished in business and industry, many managers seized upon this approach in an attempt to manipulate and control their employees. The insincerity of these men manifested itself in hand-shakes, friendly back slapping, and having lunch with the boys. In short, it took a simplistic view of human nature. As a result of this type of activity, the human relations school came under heavy criticism, and much of its worthwhile research has been ignored. None the less, both the classical and human relations schools have had a dynamic impact on organizational theory.

However, neither the classical school nor the human relations school has provided an adequate basis for an integrated or complete study of the organization. The classical school has emphasized the structure of the organization and was concerned with the separation of organizational activities into parts and tasks. The human relations school attempted to retain the classical structural model while focusing attention on human morale, attitudes, and motivations.

THE SOCIAL SYSTEM SCHOOL

In *Hawthorne Revisited*, Henry A. Landsberger identifies one of the principal short-comings of the Hawthorne studies when he comments that the researchers neglected to "draw attention to the fact that the rapidly worsening Depression in all probability had an important influence on the atmosphere in the Bank Wiring Observation Room."[15] The implication of Landsberger's statement is that both the classical and human relations schools have approached the study of the organization as a *closed system* from which all outside influences were eliminated. In the case of the Bank Wiring Room, Mayo and his associates assumed that all conditions important to the subjects' working relationship would take place in the room. Anything that happened outside the room was unimportant. The researchers failed to recognize that the Depression and the concern and anxiety created by worsening economic conditions that had all but paralyzed our nation might be carried into the room by the worker-subjects.

What Landsberger was trying to point out was that when we view an organization as a closed system, we gather all relevant information about the organization from within the organization. We study each part in isolation and avoid dealing with how the parts of the organization relate to each other or how they relate to anything that takes place outside the organization's boundaries. As a result of viewing an organization as a closed system, we neglect to consider how the organization affects and is

[15]Henry A. Landsberger, *Hawthorne Revisited*, Cornell, Ithica, New York, 1958.

affected by the environment in which it exists. Organizations cannot be realistically studied as closed systems, for they do interact with their environment.

Increasing attention is being focused on the organization as a social system. "General systems theory implies an inter-connected complex of functionally related components or parts."[16] In other words, all parts affect the whole and an action that occurs in one part of the organization is felt throughout the entire organization. According to Chester J. Barnard, if there is a change in the relationship of one part of the organization to any or all of the other parts, there is a change in the system.[17] For example, a sales clerk in the men's department of Richdales gives notice that his last day will be the fifteenth of the month. On the twelfth, the personnel department hires a new sales clerk; however, company policy states that only the training department can train and process new employees. The training department manager is ill from the thirteenth through the sixteenth. As a result, on the sixteenth all of the clerks in men's furnishings must cover the unattended area. The added burden makes them late in clearing their cash registers at the end of the day. This delays the floor manager's normal closing routine (he is personally responsible for carrying all of the cash register receipts to the accounting department) which delays the store closing process and, as a result, the people in the accounting department have to work late. Let's look at another example that demonstrates the same principle but outside of the organizational setting. A car stalls on the expressway during rush hour traffic. Traffic backs up the access ramp leading to the expressway and blocks traffic on Main Street, which means that all the workers parked in lots on Main Street will be late for supper. As Redding has so aptly pointed out, "changes in any one part of the organization inevitably (regardless of how subtly) produce changes in the rest of the organization."[18] If you have ever dropped a pebble into a pool of water and watched the ripples extend from the point of disturbance to the outer limits of the pool, you have a reference point for the social system concept. In viewing an organization as a social system, we accept the fact that the organization will be affected by structural, functional, and human issues. Questions of division of labor, span of control, and chain of command become as important as, and interact with, questions of morale, attitude, and personality.

To summarize, the parts of the system that are of strategic importance are the individual, the formal structure, the informal structure, and the physical surroundings of the worker. These parts are woven together in such a manner that an action at any one level causes reactions throughout the entire system. When the organization is viewed as a social system, we can no longer divorce the job function of a cameraman from the successful functioning of the entire television station. Nor can a manager afford to focus his attention only on his own department without considering the effects that his decisions and the actions of his workers have on other departments and, ultimately, on the prosperity of the organization.

---

[16] Richard A. Johnson, Fremont E. Kast, and James E. Rosenzweig, *Theory and Management of Systems,* McGraw-Hill, New York, 1963, p. 37.

[17] Barnard, op. cit., p. 78.

[18] W. Charles Redding, "The Organizational Communicator," in W. Charles Redding and George A. Sanborn (eds.), *Business and Industrial Communication: A Source Book,* Harper & Row, New York, 1964, p. 33.

Obviously organizations are not isolated from their environments as the following example illustrates. The recent oil crisis (the Administration referred to it as a problem) caused the price of gasoline to increase markedly (environmental and inflationary). In reaction to the increased gasoline prices, the buying public started purchasing automobiles that consumed less gasoline (response to environment). Automobile manufacturers sold fewer of their large sedans and found sales of their compacts far ahead of production (organizational problem precipitated by environmental conditions).

In response to this situation, the automobile manufacturers laid off hundreds of workers from those plants producing large sedans and all but forced overtime on the workers in plants producing compact cars (environmental and inflationary). The government had to pass emergency legislation to extend welfare benefits to those workers who had been out of work for an extended period (environmental problem precipitated by organizational problem). Ludwig von Bertalanffy has defined closed systems as "systems which are considered to be isolated from their environment."[19] "Organizations are," according to Katz and Kahn, "flagrantly open systems in that the input of energies and the conversion of output into further energic input consists of transactions between the organization and its environment."[20]

Organizations may therefore be defined as *open systems* when they generate energy outputs for environmental consumption and consume environmental output in the form of organizational inputs. Some of the characteristics basic to open systems are:

1 *Import of energy.* Open systems import various forms of energy from the outside world. Organizations require resources such as people, raw materials, power, marketing information, etc., in order to maintain themselves. Richdales needs selling floor space, lights, personnel, hard goods, soft goods, and support services. WDTN needs cameras and mikes, sponsors, personnel, lights, and an intense electric supply.

2 *Change.* The process by which the imported energy is transformed into an output. Open systems create new products from raw materials. A glass manufacturer changes sand to glass, while a vocational college changes the unknowledgeable student into a welder, aerospace technician, or practical nurse.

3 *Output.* The product or service the system trades with its environment for new imports. Automobile manufacturers export cars; hospital services help reduce illness. The principal objective of the organization is often manifested in its environmental outputs.

4 *System cycles.* The repetitive act of trading output for import that provides the organization with new energy sources, i.e., money or goods that are traded for raw materials and labor.

5 *Information import and negative feedback.* There are two types of import: *energic* and *information.* We have previously discussed energic imports. Information imports provide information to the system about its environment and about its functioning in relation to its environment. Feedback occurs when system outputs are sent back into the system as new imports. Information of a negative nature fed back into the system allows the system to correct its deviations from course. When we adjust the

---

[19] Ludwig von Bertalanffy, *General System Theory*, Braziller, New York, 1972, p. 30.
[20] Daniel Katz and Robert Kahn, *The Social Psychology of Organizations*, Wiley, New York, 1966, p. 16.

thermostat in our homes, we are giving the boiler negative information about the temperature of the house. The boiler corrects the problem. If you complain to the dry cleaner about her service, she can make the necessary adjustment and retain you as a patron.

6 *Equilibrium.* Equilibrium refers to a state of balance between energy imports and output. This is not a state of balance in the true sense of the word for systems attempt to insure their stability by importing more energy than they export. We normally see this as building permanent reserves in business, as saving up the nest egg in the family, and as the process of storing up fatty tissue by the body. At its simplest level, the steady state is one of homeostasis over time. At more complex levels, equilibrium is viewed as growth and expansion so that the basic character of the system is preserved.

7 *Interdependence.* The underpinning for systems theory is the concept of interdependence (the whole system, the parts of the system, the parts in relation to each other, and the parts in relation to the whole). Any change within the system will not only be felt at the point of origination, but also will impact on the entire system.

8 *Equifinality.* This concept suggests that it is possible for any system to achieve the same end state of existence from differing internal conditions or by taking a variety of different paths.

INDUSTRIAL HUMANISM

In our current world of "future shock" the organization is an inherent part of all of our lives. Organizations of the past were, for the most part, static and could be characterized as traditional bureaucracies. Rapid change is as much a part of today's organizations as fast food service is a part of today's lifestyle. Just as change in our lifestyle requires adaptive adjustment, change in organizations requires new systems of organization.

When change becomes frequent enough in an organization to be thought of as a standard mode of operation, reorganization ceases to be a one-time proposition and becomes a continuous and ongoing process. As we have seen, organizations do not exist in a vacuum. They interact with their environment. Organizational change is often forced by rapid change in the environment. Traditional organization structures were designed to accommodate only predictable conditions. Rapid changes in the environment could not be effectively responded to by the traditional bureaucratic model.

The unique problems brought about by rapid change necessitate larger amounts of information to resolve them than do those problems that are routine and repetitive. As a result, modern organizations require more information, and they require it faster. New systems of organization had to be developed. The system proposed by many authors as best suited to cope with dynamic change is one based on participative management. William G. Scott first classified these types of systems under the heading *industrial humanism.*[21]

[21]William G. Scott, *Organizational Concepts andAnalysis,* Dickenson, Belmont, Calif., 1969, pp. 150–151.

Prior to 1968 the industrial humanism movement did not have a synthetized body of knowledge. Scott provided a framework for that synthesis when he set forth those values associated with industrial humanism. Scott believed industrial humanists:

    1   Assume the dignity of the individual plus the need of protecting and cultivating personality on an equal rather than hierarchical basis

    2   Assume there is a steady trend in the human condition toward the perfectibility of the individual

    3   Assume that organizational gains are basically the gains of people in them, and the benefits flowing from these gains should be distributed as rapidly as possible to those responsible for them

    4   Assume that those in organizations should, in the last analysis, give their consent to those who make policy and establish controls

    5   Assume that change in organizations should be the result of full awareness of alternatives, and consensus by participants[22]

Using these principles as a guideline, it becomes possible to identify a group of writers whose works reflect these values.

Abraham Maslow's approach to the basic human needs of the individual was one of the first to be extrapolated to the organization. According to Maslow, basic human needs are arranged in a hierarchy according to their strengths. Figure 2-6 illustrates this hierarchy of needs. The physiological needs are at the bottom of the hierarchy because they are the most basic and they tend to be the strongest until they are satisfied. Each successive need then becomes the strongest until it is satisfied. Human beings are constantly striving for self-actualization. The self-actualized person has become what he or she is capable of becoming. He or she does what he or she thinks is important and receives satisfaction from the act itself.

Another early development was Carl Rogers's approach to client-centered therapy. Rogers's technique was concerned with the "independence and integration of the individual." The individual's growth, and not the problem, was the focus. The client set the goals and direction of change while the counselor only served to provide the method.

Small group research was moving in a similar direction. The development of the

---

[22]Ibid., p. 158.

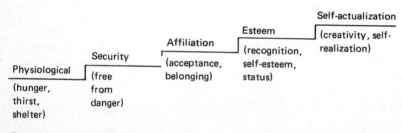

Figure 2-6   Maslow's hierarchy of needs.

National Training Laboratories and their use of T-grouping techniques closely parallels Rogers's client-centered approach. Change in the T-group was facilitated by the development of nonauthoritarian client-centered roles.

Change and the accomplishment of change is a theme readily identifiable throughout these theories. For example, in developing his power-equalizing models Leavitt indicates:

1 They are centrally concerned with effect, i.e., with morale, sensitivity, psychological security.
2 They value evolutionary, internally generated change in individuals, groups, and organizations over externally planned or implemented change.
3 They place much value on human growth and fulfillment as well as upon task accomplishment.
4 They share a normative belief that power in organizations should be more equally distributed than in most existent authoritarian hierarchies.[23]

The concepts advanced by Leavitt are operationalized at the organizational level by McGregor. In an early work, "The Human Side of Enterprise," McGregor suggests that management misconstrued human nature. They believed in Theory X. In Theory X:

1 Management is responsible for organizing the elements of productive enterprise—money, materials, equipment, people—in the interest of economic ends.
2 With respect to people, this is a process of directing their efforts, motivating them, controlling their actions, and modifying their behavior to fit the needs of the organization.
3 Without this active intervention by management, people would be passive—even resistant—to organizational needs. They must therefore be persuaded, rewarded, punished, controlled—their activities must be directed. This is management's task in managing subordinate managers or workers. We often sum it up by saying that management consists of getting things done through other people.

Behind this conventional theory there are several additional beliefs—less explicit, but widespread:

1 On the average people are by nature indolent—they work as little as possible.
2 They lack ambition, dislike responsibility, prefer to be led.
3 They are inherently self-centered, indifferent to organizational needs.
4 They are by nature resistant to change.
5 They are gullible, not very bright, the ready dupe of the charlatan and the demagogue.[24]

McGregor believed that rather than being a reflection of the individual's inherent nature, this behavior was a reflection of the "nature of industrial organizations, or

[23] Harold J. Leavitt, "Applied Organizational Change in Industry: Structural, Technological, and Humanistic Approaches," in J. G. Marsh (ed.), *Handbook of Organizations*, Rand McNally, Chicago, 1965, p. 1154.
[24] Douglas McGregor, "The Human Side of Enterprise," in K. Davis and W. Scott (eds.), *Human Relations and Organizational Behavior*, McGraw-Hill, New York, 1969, p. 8.

management philosophy, policy and practice."[25] As an alternative to Theory X, McGregor offered what he called Theory Y, which stated:

1 Management is responsible for organizing the elements of productive enterprise, money, materials, equipment, people—in the interest of economic ends.

2 People are *not* by nature passive or resistant to organizational needs. They have become so as a result of experience in organizations.

3 The motivation, the potential for development, the capacity for assuming responsibility, the readiness to direct behavior toward organizational goals are all present in people. Management does not put them there. It is a responsibility of management to make it possible for people to recognize and develop these human characteristics for themselves.

4 The essential task of management is to arrange organizational conditions and methods of operation so that people can achieve their own goals *best* by directing *their own* efforts toward organizational objectives.[26]

The principal tenet of Theory Y which associates McGregor with the industrial humanism school is the statement: "The motivation, the potential for development, the capacity for assuming responsibility, the readiness to direct behavior toward organizational goals are all present in people. Management does not put them there. It is a responsibility of management to make it possible for people to recognize and develop these human characteristics for themselves."[27]

Probably one of the most controversial theories in the industrial humanism movement has been advocated by Frederick Herzberg. Herzberg has arrived at conclusions that are consistent with those of McGregor and Maslow. In his research Herzberg found that certain factors in the work environment are very important motivators. *Motivator factors* provide opportunity for achievement, recognition, participation, and growth. Conversely, factors such as physical conditions, security, salary, and company policy were not significant motivating forces. However, this latter group, when not *maintained* at satisfactory levels, could become power dissatisfiers. These factors, often referred to as *maintenance factors*, were identified by Herzberg as *hygiene factors*. They are factors that relate to job context rather than job content.[28]

The humanist movement also provided a framework for the management theories being developed by Rensis Likert. He suggested that most management styles could be classified as belonging to one of four possible *systems*. Systems 1 and 4 respectively paralleled McGregor's Theory X and Theory Y. The other two systems fell in between these two extremes. Some of the characteristics of System 4 are:

• Superiors have complete confidence and trust in their subordinates in all matters.
• There is group participation in goal setting, improving methods, appraising progress, etc.

[25] Ibid., p. 9.
[26] Ibid., p. 8.
[27] Ibid., p. 14.
[28] Frederick Herzberg, "One More Time: How Do You Motivate Employees?" *Harvard Business Review*, 46:53–62, January 1968.

- There is extensive friendly interaction with a high degree of confidence and trust.
- Decision making is widely done throughout the organization, but is well integrated through the linking process provided by overlapping groups.
- The informal and formal organization are one and the same; hence all social forces support efforts to achieve the organization's goals.[29]

His concern for individual growth and the development of a democratic organization places Likert clearly within the industrial humanism philosophy.

In his writings Chris Argyris expresses concern for human fulfillment. In 1957, Argyris published a book called *Personality and Organization* in which he developed the point that the needs of the organization and the needs of the individual worker are in conflict.[30] Argyris feels that every normal person develops from dependence to independence as he or she matures. He believes that people grow in the direction of wanting to make more decisions for themselves, of wanting to be more responsible, of wanting to be more competent, and of wanting to demonstrate or exercise this competence. Notice the similarity to McGregor's Theory Y.) In contrast to this, Argyris says that the very structure of our formal business and industrial organizations exert pressures in directions *opposite* to those described above. That is, such organizations encourage employees to be passive and submissive to authority, to use only a few of their skills, and to allow decisions to be made *for* them. Argyris feels that this conflict results in restriction of production, increased absenteeism and turnover, high grievance rates, and the formation of informal work groups having antimanagement attitudes. Argyris observes that management has traditionally tried to solve such problems by getting tough and tightening down the screws in order to bring the employees into line. Such practices only serve to intensify the conflict through pushing the workers even further in the direction opposite to that of their normal development. Argyris sees this as a problem at all levels of the organization and he advocates two approaches as solutions.

First, he says that the sources of many of these problems lie in the area of interpersonal relations and he is in favor of training supervisors to be more understanding and sensitive in relating to their workers and to each other. He feels that this will improve communication and make people better able to work together to do a better job.

Second, he is in favor of job enlargement, that is, making jobs more challenging so that people can make more decisions, be more responsible, and use more of their skills. The purpose of all this is to help the individual "return to a basic human orientation where his own inner sense of worth is paramount."[31]

In an attempt to resolve the problem of relating personal fulfillment to organization productivity, Blake and Mouton developed a technique of integrated management. It

---

[29]Rensis Likert, *The Human Organization: Its Management and Value*, McGraw-Hill, New York, 1967, pp. 4–10.

[30]Chris Argyris, *Personality and* Organization, Harper and Row, New York, 1957.

[31]Chris Argyris, *Integrating the Individual and the Organization*, Wiley, New York, 1964, p. 260.

is commonly referred to as *the Grid*—the Management Grid. Here work accomplishment is by commitment of all organization members.

The systems we have discussed were primarily designed to deal with change and promote a democratic environment. Warren Bennis felt that a move toward democratic systems was inevitable because "democracy becomes a functional necessity whenever a social system is competing for survival under conditions of chronic change."[32] And change was to be planned change implemented by a change agent. To that end, Bennis set forth "normative goals for . . . change agents" that included:

- Effecting a change in values so that human factors and feelings come to be considered legitimate
- Improving interpersonal competence of managers
- Developing team management
- Implementation of conflict resolution in place of the exercise of pure power, suppression, denial, etc.[33]

ORGANIZATIONAL ELEMENTS AFFECTING COMMUNICATION

It should be obvious by now that the organization exerts tremendous influence upon the communication behavior of the people who come in contact with it. The very structure of the organization is designed to create a variety of communication situations and decision points as well as to determine the direction of message flow. In addition, the organization affects the communication behavior of people as individuals. These two aspects of overlapping, but mutually distinguishable, communication are referred to by W. Charles Redding as "structural and personal communication":

1 *Structural communication*—denotes those forms of communication activity not primarily associated with any individual person as sender or receiver, but representing messages required by the inherent "structural-functional" demands of the organization per se. Examples are manuals and handbooks; general, impersonal bulletins and notices of all kinds, suggestion systems; "house organs" or employee publications; directional signs, advertisements; company announcements; safety instructions; union contracts; and orientation materials for new employees.

2 *Personal communication*—denotes the speaking, listening, writing, reading, and nonverbal communication behavior of individual persons within the organizational setting. Examples: issuing orders or instructions, conducting appraisal interviews, listening to suggestions and complaints, visiting the plant premises, participating in conferences, and talking to employee groups.[34]

[32]P. Slater and W. Bennis, "Democracy Is Inevitable," *Harvard Business Review,* 42:51-59, March 1964.
    [33]W. Bennis, "Theory and Method in Applying Behavioral Science to Planned Organizational Change," in W. Bennis, K. Benne, and R. Chin (eds.), *Planning of Change,* Holt, Rinehart and Winston, New York, 1969, p. 69.
    [34]Redding and Sanborn (eds.), op. cit., p. 45.

In order that we avoid the sin of pigeonholing, let us view these two aspects of organizational communication as existing at either end of a continuum (see Figure 2-7). As we move closer to the mid-point of the continuum, we move closer to those messages that involve both structural and personal dimensions. For example, business meetings occur quite frequently in most organizations and consist of persons listening and speaking. These meetings are often affected by the organizational system in that they reflect a structured superior-subordinate relationship.

As we have learned, the very structure of the organization often determined communication. If we were to reorganize an organization, we would in effect be changing the communication paths of that organization. This occurs because organizations consist of interrelated parts (we call these parts *departments*) with communication linkages existing between and among the parts. Adjust the parts and you automatically cause change or adjustment among the interconnected linkages. Thus, we have as an outgrowth of the structure of an organization, the creation of channels of message flow (paths) and networks (interconnected paths).

The division of labor, specifically the scalar process, gives birth to the concept of vertical communication. Vertical communication consists of downward (from superior to subordinate) and upward (from subordinate to supervisor) communication. Thus, the chains of command are actually lines of authority and accountability that create the formal channels of communication. Because of the hierarchical structure of most tall organizations, the manager (i.e., decision maker) is often isolated from the people above and below him or her. In addition, communication is less spontaneous and often does not reflect the real circumstances surrounding problems.

Horizontal communication is also a function of the division of labor. It issues from the functional process, i.e., specialization, and takes place between people, units, or departments on the same level. While job specialization is essential to the efficient operation of a business or industrial organization, it leads to the separation of people by groups, by space, by role (job function), and by status. As specialization increases, each worker becomes more dependent upon his or her fellow workers. This concept may be best exemplified by an automobile production line. Before I can rivet the fender to the body you have to put the fender in place. Thus, division of labor increases employee interdependency, which often leads to the generation of strain and tension among workers. After all, how would you feel if you were on piece work and the worker who was feeding you raw material started to goof off?

Span of control determines whether we have a tall or flat organization. This in turn has a direct bearing on the number of levels the organization will have. Tall organizations increase the number of channels of communication, thus increasing the possibility of message distortion. Another feature of tall organizations is that they have few

Structural-personal

Structural		Personal
Communication	Messages	Communication
	^	

Figure 2-7 Relationship between structural and personal communication.

power and decision-making points. There is better control over decision making; however, decision making often takes longer and is less immediately responsive to emergencies. Flat organizations reduce the number of levels through which messages must travel, but often lead to information overload at the manager's office. Authority and decision making are generally spread out in a flat organization. This allows for more immediate response to emergencies, but often the right hand doesn't know what the left hand is doing.

Not only does the organization affect structural communication, but, as we mentioned earlier, it also affects the communication behavior of the individual as a person. As a member of an organization we are members of a structural set of interpersonal relationships. Each of us is assigned a role to play with specific standards or rules of conduct. Because of the role assignment within the organization, we all develop mutual expectations. Our roles determine whom we interact with, when we interact, how we interact, and indeed whether we interact. In addition, simple membership in a large complex organization creates professional, social, and personal tension that affect our daily communication.

Within organizations there are both formal and informal channels of communication. *Formal* channels are those that represent the "official" lines of communication as specified on the organizational chart and as embodied in the chains of command. Formal messages theoretically require no persuasion and are accepted by members of the organization without question. A channel that exists outside of the formal channel is referred to as an *informal* channel. The grapevine is the principal network for distribution of informal messages.

SUMMARY

If we are to survive and be successful in an occupational organization, it is necessary that we grasp the basic nature and structure of these organizations. Our communication effectiveness begins with an adequate understanding of the four principal schools of thought governing how workers are viewed and organized: the classical school, the human relations school, the social systems school, and the industrial humanism school.

The classical school is principally concerned with those structured aspects of the organization that determine size, shape, and managerial functions. Important concepts to remember are: division of labor, chains of command, span of control, line versus staff functions, and scalar function.

The human relations school developed in light of findings from the Hawthorne studies. This school was concerned with such people-oriented variables as morale, attitudes, and personality.

The social system school is predicated upon research from general systems theory. Underpinning this approach is the interdependency of the parts of the organization with the whole organization. The differences between closed and open systems were explored, resulting in the elaboration of an open system model. The interaction and exchange that transpires between organizations and their environments led to the conclusion that organizations are open systems.

Change and its effect upon the organization is the principal tenet of the industrial humanism school. Implicit in this philosophy is a concern for motivating the worker to increased productivity. In contrast with the classical school, the industrial humanism school recognizes the individual's desire for personal growth. It attempts to facilitate that growth in order to maximize the worker's desires as well as the organization's productivity.

In concluding the chapter, we briefly examined those structural and personal organizational elements that affect communication. Key concepts discussed were channels, networks, horizontal and vertical communication, and formal and informal communication.

A final caution—although we have discussed independently of each other the classical school, the human relations school, the social system school, and the industrial humanism school, it is extremely unlikely that you will find an organization that represents just one of these schools. Some organizations will reflect more of one approach than the other, but for the most part, the vast majority of organizations you interact with will reflect aspects of all four schools.

Chapter 3

Communication Networks in Organizations

One way of looking at an organization is to view the people and departments within it as information storage units. If we take this approach then the organization becomes "an elaborate system for gathering, evaluating, recombining, and disseminating information."[1] It is not surprising, in these terms, that the effectiveness of an organization with respect to the achievement of its goals should be so closely related to its effectiveness in handling information. Bavelas and Barrett highlight this relationship when they say:

> In an enterprise whose success hinges upon the coordination of the efforts of all its members, the managers depend completely upon the quality, the amount, and the rate at which relevant information reaches them. The rest of the organization, in turn, depends upon the efficiency with which the managers can deal with this information and reach conclusions, decisions, etc. This line of reasoning leads us to the belief that communication is not a secondary or derived aspect of organization—a "helper" of the other and presumably more basic functions. Rather it is the essence of organized activity and is the basic process out of which all other functions derive. The goals an organization selects, the methods it applies, the

---

[1] Thomas Tortoriello, in a lecture on Organizational Communication. Seminar 611, Miami University, Oxford, Ohio, May 1975.

effectiveness with which it improves its own procedures—all of these hinge upon the quality and availability of the information in the system.[2]

Thus, communication and control may be viewed as the decisive processes in an organization. "Communication is what makes organizations cohere; control is what regulates their behavior."[3] If the manager can identify and trace the networks by which information is carried to different parts of the organization and determine how it will affect the behavior of the organization, he or she will have a better understanding of that organization as well as a better opportunity for success.

A PERSPECTIVE

According to Katz and Kahn, "The very nature of a social system . . . implies a selectivity of channels and communication acts—a mandate to avoid some and to utilize others." For example, if 300 people were waiting to catch an overseas flight at Kennedy Airport, the number of potential communication channels would be $N(N - 1)/2$ or 44,850. By organizing these 300 individuals into a network of sixty groups of five each and insuring that each member of a five-member team had a single role while remaining interdependent with his or her team, the number of channels within the newly organized work team is reduced to ten in a completely interdependent condition. By the simple act of organizing, we have effectively reduced the available communication channels from 44,850 to 10.

By operational definition an organization requires structured communication channels that restrict and constrain random messages—messages that might inhibit organizational objectives. In addition, the closer we move to the center of the organization, the locus of control and decision making, the more pronounced the emphasis placed on information exchange becomes. Company executives make decisions predicated upon the information they receive and rarely on personal experience with the problem, whereas line managers make many decisions as a direct result of experiencing the consequences of the problem. For example, if you work for a publishing company as a department manager of shipping, you could experience, on a daily basis, the problems generated by using an undependable trucker. Your decision making about that trucking company would be a product of personal experience. However, when the president of your company makes a decision to buy his own fleet of trucks and hire his own drivers, that decision is predicated upon information supplied to him by his organization and not upon personal experience. "In this sense, communication—the exchange of information and the transmission of meaning—is the very essence of . . . an organization."[5]

---

[2] Alex Bavelas and Dermot Barrett, "An Experimental Approach to Organizational Communication," *Personnel*, 30:368, January 1951.

[3] Karl W. Deutsch, "On Communication Models in the Social Sciences," *Public Opinion Quarterly*, 12:367, Fall 1952.

[4] David Katz and Robert Kahn, *The Social Psychology of Organizations,* Wiley, New York, 1966, p. 226.

[5] Ibid., p. 223.

MESSAGE PURPOSE

In reviewing the literature, there appears to be a variety of answers available in response to the question, "What are the primary functions messages serve in an organization?" If we are to grasp the purposes that organizational messages serve, a review of some of these responses might prove useful at this time.

According to Katz and Kahn[6] the primary functions of messages in organizations are to facilitate production, maintenance, procurement and disposal, adaptation, and management. Thayer[7] identifies four functions of message flow: to inform, to persuade, to command and instruct, and to integrate. Berlo[8] talks of production, innovation, and maintenance. Finally, Redding[9] suggests three general reasons for message flow: task concerns, maintenance concerns, and human concerns, i.e., people problems.

We believe that message purpose should be determined by those subsystems that one can identify as fundamental to the organization. For our purposes we will identify six subsystems (production, maintenance, support, adaptation, managerial, and human) that support six message functions: production, maintenance, support, adaptation, managerial, and human. Most of those message purposes suggested above can be incorporated into our six categories.

Production systems are directed toward getting the job done. Task requirements are met by the line operation. They have the principal responsibility of realizing the major purpose for which the organization was created and vested. *Production messages*, or *task messages* as they are sometimes called, relate to production standards, levels of profitability, acquisition of energy inputs, the change process, outputs, system cycles, quality of service, etc. (see Chapter 2, "The Social System School"). Any information necessary for the worker to adequately handle his or her job (orientation, training, goal setting, systems, procedure) is a task message.

Maintenance systems are directed at insuring stability and predictability, or at insuring a steady state or equilibrium. As a result of this subsystem, many organizations manifest a tendency toward organizational rigidity. An example might be reflected in the statement, "Rules are rules." The folly of this statement lies in the fact that rules are only viable as long as they do what they were originally designed to do. If the cause that brought the rule into being disappears and the rule doesn't, you are experiencing the preservation of the status quo in absolute terms.

Maintenance messages would relate to the selection procedures used to select the "right personality for this organization," socialization or indoctrination practices, system rewards, policy or regulating statements. Maintenance messages are any messages that help the organization perpetuate itself.

Support systems are directed toward helping functions that insure realization of the production structures goals. *Support messages* deal with the procurement of raw

---

[6] Ibid., pp. 85–96.

[7] Lee Thayer, *Communication and Communication Systems*, Irwin, Homewood, Ill., 1968, p. 117.

[8] David Berlo quoted by W. Charles Redding in *Communication 694*, Seminar in Organizational Communication, Purdue University, March 13, 1975.

[9] W. Charles Redding, "The Organizational Communication," in W. Charles Redding and George Sanborn (eds.), *Business and Industrial Communication: A Source Book*, Harper & Row, New York, 1964, p. 43.

materials, manpower, transportation, internal food services, housekeeping, the disposal of outputs, etc.

Adaptive systems allow the organization to interface with a constantly changing environment. Maintenance systems look inward; adaptive systems look outward. *Adaptive messages* would be generated by departments and/or people involved in public relations, planning, research, and development. Adaptive systems strive to achieve environmental constancy by bringing the external world under control. An example would be the annexation of a township by a city.

Managerial systems dissect the production, maintenance, support, and adaptive systems. It is the decision-making aspect of the organization. If the organization is to survive, decisions must be made that govern internal as well as external conflict. *Managerial messages* include orders, commands, procedures, and control designed to facilitate the organization's primary objective.

Human systems are directed toward meeting the needs, desires, and wants of the personnel who comprise the organization. These systems attempt to be responsive to the individual workers and informal groups. Unlike the other subsystems that were an inherent part of the organization structure, human systems were born out of recognition of the self-actualization needs of the worker and were first identified through the Hawthorne studies. Human messages are concerned with beliefs, attitudes, values, feelings, self-concept, and morale. They can cover a wide variety of situations ranging from appraisal interviewing, positive supervisor feedback, and performance rewards, to casual conversations, rap sessions, or simple jiving. Regardless of the nature of the communication, managers are becoming increasingly sensitive to the concept that if it is voiced on the job, it is important. Because of this new awareness, each time the manager is the recipient of fresh information she will learn something new about the organization, herself, or the employee. At any rate, she should know more after the message is sent than she did before it was sent.

FORMAL COMMUNICATION NETWORKS

Communication networks or channels may be identified as either formal or informal. When message flows follow the formal structure of the organization as represented by the organizational chart, they are following *formal* communication networks. When the scalar principle of authority and hierarchy is employed, messages will flow in vertically (down and up) directions. They will flow horizontally (across) the organization if the functional principle dictates the direction.

Downward Communication

The classical school viewed the *downward* network as a tool for transmitting orders. In most modern organizations, most information still flows from top to bottom. Katz and Kahn[10] have identified five types of messages that generally flow from the supervisor to the subordinate. They are job instructions, job rationale, policy and procedure, feedback, and indoctrination.

[10] Katz and Kahn, op. cit., p. 239.

Figure 3-1 Formal and informal channels.

1 *Job instructions* attempt to explain how an assigned task is to be accomplished. For example, "Before you start to unload the truck, make sure that the truck doors are latched back and that the ramp is securely in place." The content of job instructions is directly related to the complexity of the job and the skills required to do it. Very precise job instructions can be developed for simple routine jobs that require minimal skills, whereas complex jobs that necessitate specialized skills require more generalized job instructions. Job instructions may come from on-the-job training by the supervisor, training sessions, training manuals, or written job specifications.

2 *Job rationale* attempts to provide the worker with a full understanding of his or her job and how it relates to other jobs in the organization. For example, "You are the department manager of accounts payable and before the finance department can pay our bills you must tell them what bills they are cleared to pay." Many employees know what they are doing but have absolutely no idea why they are doing it or how it affects the organization. Departmentalization and division of labor have done a lot to severely restrict a systems view of the individual job.

3 *Policy and procedures* statements acquaint workers with the practices, regulations, and benefits afforded them by their employer. For example, "After you have worked with us for 1 year you are entitled to 1 week's vacation with pay." Generally this information is contained in an employee handbook accompanied by materials from the employer's insurance company. Most large companies have a support person well versed in benefits. That person is always someone you should know.

4 *Feedback* refers to those messages that tell the worker how he is performing his job. For example, "Harold, I think you did a great job typing those eighty-five letters." For the most part academicians have tended to be unduly harsh on business and industry when talking about performance feedback. Perhaps it is a result of the archaic system they labor under, or due in part to their frantic efforts to find a system in which the supervisor (chairman) has as little input as possible. At any rate, most businesses approach performance reviews as developmental tools necessary to the growth of the

employee and crucial to building an adequate talent pool to sustain the needs of the organization.

5 *Indoctrination* messages attempt to enlist the employee's enthusiastic support of specific organizational objectives. For example, "Richdales would like every employee to contribute his or her fair share to the United Way."

There can be little doubt that the hierarchical structure of an organization is the most powerful influence on downward communication. Because of the hierarchical structure as messages pass from superior to subordinate, they demand attention and are accorded respect. The price one would pay for deliberately altering or suppressing such a message could easily be one's job.

As messages move down the organization, they tend to grow and gain substance (see Figure 2-3). At the top of the organization a concept is formed. The next level develops strategies, the next functional programs, and the last one or two levels are responsible for implementation.

Most organizations have concentrated on and accomplished only numbers 1 and 3 (*job instructions* and *policy and procedure*), while paying little attention to numbers 2, 4, and 5. An organization that only gives orders about job instructions and organizational procedures and neglects to provide information about job performance or rationale will have a negative impact on its people. Such a downward orientation is conducive to an authoritarian atmosphere that will inhibit the effectiveness of upward and horizontal channels. An organization can greatly benefit itself by communicating to its people the rationale behind their job, by pointing out the relationship of the job to the goals of the organization, and by informing its employees about subsequent job performance.

Downward messages are often disseminated through many types of media. A few examples of written media are: pay incentives, posters, bulletin boards, periodicals, letters, handbooks, manuals, company newspapers, standard reports, annual reports, and memos. Examples of oral media are: speeches, verbal orders or instructions, meetings, discussions, closed-circuit television, public address systems, and telephones.

With respect to downward communication, Shannon and Weaver remind us that "Management should judiciously choose the subjects to be communicated, determine the characteristics of the intended audience and select a restricted number of channels to reach the minds of the audience."[11]

Upward Communication

The classical organization structurally provides for vertical communication flows; however, in most organizations downward communication has traditionally dominated. Authority has prevailed over the more participative styles associated with *upward* communication. As a result, upward communication has often been stifled, misused, and ignored.

The effectiveness of upward communication in organizations has been the subject of considerable reserarch. Representative of that body of information is a study

[11] Claude Shannon and Warren Weaver, *The Mathematical Theory of Communication*, University of Illinois, Urbana, 1963, p. 264.

conducted by Ralph Nichols.[12] Nichols asked managers and employees of twenty-four plants to rank the ten most important morale factors. While the managers ranked appreciation of work done, feeling a part of things, and sympathetic help on personnel problems as 8, 9, and 10 respectively, the workers ranked these same factors as 1, 2, and 3. These results do not speak very highly of upward communication. Yet upward communication, when it takes place, has the effect of improving employee morale and creating an organizational atmosphere that facilitates increased productivity. Plantz and Markover[13] tell us it reveals the receptivity of the company to downward communication, it encourages the submission of new ideas, it facilitates acceptance of decisions because subordinates feel a part of the decision-making process, and it provides feedback to the manager about the success of his or her downward communication. Communication activities used to facilitate upward communication include:

1 *The grievance procedure* that allows an employee to make an appeal beyond his immediate supervisor. The worker is protected against arbitrary action from his boss and upward communication is encouraged.

2 *Counseling sessions and exit interviews* are generally handled by the personnel department. For example, upward communication is encouraged at Richdales through a staff of professional counselors that conduct directive and nondirective counseling sessions and hold exit interviews for those who leave the organization.

3 *Attitude questionnaires and opinion surveys* are generally administered by the personnel department, research department, or organizational development. Much valuable information about problems as well as the general atmosphere of a system or subsystem can be gained from these forms of upward communication.

4 *The open-door policy* means literally that the supervisor's door is always open to subordinates. This continuous invitation for subordinates to come in and talk over their problems can be invaluable if handled properly.

5 *Coffee breaks and rap sessions* will go a long way in providing the supervisor with information as well as toward creating a good work environment. The problem is that most supervisors want to spend that time with their superiors and not with their subordinates. As a result, one of the best opportunities for upward communication is often lost.

For the most part, upward communication supplies two types of information: first, personnel information about attitudes, ideas, and performance; and second, technical feedback about goal accomplishments—vital information needed for controlling the organization. Personnel information is generally passed from the subordinate to the superior. It consists of information about:[14]

1 What the person has done
2 What those under him have done
3 What his peers have done
4 What his problems are

[12] Ralph G. Nichols, "Listening Is Good Business," *Personnel*, 38:4, Winter 1962.
[13] Earl Plantz and William Markover, "Upward Communication: A Project in Executive Development," *Personnel*, 28:304–318, 1952.
[14] Katz and Kahn, op. cit., p. 245.

5   What the problems of his department are
6   What he thinks needs to be done
7   What his perception of his job performance is
8   What organizational policy and practices need adjusting

The second type of upward information, feedback for control purposes, is necessary if the organization is to survive. As Scott tells us, "Decision centers utilize information feedback to appraise the results of the organization's performance and to make any adjustments to insure the accomplishment of the purposes of the organization."[15] The key to successful feedback, then, is the system's ability to provide the decision centers with accurate, timely information regarding the status of the monitored activity.

As information travels up through the organization, it is subject to a tremendous number of impeding and distorting forces. Three of those forces are *filtering, status,* and *overload.* Employees have a tendency to send upward those messages that make them look good while filtering or blocking those messages that make them look bad. On the other hand, managers have a tendency to resist accepting unfavorable news for as long as possible. This might possibly explain why so many managers are reactive rather than proactive. The messages regarding the impending problem are there, but the manager chooses not to deal with them. One other possibility exists. The manager might be suffering from message overload. Message overload is simply the reception of messages in such a quantity that the receiver is inundated and unable to respond. The messages are still sitting in the in-basket waiting to be read. In addition, Read[16] tells us that the more upward mobility an employee feels she has the less information she will share with her boss.

These only represent a few of the problems that can interfere with upward communication. The very nature of the hierarchical structure presents the biggest problem—for executives are paid to direct, coordinate, and control the people below them. They are viewed as, and view themselves as, the senders of messages and as a result are less in the habit of listening to their subordinates. Conversely, the subordinate is a receiver of messages and expects to listen to his boss rather than be listened to. As we mentioned earlier, the subordinate is not likely to give his boss information that will lead to decisions that adversely affect him. Not only do subordinates tell the boss what he wants to hear, but they also tell him what they want him to know.

Koehler and Huber[17] have identified five factors that influence upward communication effectiveness. Upward communication is likely to be:

1   Used by decision centers if it is positive rather than negative
2   Used by decision centers if it is timely
3   Used if it supports current policy
4   Effective if it goes directly to the decision center who will act on it
5   Effective when it has intuitive appeal to the decision center

[15] William G. Scott, *Organization Theory*, Irwin, Homewood, Ill., 1967, p. 168.
[16] William H. Read, "Upward Communication in Industrial Hierarchies," *Human Relations,* 40:3–15, 1962.
[17] J. W. Koehler and G. Huber, "Effects of Upward Communication on Managerial Decision-Making," International Communication Association, New Orleans, 1974.

In the final analysis, the success of upward communication rests with the manager. Davis provides a valuable insight for the manager interested in meeting the challenge of facilitating good upward communication when he says:

A manager often does not realize how great the upward communication barriers can be, especially for the blue-collar worker. His status and prestige at the plant are different from the workers'. He probably talks differently and dresses differently. He can freely call a worker to his desk or walk to his work station, but the worker is not equally free to call in his manager. The worker usually lacks ability to express himself as clearly as the manager, who is better trained and has more practice in communication skills. . . . The worker is further impeded because he is talking to a man with whose work and responsibilities he is not familiar. The result is that very little upward communication occurs unless management positively encourages it.[18]

Horizontal Communication

Horizontal communication is the lateral exchange of messages by peers. As early as 1916 Fayol proposed his classic *bridge* of horizontal communication. Classical organization theorists placed little emphasis on the communication process. Indeed, communication was implicit in their managerial chain of command and their hierarchical structure, but they never fully developed or integrated communication into organizational or managerial theory. Until Chester Barnard in 1938, Fayol was about the only one who gave a detailed analysis of communication and provided a solution.

If in Figure 3-2 the formal channels were strictly followed and if F wanted to communicate with P, he or she would have to go through EDCBA, LMNOP, and back again. In other words, F would have to go through twenty people to get a message to, and receive a message from, P.

However, Fayol's *gangplank* (see Figure 3-3) would "allow the two employees F and P to deal at one sitting, and in a few hours, with some question or other which via the scalar chain would pass through twenty transmissions, inconvenience many people, involve masses of paper, lose weeks or months to get to a conclusion less satisfactory

[18] Keith Davis, *Human Behavior at Work,* McGraw-Hill, New York, 1972, p. 218.

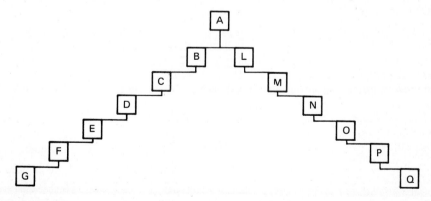

Figure 3-2 Fayol's chain of command.

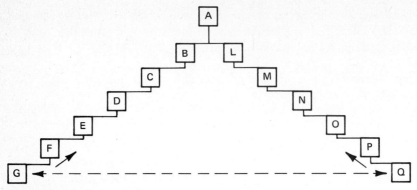

Figure 3-3 Fayol's gangplank.

generally than the one which could have been obtained via direct contact as between F and P."[19] Because the message goes through only one relay, its accuracy and speed are greatly increased. In our model, retention of the chain of command is maintained by the supervisor informing his superiors that he was contacting those below them (by memorandum) so as not to subvert their authority.

Horizontal communication is critical in most modern businesses. Many tasks cannot be so tightly structured that coordination among peers in carrying out jobs is ruled out. In addition to providing task coordination, horizontal communication also furnishes social-emotional support. The employee can more comfortably turn to a peer for social-emotional support than she can to someone above or below her. Understandably people in the same boat who share the same problems find it easier to relate. Horizontal communication can benefit the organization if the social-emotional support facilitates task coordination to achieve organizational goals. However, "if there are no problems of task coordination left to a group of peers, the content of their communication can take forms which are irrevelant to or destructive of organization functioning."[20] It is possible that horizontal communication may be entered into at the expense of vertical communication.

Goldhaber[21] has synthesized several research studies in identifying four purposes for entering into horizontal communication.

1 *Task coordination.* During a period of gas shortage, department managers in a chemical plant might meet biweekly to discuss how each department will contribute to cutting gas usage.

2 *Problem solution.* Again during a gas shortage, the foremen from a sheet metal plant may meet to determine the internal allocation of gas in order to maximize output while keeping as many people working as long as possible.

3 *Sharing information.* The research department might call a meeting with all other departments to disseminate new data. Shortly after developing a new training

[19]Henry Fayol, *General and Industrial Management*, trans. Constance Storrs, Pitman, London, 1949, p. 35.

[20]Katz and Kahn, op. cit., p. 244.

[21]Gerald M. Goldhaber, *Organizational Communication*, Brown, Dubuque, Iowa, 1974, p. 121.

curriculum, one of the authors had a meeting with all members of management to explain the new programs.

4 *Conflict resolution.* Members of one department may meet to resolve a conflict with other departments.

5 *Interpersonal rapport.* Like people everywhere, people who work in business and industry have a need to develop a basic interpersonal rapport with those with whom they interact. Your ability to develop this rapport may be the single most important factor of your success in business.

In spite of the importance of horizontal communication in today's organizations, we know relatively little about how it functions and how best to go about promoting its growth. We do know that as organizations grow in size, horizontal communication becomes increasingly important if production outputs, timing, and action plans are to be coordinated.

We have talked about the three channels of formal communication: downward, upward, and horizontal communication. When messages do not follow these channels, we call them *informal* messages.

INFORMAL COMMUNICATION NETWORKS

Messages that do not follow either scalar or functional lines are classified as *informal*. The informal system that is neither required nor controlled by management develops out of the social relationships that exist among and between employees. *Grapevine* is the term most commonly associated with the informal communication network in an organization. The history of the term grapevine can be traced back to the Civil War when telegraph lines were strung randomly from tree to tree like a grapevine. Messages sent over this network were often garbled and false information or rumor was attributed to having come from the grapevine.[22] A certain negative connotation has been carried over to modern times. The logic appears to go like this: The informal network is equated to the grapevine; the grapevine is equated to rumor; a rumor is bad. In most management circles, the next step in the sequence is to identify the informal network as being bad.

Rumors are only one type of information carried by the grapevine; however, rumor can adversely affect subsequent messages. Once a rumor is accepted, the receiver tends to distort future events to conform to the rumor. Perhaps it was this reasoning that led John Miner to say, "There is very little that can be done to utilize the grapevine purposefully as a means of goal attainment. As a result, rumors probably do at least as much to subvert organizational goals as to foster them. They may well stir up dissension."[23] The informal network can spread false rumors and destructive information or it can effectively supplement the formal downward, upward, and horizontal flow of messages.

In spite of the possible drawbacks, many organization theorists now recognize the

---

[22] Davis, op. cit., p. 261.
[23] John B. Miner, *Personnel Psychology*, Macmillan, New York, 1969, p. 259.

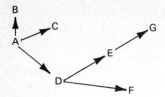

Figure 3-4 The grapevine cluster.

positive potential of the informal network. As Davis[24] has pointed out, under normal business conditions, between 75 percent and 95 percent of grapevine information is correct. In addition to being accurate, the grapevine is fast. Because it is functionally predicated upon social relationships, the grapevine tends to be much faster in disseminating information than the formal downward channels. As formal horizontal (lateral) channels are often inadequate in most organizations, the informal network is generally used to coordinate horizontal activities. It is also the informal network that most often provides information to superiors about the potential, performance, ideas, attitudes, and values of subordinates. Obviously, another advantage of the grapevine is that it can carry a great deal of information.

Since the informal organization structure will always coexist with the formal organization structure, there will always be an informal communication network in every formal organization. The grapevine is often viewed as a long chain along which messages pass from A to B to C to D, etc. This is a common misconception. Davis explains the grapevine flow (see Figure 3-4):

> A tells three or four others. . . . Only one or two of these receivers will then pass on the information, and they will usually tell more than one person. Then as the information becomes older and the proportion of those knowing it gets larger, it gradually dies out because those who receive it do not repeat it. This network is a "cluster chain" because each link in the chain tends to inform a cluster of other people instead of only one person.[25]

PERSONAL INSIGHT

Your authors are of the opinion that in order to succeed as a manager, you must be able to:

1 Find out what information is available in the organization and determine how to locate it. Be friendly and don't be afraid to ask questions. Most people enjoy the professor role. As quickly as possible familiarize yourself with as many people and as many departments as you can. Learn their purpose, function, and scope. Make friends with as many people as possible. Develop a smile and use it. It will serve you well.

[24]Keith Davis, "Care and Cultivation of the Corporate Grapevine," *Dun's Review,* **102:**46, July 1973.
[25]Keith Davis, "Management Communication and the Grapevine," *Harvard Business Review*, **31:**43–49, May 1953.

2 Determine where the information you need is stored. Is it located in only one place? Or is the information of such a nature that, say, both the advertising and research departments would have it cross-filed? Knowing where the information is stored is almost as important as knowing whether or not it exists.

3 Identify the various uses for the information. One way of doing this is to keep two sets of file cards. On one set you identify information that might be relevant to your present job. For example, as a department manager in the women's coat area, a list of customers who have purchased coats during the past few seasons could be valuable. The second set would be of a general nature. For example, a policeman might keep a list of the heads of all the various departments within the city administration.

4 Determine which information must be committed to memory for immediate recall and which you need only know where to go to option it.

SUMMARY

An organization requires structured communication channels that restrict and constrain random messages. This enables managers who make decisions predicated upon the information they receive and not on their personal experience of the problem to maximize their efforts at decision making, coordination, and control.

Message purpose is dictated by the functional subsystems of the organization. We have identified six organizational subsystems: production, maintenance, support, adaptation, managerial, and human. In most complex organizations, messages can be diffused via written and oral media. We spoke of memos, bulletin boards, etc. as written media and meetings, closed-circuit television, etc. as oral media.

When messages follow official paths derived from the organization's structure, they are flowing in accordance with formal communication networks. As a result, messages flow downward, upward, and across the organization. Downward communication refers to messages sent from superior to subordinate such as orders, commands, etc. Upward communication refers to messages sent from subordinates to supervisors for the purpose of inquiry, clarification, feedback, etc. Horizontal communication is the lateral exchange of messages among people on the same organizational level. These messages generally pertain to coordination, problem solving, conflict resolution, information sharing, and development of interpersonal rapport.

When messages deviate from traditional channels, they are called informal messages. The informal network is often referred to as the grapevine. The grapevine is viewed by some managers as being synonymous with rumor mill, but most recently organization theorists have recognized its value. The grapevine is accurate, fast, can be used to supplement horizontal and vertical channels, carries a lot of information, and disseminates information through clusters. The grapevine also provides managers with important feedback about employee potential, performance, ideas, attitudes, and values.

Chapter 4

Leadership and the Management of Human Resources

From the beginning of time, man has recognized that the difference between success and failure, whether in a business, a war, or a football game, can largely be attributed to leadership. Consequently, leadership has probably been researched, written about, and informally discussed as much as any other single topic. Yet, despite its recognized importance and all of the attention given to it, leadership still remains problematic. We know it exists, and we know it can have a tremendous influence on individual performance, but its specific dimensions and their interrelationships continue to elude us.

THE ROLE OF LEADERSHIP

Despite these difficulties the nature of a group's leadership clearly makes a difference to many aspects of its functioning. Early research conducted by Lippit and White[1] strongly advances the position that the same group of people will behave in decidedly different ways when functioning under leaders who behave differently. Fleishman found that the employees' leadership also is affected by the leadership of his or her

---

[1] Ronald Lippit and Ralph White, "Leadership Behavior and Member Reaction in Three Social Climates," in Dorwin Cartwright and Alvin Zandler (eds.), *Group Dynamics*, Harper & Row, New York, 1968, pp. 318–335.

superior.[2] Thus, a foreman working for a boss who expresses positive attitudes toward him is more likely to express positive attitudes toward his subordinates.

As we learned in Chapter 2, each individual in an organization is only one part of a complex system. He or she is also interdependent within that system. Thus, your effectiveness as a supervisor will not only be felt by the subsystem (department) you are functionally responsible for, but will also be indirectly felt by other subsystems within the organization.

Management will understandably be concerned about motivating employees because organizational goals such as productivity, profits, and growth are highly dependent upon the efforts of individual workers. As a manager, you should be able to foster cooperation of employees through leadership.

WHAT IS LEADERSHIP?

The meaning of leadership differs from person to person. One individual may be viewed as a leader because of the position she holds in an organization. Another because he is a "great man" and possesses inherent personal characteristics necessary for leadership. While a third may be termed leader because of that person's ability to direct the sum total of his or her behavior to successful relations with subordinates.

Apparently leadership has at least three major meanings: the nature of a position, the characteristic of a person, or a category of behavior. To be a police sergeant is to occupy a position of leadership. To be a police chief is to occupy a position of greater leadership. Yet, leadership is a relational concept, for without *followers* there can be no *leader*. Since leadership is operationally dependent upon the situation and upon those to be led, a concept of leadership that is conceived solely on an ability would be misleading. If the sergeant were made chief, would his leadership ability still be operative? And if he could not lead as chief, what would have happened to his leadership abilities?

Common to many definitions of leadership are the concepts of influence, accomplishment, and communication. According to Verderber, "Leadership is exerting influence; and leadership is getting things done."[3] Tannenbaum defines leadership as "inter-personal influence, exercised in a situation and directed, through the communication process, toward the attainment of a specified goal or goals."[4] He implies that "leadership always involves attempts on the part of a leader (influencer) to affect (influence) the behavior of a follower (influencee) or followers in a situation."[5] In the organization the superior influences the subordinate to cooperate in the completion of a desirable goal. French feels that "to a large extent leadership consists of a member's ability to influence others both directly and indirectly by virtue of his position in the power structure, including the structure of legitimate authority. Thus leadership may

---

[2]E. A. Fleishman, "Leadership Climate, Human Relations Training and Supervisor Behavior," *Personal Psychology*, 6:205–222, July 1953.
[3]Rudolph F. Verderber, *Communicate*, Wadsworth, Belmont, Calif., 1975, p. 138.
[4]R. Tannenbaum, L. Weschler, and F. Massarik, *Leadership and Organization*, McGraw-Hill, New York, 1961, p. 24.
[5]Ibid.

be distributed among many members or concentrated in a few."[6] Katz and Kahn consider "the essence of organizational leadership to be the influential increment over and above mechanical compliance with the routine directives of the organization."[7] They observe that all supervisors at any given position within the hierarchical structure of the organization are created equal with respect to the legitimate power of the office. However, they do not all remain equal. While one supervisor may have an amicable personality, another may have a much better understanding of people. Some will be much more knowledgeable about the technical aspects of the line function, while others will have a much better understanding of organizations and how they function.

Types of Leadership Power

The locus of these various strengths have been discussed by French and Raven.[8] They discuss five types of power: *legitimate power* (power derived from the supervisor's

[6]John R. French, "A Formal Theory of Social Power," in Dorwin Cartwright and Alvin Zandler (eds.), *Group Dynamics*, Harper & Row, New York, 1968, p. 565.
[7]David Katz and Robert Kahn, *The Social Psychology of Organizations*, Wiley, New York, 1966, p. 302.
[8]John R. French and Bertram Raven, "The Basis of Social Power," in Dorwin Cartwright and Alvin Zandler (eds.), *Group Dynamics*, Harper & Row, New York, 1968, pp. 259–269.

Figure 4-1 All supervisors at the same level in an organization start out on an equal footing.

assigned role or organizational position), *reward power* (power based on the supervisor's ability to reward), *coercive power* (power based on the supervisor's ability to punish), *referent power* (power based on the supervisor's ability to identify with, and liking for, his or her subordinates), and *expert power* (called *informational power* by Deutsch and Gerard, power derived from the supervisor's technical expertise in a specific area).

Under normal circumstances all supervisors at the same level in an organization start out on an equal footing. For example, Richdales provides equal legitimate power for all department managers and equal access to the use of organizationally sanctioned rewards and punishments. But Nadean, a department manager in fine jewelry, utilized her legitimate power effectively to increase the volume and profitability of her department, thus maximizing her influence in the company. Rick failed to use the organizational structure to accomplish his sales goals in the sporting goods department. In this example, Nadean earned the respect, admiration, and affection of her superior, peers, and subordinates (increasing her referent power) because she had *demonstrated* her ability to use legitimate power to motivate workers to achieve organizational goals.

Nadean's expertise in technical matters also provided increased acceptance of her suggestions and directives. Nadean knew all aspects of fine jewelry and what she didn't know she quickly learned. In addition she had a working knowledge of all systems and subsystems that impacted on her department. In short, she knew the organization and how it worked. If, for example, a shipment of 20 dozen bracelets had been delayed while being transferred from the downtown store to her department at the branch, Nadean would have known the fastest method of tracking and locating the goods.

Referent and expert power cannot be conferred by the organization and yet both play an integral part in getting organizational work done. To the extent that they develop within a group, expert and referent power represent additions to the power that may be assigned by an organization. They can quite literally provide an increase in the total amount of supervisory control over subordinates. Tannenbaum has shown this to be a persistent factor in increased organizational performance.[9] Moreover, expert and referent power can be used in place of other types of power. As substitutes for coercive power, expert and referent power are free of unintended and undesirable organizational consequences. The television technician who complies with his supervisor's wishes for fear of punishment may plan for the day when he can get back at his supervisor or at the station as well. Perhaps he subtly sabotages his supervisor by turning in poor inventory control counts or gets even with the station by airing the wrong commercial, costing the station thousands of dollars. On the other hand, the person who complies for rewards may actively seek ways of obtaining the reward without producing the necessary quality and quantity of work. The anxiety, fear, frustration, uncertainty, and doubt that are often by-products of coercion and reward power are often counterproductive for the organization.

Because expert and referent power are available to all members of an organization,

[9] A. S. Tannenbaum, "Control in Organizations," *Administrative Science Quarterly*, 7:236–257, September 1962.

they represent potent additions to organization effectiveness and control. They are more dependent on personal and group properties than on the formal structure of the organization. As a result, they can be effectively used by employees as well as by supervisors. The entire industrial humanist emphasis in organizational leadership may be approached as an attempt to promote referent power in addition to, and to some extent instead of, power based on rewards, coercion, and the mandate of organizational law.

Approaches

The theories of Argyris, Likert, and McGregor approach the function of leadership as one of modifying the organization to provide an opportunity for the employee to fulfill his or her own expectations while contributing to the attainment of organizational goals. Argyris[10] suggests that organizations will maximize goal attainment only when their supervisors (leaders) provide a means for employees to make contributions to the organization that are a product of the employees' need for self-expression and personal growth. Likert[11] believes that if a supervisor (leader) is to be effective, he or she must reflect behaviors that the employees perceive as supportive of their welfare. Because people have a tendency to more actively support policies and procedures they have helped to formulate, Likert encourages participative decision making and free upward communication. In this way, the supervisor will develop both group cohesiveness and concern for organizational goals. McGregor advanced two underlying beliefs about human nature that influence managers and their leadership; these are known as Theory X and Theory Y.[12] Theory X is based on the assumption that people have an inherent dislike of work and will avoid it whenever possible. Thus, the supervisor (leader) must direct and control with punishment if management is to get workers to put forth adequate effort toward the achievement of organizational goals. Theory Y is based on the assumption that the expenditure of physical and mental effort in work is as natural as it is in play or rest. According to this theory the capacity to exercise a relatively high degree of imagination, ingenuity, and creativity in the solution of organizational problems is also inherent in most people. Thus the supervisor (leader) need only arrange organizational conditions to facilitate the fulfillment of employee needs. If we closely examine the basic tenents of these theories, we will see that while the organization is by nature structured and controlled, it is the leader's primary task to direct and modify employees' behavior to conform to organizational expectations and goals.

THE NEED FOR LEADERSHIP

Why does a mature organization require leaders and leadership? The need for leadership in an organization stems from four principal sources:[13]

---

[10]Chris Argyris, *Integrating The Individual and The organization,* Wiley, New York, 1964.
[11]R. Likert, *The Human Organization,* McGraw-Hill, New York, 1960.
[12]Douglas McGregor, *The Human Side of Enterprise,* McGraw-Hill, New York, 1960, pp. 8–12.
[13]Katz and Kahn, op. cit., pp. 304–308.

1 Its basic imperfection as a formal abstract entity
2 The changing external environmental conditions that affect all organizations
3 Changing internal dynamics fostered by subsystems within the organization
4 The nature of the human being occupying organizational positions

Imperfection of the Organization

It becomes apparent that the dynamic interactive nature of the organization is not adequately reflected whenever the organization chart or the policies and procedures manual are compared to the real organization. But then this is common knowledge to most people. That's why a new employee, after being told the official version of his job and what policies he is expected to follow, will ask members of his work group what things are really like. He is seeking those unwritten but ever-present facts about organizational life that can often make the difference between just getting along and really enjoying your job. For example, when one of the authors was a new employee at the Connecticut Valley Candy Co. his boss told him to feel free to ask "anything, anytime." Rather quickly he learned that what the boss meant was "ask anything, anytime after I've had my morning coffee and time to catch up on my messages."

One of many possible examples of the ineffectiveness of the formal organizational design is following the letter of the organizational law.

Earl Brooks describes an episode which is a vivid example of such behavior. In the course of a study which he was doing of a railroad, he spent some time one afternoon observing and interviewing a man in a switching tower, who was separating and recombining trains of freight cars. The electrical controls and relays were so worn that they failed to slow the cars appropriately, and the violence with which they coupled led the researcher to inquire whether the cargo might not be seriously damaged. The switchman agreed that it might. "And shouldn't some of the equipment be replaced?" continued the researcher. The switchman agreed that it ought. "Then," said the researcher, "why don't you tell the regional office about it?"

The switchman's reply was oblique. "About how hot would you say it was in this tower?"

"It must be over 100," said the researcher, looking at the afternoon sun beating in the west bank of windows, "but what has that got to do with it?"

"I've been trying for six months to get a Venetian blind for that window," said the switchman. "They told me that my job was to switch trains, and they would make decisions about equipment. When they get around to that blind, I may get around to telling them about the relays in those braking controls."[14]

Changing External Environmental Condition

As we indicated in Chapter 2, by nature organizations are open systems. As such they affect, and are affected by, the environment in which they function. As the environment changes as it adjusts to new technologies, laws, values, etc., so must the organization change if it is to maintain its stable relationship with the environment. A natural

---

[14]David Katz and Robert Kahn, *The Social Psychology of Organizations*, Wiley, New York, 1966, pp. 304–305. Reprinted with permission of the publisher.

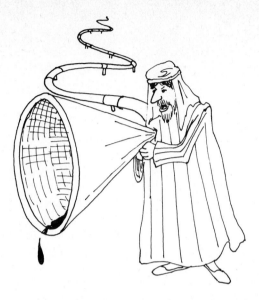

Figure 4-2 "No more oil for you!"

gas shortage and an extremely cold winter, for example, have made it necessary for many businesses that heat by gas to cut back on gas consumption or to convert to alternate energy sources. Those companies that adjusted to the gas shortage (environmental change) survived. Those that neglected to adjust and used more gas than they had been allocated were forced to close down. Thus, a relationship that is initially supportive of both organization and environment may become inefficient or unfeasible.

Changing Internal Dynamics

Within the organization, subsystems are constantly striving to do a better and more efficient job, thereby gaining influence and power. For that is what growth means in an organization. Some subsystems are successful and some are not. In some instances the growth of one subsystem (department) forces the growth of another subsystem. Take the case of the computer center of a local police department that expanded its LEADS (Law Enforcement Automated Data System). As a result of the computer center expansion, the physical department had to hire a new technician and two new maintenance men. On the other hand, subsystems often find themselves responding to antagonistic organizational goals. The personnel department is responsible for keeping the organization functioning at its maximum potential with a minimum work force, yet production departments tacitly resist manpower cutbacks. Changing internal dynamics are ever present. (See Figure 4-3.)

Human Beings in Organizations

A final reason why organizations once established do not continue unmodified lies in the nature of human membership in organizations. "Human membership in an organization is segmental in nature; it involves only a part of the person."[15] Other organiza-

[15] Ibid., p. 307.

Figure 4-3 Changing internal dynamics.

tions and activities make demands on the worker's time and energy, gratify his or her needs, and provide satisfaction and comfort. These other organizations, these other aspects of the individual's life, impact on him or her as a social being and as a working person. If such behavioral changes are disruptive to required modes of organizational behavior, adaptive change within the organization is required. If, for example, a TV cameraman comes to work emotionally distressed because his wife left him, someone must decide whether to allow him to work or not. If he is allowed to work, his impact on fellow workers must be gauged. If he is sent home, a suitable replacement must be located and paid.

In addition, people are constantly joining the organization and leaving it. Each person is unique and affects the work group differently. A supervisor with a humanistic background in social psychology may have a different approach to subordinates and production than his or her replacement who may be a supervisor with a systems engineering background. To some degree, every event of departure and replacement has an effect on the organization as well as on the people involved.

If there were not inherent imperfections in organizations, if external environmental conditions did not change, if internal conditions were static, and if human beings, with all their problems, were not a part of our organizations, then, perhaps, leadership would be unnecessary because once established our organizations would run by themselves. This condition will, in all probability, never exist, therefore leadership is necessary.

Figure 4-4 People are constantly joining and leaving the organization.

LEADERSHIP THEORIES

The Trait Theories

The *personality* or *trait* approach to leadership grew out of the assumption that leaders were born, not made. At least that's what the early Greeks and Romans believed when they first began philosophizing about leadership. This *great man* theory of leadership suggested that a person was either born with or without the traits necessary for leadership. The great man theory evolved into a more realistic trait approach that accepted the position that leadership traits are not completely inborn but could also be acquired through learning. The 1940s and 1950s saw a serious attempt to use personality tests to identify the human characteristics most likely to be associated with managerial success. Personality inventories, self-ratings, and checklists were widely used. The goal was to isolate the traits and then work out a test that would determine whether a person could or should be a leader. The results of this voluminous research were generally very disappointing, leading researchers to conclude that a trait approach to leadership was not going to provide a singular method for identifying or predicting leaders. Davis asserts that, "In spite of the disagreement regarding leadership traits and the measurement difficulties involved, there is a fairly uniform agreement that some traits are related to leadership."[16] Recognizing that there are no cause and effect relationships, Davis suggests that the following traits appear to impact on leadership:[17]

1 *Intelligence.* The leader generally possesses higher intelligence than the average intelligence of his followers; however, the intellectual ability of the leader cannot be exceedingly greater than that of the follower.

2 *Social maturity.* Leaders are emotionally stable, mature, and have a positive self-concept. They also tend to have a broader spectrum of interests and activities than the follower.

[16] Keith Davis, *Human Relations at Work*, McGraw-Hill, New York, 1967, p. 105.
[17] Keith Davis, *Human Behavior at Work*, McGraw-Hill, New York, 1977, pp. 103–104.

3 *Inner motivation (initiative).* Leaders have relatively intense motivational drives expressed as a desire to accept responsibilities or to accomplish.

4 *Human relations attitudes.* A leader recognizes the worth of his or her followers. The Ohio State leadership studies called it "initiating" and "consideration," while the Michigan studies referred to it as "employee orientation" rather than "production orientation."

Remember, the possession of one or more of these traits does not mean that you will be the leader of the group. But it is highly unlikely that you will be the leader if you do not exhibit these traits to a greater degree than others in the group.

The Situational Theories

More widely accepted today than the trait theories are the situational theories. The *situational* theories of leadership emphasize that leadership roles, skills, and behaviors are dependent upon the situation. According to Davis, "The leader and his group interact not in a vacuum, but at a particular time and place within a specific set of circumstances. This is their situation."[18] In a review of the literature Filley and House identified the following situational variables as those that affect leadership:

1 The previous history of the organization, the age of the previous incumbent in the leader's position, the age of the leader, and his or her previous experience
2 The community in which the organization operates
3 The particular work requirements of the group
4 The psychological climate of the group being led
5 The kind of job the leader holds
6 The size of the group led
7 The degree to which group-member cooperation is required
8 The cultural expectations of subordinates
9 Group-member personalities
10 The time required and allowed for decision making[19]

Unfortunately, most of the variables mentioned by Filley and House have not been validated by further research. An exception is the promising work being done by Fred E. Fiedler.

Fiedler's Contingency Model

Fiedler combined the trait and situational approaches in the development of his *contingency* model of leadership effectiveness.[20] The theory, which has been developed over the past 25 years, suggests that group or organization effectiveness depends on two interacting or contingent factors:

[18] Davis, *Human Relations at Work*, p. 109, op. cit., p. 109.
[19] Alan Filley and Robert House, *Managerial Process and Organizational Behavior*, Scott, Foresman, Glenview, Ill., 1969, p. 409.
[20] Fred E. Fiedler, Martin Chemers, and Linda Mahar, *Improving Leadership Effectiveness*, Wiley, New York, 1976.

1 The personality of the leaders that determine their leadership style.

2 The amount of control and influence that the situation provides the leaders over their group's behavior, the task, and the outcome. This factor is called *situational control*. Since Fiedler's interpretation of *leadership style* and *situational favorableness* are unique to his model, a description of each would appear to be in order.

Leader Personality Fiedler developed a unique operational method for measuring leadership style. It is referred to as the *Least Preferred Coworker* (LPC) scale. The score is obtained by first asking an individual to think of all coworkers he has ever known. Then he is asked to describe the person he least preferred as a coworker. The LPC score is the sum of the individual's responses to eighteen bipolar adjective scales such as the one shown in Figure 4-5.

The score may be high (8 × 18), it may be low (1 × 18), or it may tend to vary across the bipolar adjective scales. The directionality (high or low) of the score is important.

Relationship-motivated leaders The *human relations* or *lenient* style is associated with the leader who does not discern a great deal of difference between the most and least preferred coworkers. He or she gives a relatively favorable description (LPC score of 64 or above) of the least preferred coworker.

Task-motivated leaders The *task-directed* or *hard-nosed* style is associated with the leader who perceives a great difference between his or her most and least preferred coworker and gives a very unfavorable description (LPC score of 57 and below) of the least preferred coworker.[21]

Situational Control This is the variable that mediates the relationship between leadership style, as determined by the LPC score, and group or organizational performance. It has been defined as the amount of control or influence that the situation provides the leader over the group's behavior. Situational control is described by Fiedler in terms of three dimensions:

1 *The leader-member relationship* is the single most important element in situational control. It is the amount of loyalty, dependability, and support the leader receives.

2 The second most important dimension is *task structure*. This is the degree to which a given task is structured. For example, building a car would be a highly structured task whereas a school dance can be organized in a variety of ways.

3 The leader's *position power* is the third dimension. This was referred to earlier as legitimate power, the power the organization vests in your organizational position for the purpose of directing subordinates.

[21]Fred E. Fiedler, *A Theory of Leadership Effectiveness*, McGraw-Hill, New York, 1967, pp. 143–144.

Pleasant ___ ___ ___ ___ ___ ___ ___ ___ Unpleasant
          8   7   6   5   4   3   2   1

Figure 4-5 LPC Scale.

The leader has situational control if all three of these dimensions are high. If the leader is generally accepted by his or her followers, if the task is highly structured, and if extensive power and authority is formally assigned to the leader's organizational position, the situation is very favorable. If the opposite is true, the situation will be very unfavorable for the leader.

The contingency model predicts that under very favorable or very unfavorable situations the task-motivated or hard-nosed leader would be effective; however, it also indicates that the relationship-motivated or lenient leader would be most effective when the situation was only moderately favorable or unfavorable.

LEADERSHIP STYLES

In light of our previous discussion, it is apparent that leadership may be viewed in terms of different approaches the leader takes when dealing with his or her followers. White and Lippit[22] identify three basic styles: authoritarian, democratic, and laissez-faire. *Autocratic* and *democratic* styles are opposite kinds of leadership behavior and represent different views as to the nature of leadership behavior. Each represents an absolute and as such each falls at the opposite end of the leadership continuum (see Figure 4-6). All other styles of leadership (supervision) fall someplace between these polar ends. Pure autocratic or democratic leadership is rarely, if ever, found in most organizations; therefore, leadership styles will be approached in terms of their tendency toward autocratic or democratic.

Autocratic

Effective management of the organization's human resources rests on some basic assumptions concerning human nature. McGregor has pointed out that inherent in the traditional management approach (scientific management) was the assumption that workers behave in accordance with what he called Theory X (see Chapter 2, p. 41). This theory holds that people inherently dislike work and want to avoid responsibility; employees must therefore be closely directed and controlled if productivity is to be maximized. An autocratic supervisor gives orders and expects them to be carried out. He believes that the only way to get conscientious performance is to expect and secure discipline and immediate acceptance of all orders. The personal needs of his subordinates are secondary, if that. He believes that the employee is being paid to work and that is all he or she needs. This supervisor leaves little room for subordinates with self-actualization needs.

One police department for which one of the authors consulted provides a good example of the autocratic approach. Sergeant Smith had six police officers working on his shift. Smith believed that every man should pull his own weight and do his fair

[22]Ralph White and Ronald Lippit, *Autocracy and Democracy*, Harper & Row, New York, 1960, p. 4.

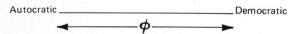

Autocratic _____ Democratic

Figure 4-6 Leadership continuum.

Figure 4-7 Theory X: The "carrot and stick" routine.

share. He expected all of his men to participate equally in every aspect of their work, i.e., vacant house checks, speeding citations, parking tickets, field interrogation of suspicious characters, preventive patrol (locating street hazards), investigation of property damage and/or personal injury accidents, etc. Patrolman Dixon didn't particularly like making vacant house checks and avoided them with a passion, much to the dismay of Sergeant Smith. Smith tried to beat Dixon into carrying his load by giving him the oldest patrol car, and by assigning him to the worst part of town. It didn't work. Next Smith tried to bribe Dixon by promising him soft duty posts. That didn't work either. Nothing worked. What Sergeant Smith didn't recognize was that Dixon disliked doing vacant house checks as much as Patrolman Bradley disliked writing speeding citations. Dixon had, for years, written more speeding citations than anyone else in the department and Bradley had always preferred vacant house checks to laying in wait for speeders. The solution was obvious, only Sergeant Smith couldn't see it, because his way was the right way. Why? Because he said so.

Democratic

Theory Y provides a more positive view of human nature (see Chapter 2, p. 42). In essence, it indicates that many people in organizations can exercise self-direction and self-control and can be made eager to accept new responsibilities. *Democratic* leadership is supportive of participative decision making and goal setting. The democratic supervisor endeavors whenever possible to share with her subordinates the decision making about work planning, assignment, and scheduling. When a decision must be made by the supervisor, she helps the work group clearly understand the basis for her decision. She is careful to develop participation, opinion giving, and decision

Figure 4-8 Theory Y: Partnership in decision making.

making, as well as a feeling of responsibility for the success of the work on the part of everyone. As people have a tendency to support decisions they have had a part in making, this is not that difficult to do. The democratic leader fully understands that although the entire work group may make a particular decision, she alone is responsible to the organization. The supervisor can delegate responsibility for decision making; she can never delegate accountability for the decision.

Alice Cohen, the department manager of junior dresses, utilizes the democratic approach. Alice feels that her sales clerks are responsible, capable people and she trusts their judgment. It is her practice to allow her salespeople to schedule their own hours. Alice does establish general parameters within which her people must operate. They are (1) the department must be covered at all times, (2) the amount of coverage must be consistent with customer traffic, and (3) everyone must take their lunch and coffee breaks. The sales staff work out their own schedule. They decide who's off and when, etc. Alice believes that because her people are involved in running the department, they are more productive and enforce standards much more enthusiastically.

Laissez-faire

The *laissez-faire* leader plays a completely passive role, leaving complete freedom for individuals or groups to decide activities and procedures. The leader, if he or she can be called that, supplies information, helps when asked, and is friendly, but otherwise plays no active part in the work group. Laissez-faire is essentially nonleadership. If this approach is to work, success is dependent upon the quality of the subordinate group. Under ordinary circumstances the laissez-faire style would be of questionable value.

When the autocratic and democratic styles are compared for productivity, Lippit and White noted that the autocratic groups were higher in quantity, while the democratic groups were higher in quality. Autocracy appears to create aggression and discontent, even though the discontent may not appear on the surface. There is more dependency and less individuality in autocracy. Shaw has observed that it is easier to

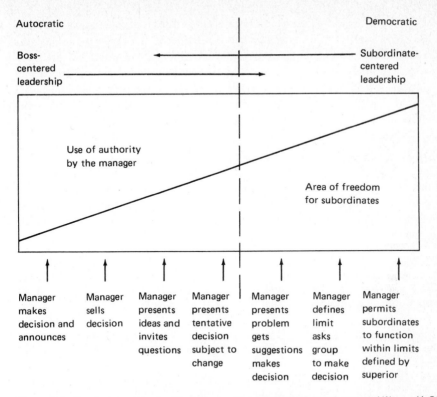

Figure 4-9 Continuum of leadership patterns. (From Robert Tannenbaum and Warren H. Schmidt, "How to Choose a Leadership Pattern, *Harvard Business Review,* May–June 1973, Copyright © 1973 by the President and Fellows of Harvard College; all rights reserved.)

be a good autocratic leader than a good democratic leader. He suggests that "it is easy to issue orders, but difficult to utilize effectively the abilities of the group members. If a leader doubts his ability to be an effective democratic leader, then he probably is well advised to play the autocratic role."[23]

LEADERSHIP PATTERNS

If we extend the leadership continuum in Figure 4-6, we can observe the range of possible leadership styles available to a manager. Each style is related to the degree of authority used by the supervisor and to the amount of freedom the subordinates enjoy in decision making. The continuum in Figure 4-9 shows an absolute autocratic leader at the extreme left-hand side of the range. Here the emphasis is on the manager—on what he is interested in, how he sees the problem, and on how he feels about it. As we move from the left to the right, autocratic behavior decreases and democratic behavior increases. The center of the range is the point at which autocratic tendencies change to democratic tendencies. The principal difference between the left and right side of the mid-point is that on the left side the leader presents *his decision* for consideration, while at the right he presents *the problem* for consideration. This repre-

[23] Marvin Shaw, *Group Dynamics*, McGraw-Hill, New York, 1971, p. 274.

sents the point of transformation from a leader-centered form of supervision to a work group-centered form. At the extreme right-hand side of the range is the absolute democratic leader. Here the emphasis is on the subordinates—on what they are interested in, on how they see the problem, and on how they feel about it. Thus, as we move from left to right on the continuum in Figure 4-9, the leadership pattern changes from the traditional bureaucratic model inherent to the classical school to the democratic model advanced in the industrial humanism school.

VARIABLES AFFECTING LEADERSHIP STYLE

Up to this point we have looked at the available range of leadership styles most commonly found in business and industry. Now let's look at three major forces advanced by Tannenbaum and Schmidt[24] that will determine the appropriateness and desirability of the style to be selected.

Forces in the Manager

A manager's personality and cultural background will determine how he views his leadership problems. Important internal forces that will affect him are:

1 His value system—his beliefs about the freedom of others to determine their own fate; the relative importance he attaches to organization efficiency, personal growth of subordinates, and company profits.[25]

2 His confidence in his subordinates—his confidence in their loyalty, technical knowledge, competence, emotional stability, i.e., the degree of trust he has in them.

3 His own leadership inclination—some supervisors feel more comfortable as highly directive leaders, others prefer a team role.

4 His feeling of security in an uncertain situation—largely determined by his tolerance of ambiguity. If the manager relinquishes control over the decision-making process, he reduces the predictability of the outcome and ambiguity may increase proportionally to decreased predictability.

Forces in the Subordinate

The manager will want to consider a number of forces affecting her subordinates' behavior prior to determining how to lead them. Her subordinates are influenced by personality variables and cultural background in much the same manner she is (see above).

In addition, they carry with them expectations with regard to the roles of leader and follower.

1 The subordinate's personality—he has his own set of values, his own cultural background, and his own distinct personality. Some personality types function well

---

[24] Robert Tannenbaum and Warren Schmidt, "How to Choose a Leadership Pattern," *Harvard Business Review,* 51(3):162–172, May–June 1973.

[25] Chris Argyris, "Top Management Dilemma: Company Needs vs. Individual Development," *Personnel,* 34:123–124, September 1955.

under autocratic leaders, others do not. Some have a high tolerance for ambiguity, others do not. Some have the ability to solve complex problems, others do not. Different subordinate behaviors call for different leadership styles.

2 The subordinate's expectations—all employees have expectations about their supervisors and the company that employs them. Expectations will differ among subordinates, but generally they deal with: treatment, pay, fringe benefits, working conditions, attitude, etc. Different subordinate expectations call for different leadership styles.

Forces in the Situation

Critical environmental pressures that affect the manager are often ignored or deemphasized. They are:

1 The type of organization—the values, traditions, and managerial philosophy of the organization. The newcomer quickly learns which behaviors are approved of and that if he deviates radically from them he is likely to create problems for himself. The fact that his superiors have a preconceived notion of what the good executive should be will create pressure pushing the manager toward that end of the behavior range (autocratic $\leftrightarrow$ democratic) which is consistent with their notion. In addition, factors such as the size of the work unit, their geographic distribution, and the degree of inter/ intra organizational security may limit the manager's ability to function in a flexible manner.

2 The effectiveness of the group—before turning the decision-making process over to a work group, the supervisor should assess the employees' ability to function as a unit. Relevant factors to be considered are: the degree of confidence that the members have in their own ability to solve problems as a group, their past success in solving problems, cohesiveness, mutual acceptance, and commonality of purpose.

3 The problem itself, and 4 the pressure of time—these two variables have been combined because of their interdependent nature. Problems are always confronted in terms of the time constraints impacting on them. Time is often a predominant variable in determining what supervisory style is appropriate for handling a specific problem. The more the supervisor feels the need for an immediate decision, the more likely he is to make the decision himself, thus eliminating the opportunity for participative decision making.

If leadership is to be successful, it must be flexible enough to accommodate forces in the supervisor, the subordinate, and the situation. While predictability in supervisory behavior is important so expectations can be consistently responded to and normalcy established, it must also be flexible enough to allow for necessary shifts in leadership style.

COMMUNICATION AND LEADERSHIP

"The quality of communication skills possessed by managers or administrators and organized personnel determines the degree of achievement motivation that can be generated for desired organizational behavior."[26] The principal responsibility of

[26] A. Rice, *Learning for Leadership*, Tavistock, London, 1965, p. 141.

management (leadership) may be viewed as the coordination and control of relations between the organization and its internal environment in order to optimize
organizational goal achievement.

Just how a manager will communicate within the organization will depend largely
upon the leadership style he or she is employing at any given point in time. The leadership style and corresponding communication pattern is extremely important because,
according to Marlick and Van Ness, "to a considerable extent the holders of power in
an organization hold their power because they are able to get their definition of the
situation accepted by others."[27] Communication serves two main purposes for the
organizational leader:

1 It provides a vehicle through which he can implement his plan of action.
2 It provides a means by which members of the organization can be motivated
to execute the plans.[28]

It is important that the supervisor be sensitive to the needs and wants of the employees, demonstrate a concern for their welfare as well as production, and impart
understanding of the reason for work and the value to be derived by the employee.[29]

Redding has drawn a number of conclusions regarding good communication and
effective leadership:

1 The better supervisors tend to be more communication-minded; e.g., they enjoy
talking in meetings; are able to explain instructions and policies; enjoy conversing with
subordinates.
2 The better supervisors tend to be willing, empathic listeners; they respond
understandingly to so-called silly questions from employees; they are approachable;
they will listen to suggestions and complaints with an attitude of fair consideration
and willingness to take appropriate action.
3 The better supervisors tend to ask or persuade in preference to telling or de-
manding.
4 The better supervisors tend to be sensitive to the feelings and ego-defense needs
of their subordinates, e.g., they are careful to reprimand in private rather than in
public.
5 The better supervisors tend to be more open in passing along information; they
are in favor of giving advance notice of impending changes and explaining the reasons
behind policies and regulations.[30]

What follows is a laundry list of dos and don'ts that have direct bearing on you as a
leader communicating in an organization:

[27]S. Marlick and E. Van Ness, *Concepts and Issues in Administrative Behavior*, Prentice-Hall,
Englewood Cliffs, N.J., 1962, p. 112.
[28]E. Flippo, *Management: A Behavioral Approach*, Allyn and Bacon, Boston, 1970, p. 385.
[29]See C. R. Walker and R. H. Guest, *The War on the Assembly Line*, Harvard, Cambridge, Mass.,
1952, p. 178 and E. Flippo, op. cit., p. 386.
[30]W. Charles Redding, *Communication Within the Organization*, Industrial Communications
Council, New York, 1972, p. 443.

1 Do make yourself available for frank, unhurried discussions of employee problems or complaints.

2 Don't attempt such discussions between phone calls or on the run.

3 Say "no" tactfully and always explain why.

4 Don't belittle or criticize an employee in front of others and never in front of fellow employees.

5 Do consider timing for corrective counseling. An evening criticism, for example, is exaggerated by darkness and day-end fatigue. A Friday counseling session destroys the weekend. An employee will accept criticism with less resistance and hostility if it is (a) prefaced with a sincere compliment for something the associate did well; (b) if you show the other person how he or she can do it better; (c) if you limit the criticism to one subject at a time, rather than a barrage of fault-finding that covers many problems; (d) prior to the counseling session if you make notes of what you want corrected and ways in which to correct it, it will help focus the session and contribute to constructive improvement.

6 Don't play favorites even though they may be your most productive employees. You can reward the best employee through the annual wage review system and with recommendations for promotions.

7 Don't show up or put down an employee by doing a particular job better or faster than the employee. You may indeed hit the home run and lose the ball game.

8 Do be sensitive to little things. The death of Mrs. Picozzi's pet cat may not generate a great deal of concern on your part, but it could seriously affect her productivity for a number of days. Remember the employees' birthdays and their anniversaries with the company.

9 Do give praise when appropriate. *This could well be your most effective management tool.*

10 Try to spend 50 percent of your time as a manager listening. Ask for and listen to employees' ideas and opinions.

11 Do delegate as much as possible. The key to participatory management is the delegation of responsibility and authority. An employee's sense of self-worth increases proportionately to the trust you place in him or her.

12 Do review the performance of your employees on a regular basis. They want and deserve the feedback.

13 Only make promises that you can keep.

14 Don't take yourself too seriously.

LEADERSHIP IN MEETINGS AND CONFERENCES

Today the average supervisor spends as much as 40 percent of his or her work week in meetings and conferences. As the concept of participative management gains wider acceptance, the use of group discussion will become more widespread in organizations. Some large organizations such as Richdales have instituted training courses in *conference leadership*. Because of the dynamic, fast-paced nature of retailing, quality decisions about trending merchandise, trafficking of goods, advertising, etc. have to be made under tremendous time pressures; therefore, effective group meetings are an essential part of the business. Understanding group leadership is becoming increasingly important to the businessperson.

Types of Groups

The various types of groups will be discussed in Chapter 8. From the standpoint of leadership, we can identify two types: directive and nondirective. These types are similar to the autocratic-democratic leadership styles illustrated in Figure 4-6.

The *leader-based* or *directive* approach is autocratic in nature and utilizes content control and a tight adherence to procedure. The leader *runs* the meeting. He or she exercises absolute control over the participants, the subject matter, and the outcome of the meeting. Sattler and Miller have identified twelve characteristics common to authoritarian leaders. They are:

Procedural control
1 He (or she) gives many orders and directives about how the conference is to be conducted.
2 He specializes in questions directed to specific persons such as "Jones, give us your report." He uses open questions that any person in the group may answer much less frequently.
3 He interrupts conferees very often.
4 He keeps the group in a strait jacket. Conferees are not permitted to initiate conversation on related phases of the problem unless the transition to the new phase happens to suit the authoritarian leader's purpose.
5 He lavishes praise upon those who are especially obedient.
6 He sometimes deliberately encourages irrelevant discussion prior to announcing a particular decision.

Content control
7 He arbitrarily decides what problems are to be discussed, including the exact problem statement.
8 He uses many questions that are slanted in order to give conferees a tip regarding the right answers.
9 He is quite willing to draw unfair inferences from the data others have given.
10 He approves and disapproves the views given by group members with a "You are right" and "You are wrong."
11 He occasionally attempts to prove his beliefs by saying that a high authority believes as he does. In doing this, he is likely to talk in paragraphs while others are required to present their remarks in a few short sentences.
12 He makes many forceful summaries with little or no effort to discover whether the group as a whole concurs.[31]

The *group-based* or *nondirective* approach is democratic in nature and, although there may be procedural structuring, there is limited control exercised. The leadership function is to facilitate the group's discussion, integrate contributions made by the group, and help the group arrive at a mutually agreed upon decision. There are six characteristics common to the democratic leader. They are:

1 He (or she) is interested in having all participants show initiative.
2 He realizes that conference discussions should be understood as group achievements.

[31]William Sattler and N. Edd Miller, *Discussion and Conference*, Prentice-Hall, Englewood Cliffs, N.J., 1954, p. 141. Reprinted with permission of the publisher.

3 He believes that intragroup communications are important.

4 He is interested in having participants satisfy personal needs.

5 He is informal and friendly in his manner.

6 He shows that he has confidence that the group members can solve the problem under consideration.[32]

LEADERSHIP RESPONSIBILITIES AND FUNCTIONS

As a leader of a meeting or a conference, you have three basic responsibilities: to guide, stimulate, and control.

Guiding. You guide by organizing an agenda, by introducing the topic, and by directing the flow of the discussion.

After the leader has studied the problem carefully, he should prepare an agenda or leader's outline that he can refer to during the discussion. The agenda is simply a sketch of those things that need to be accomplished. If the purpose of the meeting is to accomplish a single task, the agenda should incorporate a procedure for handling the task in a logical manner. For instance, you are a police instructor at the police academy and your group is responsible for planning a training program for new police officers. Granted the general knowledge you have may assure the generation of some ideas on the part of the group members, but think of how much more productive they would be with an agenda:

> Goal: Selection of a training program
>> What have we done in the past?
>> Which programs seemed to produce better, more alert officers?
>> What state requirements have to be included in a basic training program?
>> Suggestions for the training program:
>>> Can our personnel handle it?
>>> Can we afford it?
>>> Does it meet our needs?
>> Selection

As you can see, the agenda does not dictate what will be done, rather it suggests the kinds of questions that need to be thought about if the group is to find the best solution.

If you are dealing with an ongoing group that meets regularly to conduct organizational business, a more formal agenda is necessary:

> Calling the meeting to order
> Reading of the minutes
> Reports of officers and committees
> Old business
> New business
> Announcements
> Adjournment

A carefully planned agenda will assist the leader in conducting an orderly meeting. The agenda should be in the hands of the group several days prior to the meeting. This

[32] Ibid., pp. 142–149.

gives the group an opportunity to think about the task beforehand and to prepare if they so desire. Keep in mind that people have a greater feeling of commitment to decisions in which they have a part. The results of not planning an agenda are usually participant frustration, aimless wandering, and general dissatisfaction.

It is important that the leader properly introduce the topic. At the beginning of the group's existence, there will probably be varying degrees of commitment to the task as well as to the group. The good leader will start the group out by aligning expectations, establishing the mission, identifying time parameters, and discussing the responsibilities of each group member.

The greatest challenge that any group leader has is directing the flow of the discussion. In order to do this the leader must first keep the interaction balanced. He or she must accept the responsibility of determining who talks and of facilitating the flow of interaction. The quality of the discussion will be directly affected by the nature of the interaction. The leader must make certain that all have the opportunity to participate by inviting silent members to join in, and by raising appropriate and clear questions. Poor interaction often leads to rigid, formal, and awkward discussions. If three out of twelve people dominate the conversation, in all probability the conclusions will not represent group thinking. Second, the leader must keep the discussion on the topic. When the agenda requires the leader to explain, instruct, or inform, he or she should plan for this even to the point of making a short speech. There is nothing wrong with this as long as information-giving is the goal and purpose. Remember, all key ideas must be discussed without straying too far from the subject. (Some tangents can be productive so don't hold too tight a rein.)

Stimulating. You stimulate by creating an atmosphere in which others will feel they want to participate. The leader is in charge of such physical matters as room size, seating, heating, lighting, and ventilation. The room should be sufficiently large enough to comfortably accommodate the group, yet not so large as to swallow them up. Seating arrangements should be conducive to free interaction. Often seating is either too formal or too informal to produce the best discussion. The room should have adequate lighting and be properly ventilated. We've witnessed meetings when the group members have actually gone to sleep because the room was too warm and poorly ventilated. Sound familiar?

Controlling. A leader must maintain control regardless of his or her personal style. You control the meeting by seeing to it that the purpose of the meeting is accomplished. To do this, you may have to exercise your authority. Group members often need to feel that someone is in charge. If the group has established formal rules for its governance, make sure they are followed. If Tom starts to monopolize the discussion, it is up to you to control him. If Jane and Mary are carrying on a distracting side conversation, stop them. And as you do all these things with tact and finesse, you must be careful not to dominate the discussion.

SUMMARY

In describing organizations, perhaps no word appears in the literature as often as leadership. It is assigned a variety of meanings and is often discussed as an attribute of personality, as a characteristic of a position, or sometimes as an attribute of behavior. The latter seems to us to be the most fruitful approach.

The essence of leadership can be found in its influential capacity. We have identified five types of power: legitimate power (power derived from the supervisor's assigned role or organizational position), reward power (power based on the supervisor's ability to reward), coercive power (power based on the supervisor's ability to punish), referent power (power based on the supervisor's ability to identify with, and liking for, his or her subordinates), and expert power (power derived from the supervisor's technical expertise in a specific content area).

Development of leadership theory for management began with the first identification of the trait approach; however, the trait approach proved to be much too simplistic. The approach offered by Fred E. Fiedler proved to be much more useful. Fiedler's contingency model incorporates the leader and the situation. The favorableness of the situation dictates which leadership style will be most effective. Perhaps the most comprehensive approach would be to recognize the leader, the situation, and the group being led. These three variables can be integrated to produce a correct leadership match. Thus, there are a variety of leadership patterns ranging from pure authoritarian to pure democratic which are available to the sensitive and versatile leader. Finally, we concluded this chapter with a discussion of leadership in meetings and conferences.

Part Three

Formats for Communicating Within the Organization

Peter Drucker, the economist and perhaps the single most widely recognized expert in managerial consulting, wrote that, "Colleges teach the one thing that is perhaps most valuable for the future employee to know. But very few students bother to learn it. This one basic skill is the ability to organize and express ideas in writing and speaking."[1] Drucker is speaking of your ability to communicate in a variety of situations. As our organizations become increasingly complex, the need for you to be able to communicate from a multidimensional approach becomes correspondingly greater (see Chapter 1, p. 14). In the following five chapters we have attempted to encapsulate those communication settings most commonly encountered by the manager. We begin in Chapter 5 with a consideration of interpersonal relationships and their effect on individuals and the organization. Chapter 6 focuses on nonverbal communication and its application in a multiplicity of settings. Chapter 7 examines the interview and the interviewing process while Chapter 8 discusses the dynamics of groups at work. We conclude in Chapter 9 with the vital skills and strategies necessary to be a successful public speaker.

After reading this part of the book, the reader should be able to:

[1]Peter Drucker, "How to Be an Employee," *Fortune,* 50:126, May 1952.

1 Identify the five axioms of interpersonal communication

2 Discuss trust and the three types of feedback associated with interpersonal communication

3 Discuss the functions of nonverbal communication

4 Identify and discuss the implications of the three basic principles that summarize the use of personal space in organizations

5 List practical guidelines that can be used in planning and conducting an employment interview

6 List alternative ways in which the interviewer can guide and direct the interaction

7 Identify those variables affecting group anatomy

8 Analyze the interviewing variables affecting group interaction

9 Demonstrate effective research techniques

10 Prepare and present a message to an audience in an effective manner

Chapter 5

Interpersonal Interactions

One of the authors recently worked with an organization funded primarily through federal grants. The institute is well known for its work in the development of new educational tools and processes and it seems to have an unending supply of funds with which to carry on this work. Despite the success of some of its end-products, employees seem frustrated and angry most of the time. One source of frustration is a group of about fifteen women within the organization all of whom have been with the institute for a number of years and who have been passed by for promotion in favor of men they see as less qualified than themselves. Interpersonal relationships between these women and many of the top-level executives are deteriorating. Another source of difficulty cuts across sex roles and instead divides the group into scientists and humanists. This division is expressed in jealousy, misunderstandings, and mistrust. This organization often acts successfully as a consultant body to other institutes on collaborative processes and yet can't solve its own interpersonal dynamics.

For years the classical theory of organizations held that the "organization man" was motivated by money alone. With the advent of the human relations school, focus began to shift to interpersonal concerns as motivational factors. Only when the industrial humanism school of thought became popular were interpersonal relations viewed as a dynamic motivator for organizational as well as individual success. Yet, we are often still beset with the kinds of difficulties experienced by the earlier organizations. These difficulties not only remain on the job, but also permeate our everyday lives.

The bottom line is this: increasing your effectiveness at analyzing and coping with the dynamics of interpersonal communication in the organizational setting will also improve your ability to relate to persons in your home and social environments as well.

The intent of the present chapter is to discuss the effect of several interpersonal communication variables on the success or failure of persons to relate to one another in a meaningful way. These various factors include: perception of others, interpersonal needs, self-concept and self-disclosure, trust building, verbal barriers, feedback, active listening, conflict management, and the helping process.

DEFINITION

When we focus on interpersonal communication within the organization we are not concerned with groups of three or more people nor are we interested in the more public setting of one person communicating to a large number of other people. We are concerned with *two people who interact face-to-face for any length of time who assume the roles of sender and receiver of messages simultaneously*. Compared to a small group the *"dyadic nature of interpersonal relationships provides each participant with more involvement, more satisfaction, and more participation."*[1] It is also different from *intra*personal communication or communication with oneself.

Interpersonal relationships in the organization may take two forms: organizational or personal. An *organizational* interpersonal relationship is formed due to a structural characteristic of the organization. For example, two women are assigned to work on some particular project for the organization. Because the organizational structure has forced them to spend time together on some mutual task, they are participating in a dyadic relationship. This relationship may remain mostly task-oriented or may move outside that immediate task concern and become a personal relationship. The relationship develops because two people choose to spend time with each other due to mutual emotional needs.

Often interpersonal relationships form because individuals simply have more opportunities to interact with some individuals than with others within the organizational setting. The research on *proxemics* (the distance we place between ourselves and others) provides a strong indication that we develop our friendships based on which individuals happen to share our same space. In the organization, persons are more likely to develop relationships with those with whom they are in constant contact than those with whom they have little contact. One interesting example of this has been found in the hospital setting. In one particular study middle-management persons (in this case nurses) had more frequent contact with their immediate superiors (in this study nursing supervisors) and immediate subordinates (nursing assistants) than with their own peers (other nurses).[2] This was due primarily to the fact that

---

[1]William W. Wilmot, *Dyadic Communication: A Transactional Perspective*, Addison-Wesley, Reading, Mass., 1975, p. 18.

[2]Daniel N. Braunstein, "Interpersonal Behavior in a Changing Organization," *Journal of Applied Psychology*, **54**(2):184–191, April 1970.

these persons had more opportunities during a regular work day to be in each other's presence. This study also lends support to the theory that there is a positive correlation between agreement with organizational goals and the extent of a member's interaction with others in the organization. In other words, the more a person supports and accepts changes or goals expressed by the organization, the more that person will be likely to interact and form relationships with others in the organization.

AXIOMS

The now classic work of Watzlawick, Beavin, and Jackson[3] identified some *axioms* of communication that apply most appropriately to interpersonal communication in the organizational setting.

1. It is impossible not to communicate. There is no such thing as nonbehavior. We cannot say that communication only takes place when it is intentional, conscious, successful, or when mutual understanding occurs. Consequently, when the manager makes a comment more to himself but which is heard by others, he has communicated that message whether he intended to or not. Chapter 6 emphasizes the importance of nonverbal cues to the interpretation of our messages even when we are unaware of these cues ourselves.

2. Communication not only conveys information but at the same time imposes behavior. The *content* of the message conveys information. It may be about anything that is capable of being communicated. The second level of communication is sometimes referred to as the *command* aspect or the *relationship* level of communication. This refers to what sort of a message it is and ultimately defines the relationship

[3] Paul Watzlawick, Janet Beavin and Don D. Jackson, *Pragmatics of Human Communication,* Norton, New York, 1967, pp. 48–54.

I'll show this guy—there's no way I'm going to communicate anything to him.

Figure 5-1 Even when we don't communicate, we are communicating.

between the two individuals. Here the person is saying, "This is how I see myself" or "This is how I see you in our relationship." Information about the communication process itself or about the relationship is referred to as *metacommunication*. For example, in one company where two individuals were working together on a joint project, one individual made it clear he saw their relationship as unequal while talking about a content area. Jim told his coworker Bob that they needed to finish this project by the end of the week. The content of this message seemed simple enough; however its timing and presentation also made a clear statement about their relationship. Jim's stern tone of voice, frowning expression, and the fact that *he* had chosen the date for completion made it clear that, as far as he was concerned, he was the dominant person in this relationship and would make most decisions by himself. He was communicating on two levels: one dealt with the subject matter and the other established some rules for their relationship.

3. Communication is "punctuated" into a sequence of events. Individuals will punctuate a conversation much as we use punctuation in written communication so that it will appear that one or the other has initiative, dominance, or dependency. Punctuation in oral communication may take the form of vocal pauses, head nods, and similar nonverbal cues as well as verbal statements indicating who began the conversation. Labor and management may get into a disagreement as to *why* they are disagreeing: management says it's because labor would not negotiate when their contract ran out and thus they had nothing to negotiate, while labor claims that the reason they are now striking is because management would not negotiate. The way in which they punctuate this disagreement may imply who is at fault.

4. There are two types of communicating: digital and analogic. Digital refers to the use of language to communicate messages and *analogic* is all nonverbal communication: posture, gesture, facial expressions, voice inflection, and distances. Chapter 6 provides a detailed account of analogic communication.

5. Relationships can be symmetrical or complementary. If the relationship is *symmetrical* then individuals tend to mirror each other's behavior. Equality is maintained in terms of their behavior. In a *complementary* relationship one person's behavior complements that of the other. Thus this second type of relationship is based on a maximization of differences between the two people. Here one plays the "one up position" and the other plays the "one down position." In most relationships the individuals shift in and out of these roles at various times.

All five of these axioms provide a base for understanding the transactional nature of the interpersonal relationship. They lead to a consideration of one of the primary variables influencing the outcome of any interaction: our perception of the other person.

PERCEPTION

How we view the other person influences to a great extent how we will interact with him or her. Each of us will perceive the same person in a different way based on our own insights, self-knowledge, and previous experiences with this person. Consequently, your idea of a trusted person may be someone else's idea of someone who is dishonest and sneaky.

	Police chief:	**Switchboard operator:**
direct perspective →	"I like the new equipment."	"I don't like the new equipment."
metaperspective →	"I think the operator likes it too."	"I think the chief likes it."
meta-metaperspective →	"I think she thinks I like it."	"I think he thinks I like it."

Figure 5-2 The influence of personal perspectives on interpersonal communication.

Laing, Phillipson, and Lee[4] attempt to explain this phenomenon with their *interpersonal perception method*. This approach suggests that each individual has three perspectives that can be analyzed: *a direct perspective* (person A's view of object X), *metaperspective* (person A's view of person B's view of object X), and *meta-metaperspective* (person A's view of person B's view of person A's view of object X). Obviously there are many chances for misunderstandings to occur. For example, the Oakwood police chief thinks that the new telephone equipment that has recently been installed at the station will be a great assistance in improving communication between the main office and patrol cars. He also thinks that the switchboard operator is pleased with the addition as it will speed up her job as well. He assumes that she thinks he is pleased with the new equipment. The operator, on the other hand, is not pleased with the new equipment since she doesn't know how to run it, was given little instruction when it was installed, and must constantly refer to the service manual. She accurately perceives the chief's pleased feelings and is hesitant to complain. She knows that he is unaware of her true feelings. In this situation, one person (the switchboard operator) is *accurately* perceiving the other individual at both the metaperspective (her view of how the chief feels about the equipment) and meta-metaperspective (her view of how the chief thinks she feels about it) levels. The problem exists with the chief who has *inaccurately* perceived the operator at the metaperspective level (his view of how she feels about the new equipment). As long as the police chief operates and behaves toward the operator under this misunderstanding, the more difficult her job will become and the more tense the relationship between them will be. Figure 5-2 visually identifies these levels.

There are three additional factors that contribute to our inaccuracies in perceiving others: imposition of structure, halo effects, and leniency effects.[5] *Imposition of structure* means that we take incomplete information that we have gathered about a person and apply some structure to that information in order to obtain a more complete picture of his or her personality. Because we are unable to cope with an abundant amount of information about various people we also tend to simplify information or stereotype. In either case, our perception about the other person may be based on limited and inaccurate information. For example, Bill, the head sales clerk at Richdales department store, meets George, the new vice president in charge of public relations, for the first time at lunch on Monday. During their hour together Bill notices that George seems to be in a hurry to finish his lunch since he talks quickly and looks at his

[4] R. D. Laing, H. Phillipson, and A. R. Lee, *Interpersonal Perception*, Perrenial Library, Baltimore, 1966, pp. 49-72.
[5] Albert H. Hastorf, David J. Schneider, and Judith Pohefka, *Person Perception*, Addison-Wesley, Reading, Mass., 1970, pp. 19-25.

watch often. George says that it's taking him a little time to become adjusted to Rich-dales's store policies but that he thinks he'll like working with the company. Just as he's leaving he mentions that he'd like to have a talk with Bill sometime in the next week about a complaint he's received concerning the sporting goods department. Based on this limited information Bill forms some kind of impression of George that will affect how he will interact with him in the future. He decides that he doesn't like him because he appears to be a young man trying to push his way to the top of the executive ladder and will do it the fastest way he can. Actually, this may be the result of Bill imposing the structure of the young, aggressive junior executive on George's behavior. In reality George may just be having a tough day with little time to relax when what he'd really like to be doing that afternoon is playing golf.

The *halo effect* is just the opposite. Here we assume that because someone is good at one thing he or she will also be good at something else. We generalize a positive impression about someone to all aspects of his or her personality. This has been popu-larized in the *Peter Principle*.[6] The Peter Principle states that within an organization those individuals who perform well at one level of the organization will be the ones promoted to the next level as it is assumed that they will also perform well there. The difficulty is that just because someone is good at selling merchandise doesn't necessar-ily mean that that same person will have what it takes to be a good buyer. We assume (sometimes with disasterous results!) that the characteristics that make a person good in one situation will automatically make him or her good in another situation.

Leniency effects are similar to the halo effect in that we generalize about an indi-vidual's capabilities. We tend to judge people too high on favorable traits and too low

[6] Laurence J. Peter and Raymond Hull, *The Peter Principle: Why Things Always Go Wrong*, Morrow, New York, 1969, p. 26.

Figure 5-3 The halo effect.

on unfavorable traits. It may be that the operation of leniency in judgments is what sustains dyads in early phases of their transactions. When you have only limited information about the other person, it is not easy to reject him out of hand.[7] All of these possible errors in judgment influence the direction and outcome of an interpersonal relationship. One theory developed in an attempt to further explain this process is attribution theory.

Attribution theory deals with the process by which people attribute actions or attitudes to each other. We make conclusions about others based on what they say and do. Swensen[8] identifies two dimensions of attribution: personal causation and situational causation. I can either believe you did an act because of personal characteristics you possess *or* because you had no control over the situation and you were forced to act the way you did. In other words, I may choose to believe that the situation itself demanded a certain response from you. We need to assign some cause to actions because it helps us put order into our perception of the world. If we attribute a person's behavior to the situation then we don't hold him or her responsible as much as if we felt it was a personal causation. On the other hand, we tend to view our *own* actions differently from the way we view others. In our own case, it is the situation, not ourselves, that causes us to act in unacceptable ways. If my boss is difficult to get along with I tend to say it's because of her personality, which is too domineering. When she is easy to get along with, however, I say it's because I have learned to handle her well!

Within the organizational setting the roles individuals must play in order to maintain the structure of the organization contribute to others' perceptions of them. *Roles* are parts that are played in certain interactions with prescribed words and actions. A role transcends the individual person or exists independently of the actor. This role serves the function of placing a person in the social order and prescribes to a certain extent how a given person will interact with another person who occupies a different place in the social order. Consequently, one person's perception of another individual may be a function of the role that person is to play rather than an analysis of his or her own traits and characteristics. For example, Bill's perception of George was in part based on his perception of the role a public relations director should play in an organization. This individual must be careful that the image of the organization remains intact and, consequently, any department that causes poor public relations may suffer the consequences. He may see George as aggressive because he assumes that someone in that role is supposed to be aggressive. In order to change our perceptions of others' roles we must either redefine their role position or switch our attention from assumed role traits to personal characteristics.

One state agency whose function is to provide crisis intervention training for organizations consistently faces a problem with role definition. Often organizational members are hostile and defensive in their initial interactions with the agency representatives. This is due in part to the organizational members' assumptions that the role

[7]Wilmot, op. cit., p. 67.
[8]Clifford H. Swensen, *Introduction to Interpersonal Relations*, Scott, Foresman, Glenview, Ill., 1973, pp. 100–111.

these agency representatives are playing is a punitive one. They assume, incorrectly, that top-level management in their organization has indicated to the agency that their workers have particular deficiencies that need correction. The agency spends much of the time during initial contact redefining its role from a punitive to a collaborative one.

One interesting example of the effect of organizational roles on the individual's level of tension, job satisfaction, and internal control is a study that was conducted within a government organization (the Internal Revenue Service). The authors of the study conclude "The less rigid role expectations for incumbents of management positions contributed to favorable rather than to unfavorable relative adjustment. Specifically, in organizations like the IRS, members of management have a great deal of freedom to define their own roles as well as the roles of those below them. When this advantage is coupled with the job security provided by the civil service system, managers are apparently rendered less susceptible to the job-related tensions characteristic of management in private, competitive enterprises."[9]

These authors compared their results against those of others who have attempted to claim that the higher one goes in the organization, the greater the amount of achievement expected, and thus executives would be more susceptible to the role stresses involved in performing their supervisory and problem-solving functions. This data would suggest that this is not true in a bureaucratic structure where pressures for production are presumably less intense than those in private industry.

We will continue to perceive others in each encounter we have, no matter how brief that encounter is. While we cannot stop this process we can become more aware of some of the factors influencing that perception. Misperception at the metaperception level, the halo, leniency, and structure effects, as well as the attribution process and role definition limitations, all function to interfere with accurate composite pictures of others. We *can* work at *limiting* their effect.

INDIVIDUAL NEEDS

The extent to which an individual's needs are satisfied in any interpersonal relationship will determine the life span of that relationship as well as how much time and energy each individual is willing to devote to its development.

Abraham Maslow[10] developed a hierarchy of needs that helps determine what needs should be satisfied first before a person may move to a higher level of needs (see Chapter 2, Figure 2-6). He says that people have five sets of basic needs: *physiological* (hunger, thirst, sex), *safety* (protection against danger, threat, and deprivation), *social* (belonging, being accepted by others, and giving and receiving friendship and love), *ego* (self-esteem, achievement, status, and recognition), and *self-fulfillment* (reaching the very limits of your abilities, realizing your potential). These needs exist in a hierarchy so that physiological needs must be satisfied first before one can expect

---

[9] Cary M. Lichtman, "Some Intrapersonal Response Correlates of Organizational Rank," *Journal of Applied Psychology*, **54**(1):77–80, 1970.

[10] Abraham H. Maslow, *Motivation and Personality*, Harper & Row, New York, 1954, pp. 1–100.

to achieve higher needs. Maslow feels that individuals should strive for the highest need: self-fulfillment. Those who are able to achieve this fulfillment need are, according to him, the healthiest individuals in the society. Within the organization, individuals are often threatened by the loss of the safety need when they are in fear of losing their job. If an individual is in danger of being fired because of low production, that individual will not be interested in his or her status within the organization since a lower safety need has been threatened. As an interpersonal communicator it is important for individuals to recognize that others may be at different need levels and that this will affect the relationship. The station manager at WDTN-TV may be baffled when a popular disk jockey appears uninterested in his nomination for an outstanding community service award unless she understands that the fact that his job is in jeopardy places him at a lower level on the need hierarchy. As one author explained it, "You cannot pass information effectively to a man under stress even if that stress is only a full bladder, as every lecturer knows. Under stress, a man rejects everything but the information that he needs for survival."[11] Once a need has been satisfied it no longer is a motivating factor in the person's behavior.

Another approach to analyzing interpersonal needs in any relationship has been suggested by William Schutz.[12] It is his belief that in any encounter each individual is expressing three different needs to some degree: the need for affection, the need for inclusion, and the need to control others. First we have a need to feel included by others—to feel like a full partner in a relationship. Second, all of us have a need to give and receive affection from others as well as to control and to be controlled by others. Each individual has different levels for each of these needs. For example, some people have a stronger need to control others while some need to *be* controlled. Schutz's hypothesis is that the better the fit between individuals and their respective needs, the more productive the relationship will be. If one person has a high need for affection, his or her best relationship will be with someone who has a high need to give affection to others.

There appear to be conflicting results from tests of the applicability of Schutz's theory to the organizational setting. Underwood and Krafft[13] had industrial supervisory members complete Schutz's inventory forms on each of the three interpersonal needs. These forms then indicated a compatibility rating for pairs of workers within that setting. Two additional measures of interpersonal work effectiveness were also completed and compared to the first results. The hypothesis derived from Schutz's theory, that the more compatible two individuals' needs are in terms of affection, inclusion, and control, the more likely it is that the individuals will attain the goal of their relationship, was not proven in this industrial setting. The authors' conclusion is important. "In industry, the predominant content of interpersonal activity regards materials, costs, schedules and less personal information. Such a context may not

---

[11] Alec Irvine, *Improving Industrial Communication,* Gowen, London, 1970, pp. 177–206.

[12] William C. Schutz, *The Interpersonal Underworld: A Three-Dimensional Theory of Interpersonal Behavior,* Science and Behavior Books, Palo Alto, Calif., 1966, pp. 13–34.

[13] William J. Underwood and Larry J. Krafft, "Interpersonal Compatibility and Managerial Work Effectiveness: A Test of the Fundamental Interpersonal Relations Orientation Theory," *Journal of Applied Psychology,* 58(1):89–94, March 1973.

evoke interpersonal needs to the degree necessary to make the aim of their satisfaction a salient goal."[14] On the other hand, Reddy and Byrnes[15] in another study found that matching individuals according to their interpersonal needs (thus causing high compatibility in Schutz's terms) increased problem-solving abilities in groups. This study was done with middle managers of a medium-sized industrial firm. Although the issue has not been satisfactorily solved by research, it would appear that the interpersonal communicator should be aware of others' needs and be willing to recognize their possible influence on the life of the relationship.

One final approach to interpreting how individuals satisfy their interpersonal needs is Thibaut and Kelley's *social exchange theory*.[16] This theory states that social interactions are regulated by the individual's desire to get the maximum pleasure and minimum pain from the other person. Individuals are most attracted to persons who provide the highest ratio of rewards and the lowest amount of costs. A basic premise is that behavior will not be repeated unless it is rewarded in some way. Consequently, an individual who is requested to spend time training a new employee whom he or she does not like and will get no extra compensation for, will not be satisfying any of his or her own interpersonal needs. The cost in time and energy exceeds any benefits to be derived from the relationship, and thus the trainer will attempt to end the relationship as soon as possible.

SELF-CONCEPT AND SELF-DISCLOSURE

Self-concept refers to the way a person sees him- or herself and *self-disclosure* refers to how much of that view of self is shared with other people. Interpersonal relationships are developed through one's self-concept and self-disclosure.

Usually people are concerned with defending and enhancing their self-concept. Commonly used defenses to protect one's self-concept are rationalization and repression. When we *rationalize* we attempt to find ways to reason away observations that do not fit into our picture of ourself. *Repressing* is a way of ignoring reality. Organizational leaders need to be aware of behaviors on their part that threaten others' self-concept and cause them to become defensive.

One interesting behavior we use to maintain our self-concept is called *selectivity*. "Selectivity takes many forms, all of which serve to give some stability to one's self-concept. In general, (1) we can selectively expose ourselves to individuals who support our self-concept, (2) we can selectively interpret either our or the other person's behavior, and (3) we can selectively choose the goals we wish to achieve."[17]

An excellent example of how our self-concept influences how we interact with others in an interpersonal relationship is explained by Thomas Harris[18] in his popular

---

[14]Ibid., p. 93.

[15]Brendan W. Reddy and Anne Byrnes, "Effects of Interpersonal Group Composition on the Problem-Solving Behavior of Middle Managers," *Journal of Applied Psychology*, 56(6):516–517, March 1972.

[16]J. W. Thibaut and H. H. Kelley, *The Social Psychology of Groups*, Wiley, New York, 1959, pp. 1–50.

[17]Wilmot, op. cit., p. 52.

[18]Thomas Harris, *I'm O.K., You're O.K.: A Practical Guide to Transactional Analysis*, Harper & Row, New York, 1967, pp. 37–54.

transactional analysis book. Harris states that there are four possible positions held with respect to yourself and others. They are:

1 *I'm Not O.K., You're O.K.* "Somehow everyone else seems to have things going for them—it's just me who is out of line." When a person is in this position he communicates to others that he has rejected the personal self and needs others' acceptance and support before feeling O.K. about his own self.

2 *I'm Not O.K., You're Not O.K.* A person in this position has given up hope of developing meaningful relationships since he can neither give nor receive help from others. This person communicates both rejection of the self as well as rejection of others.

3 *I'm O.K., You're Not O.K.* This person feels that she can support her own self-concept without anyone's help. She is ultraindependent and rejects others' support. She communicates to others that *she* is fine; it's everyone else who is not.

4 *I'm O.K., You're O.K.* According to transactional theory this is the healthiest approach. Here the individual has a strong self-concept and also accepts others in positive ways. She sees herself and others as worthwhile and consequently is able to develop close personal relationships.

This approach demonstrates the interrelatedness of our perception of our self and others. Everytime we communicate with others we communicate a part of ourselves. The degree and depth of that disclosure is dependent in part on how positively we feel about our own self.

In any setting, and particularly in the organizational setting, there are appropriate and inappropriate times when one is expected to self-disclose. Too little or too much are both seen as destructive to the interpersonal process. Part of the reason is that self-disclosure develops in reciprocal stages and when one person moves faster than another she violates this principle.

Recent researchers have emphasized the multidimensional nature of self-disclosure. Gilbert and Whiteneck[19] have studied not only the amount of self-disclosure between persons, but also the level of intimacy, positiveness and negativeness, timing of disclosure in a relationship, and the effect on the recipient. They found that the more personal the disclosure statements the later in a relationship they are likely to be discussed, and the more positive the disclosures the earlier they are made in a relationship. Thus, the new training director for Richdales is more likely to reveal positive and less-personal information about himself in the initial stages of building relationships with his staff. Personal disclosures will come at a much later stage of the relationship, and such disclosures will often be made outside of the working environment.

TRUST BUILDING

The importance of trust to the interpersonal relationship has been discussed by numerous authors. Its value in the business world has been debated and argued. And yet our concept of this dimension of communication is often vague and still needs definition.

[19] Shirley J. Gilbert and Gale G. Whiteneck, "Toward a Multidimensional Approach to the Study of Self-Disclosure," *Human Communication Research*, 2:324–355, Summer 1976.

Giffin and Patton define trust as "reliance upon communication behavior (speaking and/or listening) of another person while attempting to achieve a desired but uncertain objective in a risky situation."[20] Risk in this case means that a person's potential loss if trust is violated is greater than the potential gain if it is fulfilled. One young woman was hired in an executive position for a major corporation to act as an in-house consultant to managers who had recently been released from the company. Her job was to advise them in redirecting their careers. As she explained it, this seemed a ridiculous situation: a young woman with little corporate experience, advising 40- and 50-year-old executives on career planning. She took a risk at the beginning of these relationships by saying, "Look, we both know you've had much more experience in the corporate setting than I have so I'm not going to try and act like I know more than I do. What I *do* have is access to files and career information that I can share with you. Perhaps between the two of us we can decide on the best possible course of action for your career planning." She took a risk by revealing openly her lack of knowledge, which in turn allowed her to develop a trusting environment in which to operate.

Rossiter and Pearce conclude that trust can be increased much in the way that self-disclosure is increased, "Trusting behavior on your part sometimes produces trust in the other, but distrusting behavior almost always produces distrust."[21] Consequently, they define trust as a reciprocal process, where each person suggests to the other person that the other trust him a little more than he does at that instant.

Much of the research on trust suggests that individuals have personality traits that identify people as high or low trusters. In one study the researcher found that high trusters continued to trust even after they had been deceived. These individuals will permit a mistake or two and still trust providing the mistake is admitted and an apology made. Even if they are shown clear-cut evidence that they have been tricked they will continue to extend trust.[22]

The organizational setting often seems to provide a unique environment in which mistrust is allowed to develop. In fact, some would claim that unless a person mistrusts her coworkers she may get left behind while someone else gets promoted for doing the same quality of work. In contrast, one of the authors has worked with some organizational groups in which a high level of both self-confidence as well as respect for others was exhibited. These two qualities seem to provide the foundation for a high level of trust to exist. Without a positive self-concept an individual is not able to trust others since any feedback he or she gets will be deprecated. Trust does not mean blindness.

VERBAL BARRIERS

Language is an extremely personal matter. Close friends, family members, and especially coworkers develop their own jargon and language codes that have little meaning

---

[20]Kim Giffin and Bobby Patton, *Fundamentals of Interpersonal Communication*, Harper & Row, New York, 1971, p. 150.

[21]Charles Rossiter and Barnett Pearce, *Communicating Personality,* Bobbs-Merrill, Indianapolis, Ind., 1975, p. 131.

[22]J. B. Rotter, "A New Scale for the Measurement of Interpersonal Trust," *Journal of Personality,* **35**:652–665, 1967.

outside their immediate environment. A mother and son known to one of the authors have developed a unique language system. Their half-sentences and abbreviated phrases always make sense to them but never to anyone else. In fact, they often answer each other's questions with only one or two words to hint at what the question really is! The trouble is that words do not have meanings in and of themselves but only have meanings due to the definitions we agree they will have.

Alec Irvine emphasizes the importance of the structure of our message in the organizational setting when he says, "A good deal of the operational information flow in industry and commerce is in the form of instructions—verbal, written, or best of all, written in an instruction book and explained verbally."[23] Obviously, there are both advantages and differences between the language used for written communication and oral communication. Both are necessary in an organizational setting.

There are some unique barriers in the structure of our language system that cause misunderstanding. For example, the *pseudo question* causes many of these barriers. A pseudo question is not really asking for information or an answer to the question. Rather the individual is stating an opinion or making a statement *disguised* as a question. By framing the statement in the form of a question this lowers the risk that the statement will be rejected outright in the hopes that it will force the other person to agree with it. Most questions are really indirect forms of communicating with others and in most cases could be eliminated. The result would be a clearer statement of what we're actually trying to say. Two authors[24] have identified eight types of pseudo questions:

1 The *cooptive question*, which narrows or limits the possible responses of the other person. "Don't you really feel . . . ?" or "Isn't it true that . . . ?".

2 The *punitive question*, which is when the questioner asks a question he really knows the answer to but asks it to expose the other person. For example, when someone is discussing a theory that the listener knows has not been properly researched and the listener asks the speaker what the experimental evidence indicates, they are making use of a punitive question.

3 The *hypothetical question* is usually an indirect way of criticizing or probing for the answer to a question one is afraid to ask directly. "If you were in charge of this meeting, wouldn't you handle it differently?" is an example of this type of indirect question.

4 The *imperative question* is one that actually makes a demand like, "Have you done anything about . . . ?"

5 The *screened question* asks the other person what she would like to do with the hope that she will choose the questioner's choice without the questioner having to make the choice himself. This may place the person being questioned under pressure as she may not be sure how she should answer. She wants to give the correct response and feels under pressure to guess what the questioner really wants her to say.

[23] Irvine, op. cit., p. 196.
[24] William Pfeiffer and John Jones, "An Experimental Lecture on Indirect and Direct Communication," in *The 1974 Annual Handbook for Group Facilitators*, University Associates, La Jolla, Calif., 1974, p. 203.

6 The *set-up question* maneuvers the other person into a vulnerable position, "Is it fair to say that you . . . ?"

7 The *rhetorical question* does not ask for a response but instead is intended to prevent a response and is often followed by "Right?" or "You know?" An example would be, "Don't you think it would be a good idea to finish the report tonight and have it out of the way?"

8 The *"got-cha" question* is based on one of Eric Berne's games from his book, *Games People Play*. The got'cha question isn't supposed to solicit an answer either but instead is intended to dig a pit for the respondent to fall into, e.g., "Weren't you the one who. . .?" or "Didn't I see you. . . ?"

Using these indirect verbal methods of communication causes much guesswork to occur, inaccuracy in messages sent and received, game-playing behavior, and defensiveness. The sensitive communicator will avoid using such "traps."

The problem with verbal messages is that we can, by prior agreement, make anything stand for anything else. The word is not the thing itself but only a representation of it. We have only so many words in our language with which to express millions of feelings and attitudes. Often we may find our language structure limiting. At the same time our language changes daily and words take on new meanings while older interpretations are out of date. Some years ago, S. I. Hayakawa pointed out that "The symbol is not the thing symbolized; the word is not the thing; the map is not the territory it stands for."[25]

Words may have *denotative* (dictionary meaning), *connotative* (personal reflective meaning), *informative* (literal content meaning of word), and *affective* connotations (emotional content of word). Thus one word may have four different meanings. These different meanings may derive from our cultural background as well as from our social group.

The effective interpersonal communicator will take great care to insure that she and the listener have the same interpretation for the words being used. More money is lost each year in organizations because instructions are not understood. Even the phrase, "This needs top priority" to one person may mean "attention today" and to another "attention as soon as current work load is reduced." In fact, in one corporation that exact phrase and its misinterpretation caused a major reorganization in the communication network.

FEEDBACK

Feedback may be a way of helping another person to consider his behavior or a way to reinforce his present accepted behavior. It is communication to a person that gives that person information about how he or she affects others.

Although most organizational leaders now recognize the importance of giving and receiving feedback from their superiors and subordinates, many still seem unable to effectively establish this open channel. Many have adopted what might be referred to

[25] S. Hayakawa, *Language in Thought and Action*, Harcourt, Brace, Jananovich, New York, 1949, p. 100.

as the *open-door policy*. The assumption is that if the executive's door is open employees will feel free to bring suggestions and complaints directly to their superior. "My door is always open" sounds good but do people ever, in fact, drop in? There are many executives who say that their door is open and then have it well guarded by a protective secretary. There are quite a few people who would rather go without information than go through that open door. In one case supervisors refused to approach the coordinator of the project they were working on because the environment created in that office was always one of interrogation. The implication is that if organizational leaders want feedback and open dialogue they are going to have to make more of an effort than simply opening their doors. They may have to *initiate* the informal interpersonal conversations so necessary to the continuous flow of information. This two-way communication flow will result in clearer messages, more security on the part of the listener, and a greater amount of time spent sending the message.

Basic reinforcement theory provides the foundation for the use of feedback. In the early work of Pavlov[26] it was found that stimulus-response connections are strengthened by practice and weakened by disuse and negative consequences. Feedback may deal with work performance, interpersonal relationship issues, or structured organizational information. The style of giving feedback often has a greater effect on interpersonal relations in the organization than the content of the feedback. Phelps and DeWine[27] have outlined specific guidelines for structuring feedback to maximize its effectiveness.

People give three types of feedback to others:

1 *Evaluative:* Here we observe the other's behavior and respond with our own critique of it. For example, "You are a very cold person, and I don't think that's any way to be for a person in your position."

2 *Interpretive:* Here we observe the behavior and try to analyze why the person is behaving that way. For example, "You're acting very coldly toward others, and I think it's because you're uptight about your new job."

3 *Descriptive:* Here we observe the behavior and simply feed back to the person our specific observations without evaluation; however, we do share with the person how his or her behavior affects us. For example, "Sometimes it's difficult for me to interpret your comments because you look so stern and speak so abruptly, which often gives me the impression that you're angry."

In building interpersonal relationships, try to use descriptive feedback. Also remember the following criteria for useful feedback:

1 It is descriptive rather than judgmental. Describing one's reaction leaves the individual free to use it or not use it as he sees fit. Avoiding judgmental language reduces the need for the person to react defensively.

2 It is specific rather than general. To be told that one is dominating will probably not be as useful as to be told, "Just now, when we were deciding the issue, you did not

---

[26] I. P. Pavlov, *Conditioned Reflexes*, Oxford, London, 1927, pp. 1–100.
[27] Lynn Phelps and Sue DeWine, *The Interpersonal Communication Journal*, West, St. Paul, Minn., 1976, pp. 78–79.

listen to what others said, and I felt forced to accept your arguments or face attack from you."

3 It takes into account the needs of both the receiver and giver of feedback. Feedback can be destructive when it serves only our own needs and fails to consider the needs of the person on the receiving end.

4 It is directed toward behavior that the receiver can do something about. Frustration is only increased when a person is reminded of some shortcoming over which she has no control.

5 It is solicited rather than imposed. Feedback is most useful when the receiver himself has formulated the kind of question those observing him can answer.

6 It is well timed. In general, feedback is most useful if it is offered at the earliest opportunity after the given behavior (depending, of course, on the person's readiness to hear it, and the support available from others).

7 It is checked to insure clear communication. One way of doing this is to have the receiver try to rephrase the feedback she has received to see if it corresponds to what the sender had in mind.

8 When feedback is given in a training group, both giver and receiver have the opportunity to check with others in the group about the accuracy of the feedback. Is this one person's impression or an impression shared by others?

Feedback, then, is a way of giving help, a corrective mechanism for the person who wants to learn how well his behavior matches his intentions, and a means for establishing one's identity—for answering the question, "Who am I?"

In an early study by Dahle[28] the importance of providing feedback in a number of medias was tested. In an industrial setting the researcher sent messages to a total of 612 employees through oral messages only, written messages only, oral and written messages, a bulletin board, or the functioning grapevine. The combination of both oral and written messages occasioned more accurate content retention than did the use of oral messages alone, written messages alone, a bulletin board, or the grapevine. As a result we might say that the use of several modes of communication are more effective in sending feedback to others in the organizational setting than the use of any mode by itself.

In a fairly simple experiment two researchers[29] had leaders describe four geometrical patterns to subjects under four different conditions: no feedback allowed by

Table 5-1 Feedback Summary Chart

Do make feedback	Don't make feedback
Descriptive	Judgmental
Specific	General and vague
Relevant to both persons' needs	Irrelevant to either
Directed toward behavior	Directed toward personality
Well timed	Inappropriate for the setting or occasion

[28] Thomas L. Dahle, "An Objective and Comparative Study of Five Methods of Transmitting Information to Business and Industrial Employees," *Speech Monographs*, 21:21–28, March 1954.
[29] Harold J. Leavitt and Ronald A. H. Mueller, "Some Effects of Feedback on Communication," *Human Relations*, 4:401–410, 1951.

listeners, listeners were visible to leaders but were not allowed to ask questions, listeners could ask only yes–no type questions, and a free feedback condition. Drawings were more accurate under the free feedback condition. In addition, subjects' estimates of their accuracy under this condition were more accurate. Free feedback takes shorter amounts of time with each successive trial.

Another researcher[30] measured the amount of productivity increase as the communication of results increased. The researcher had the management of an organization communicate to its employees their production efficiency via group meetings, bulletin boards, supervisor contact, and outside employee's activities. In essence, management rewarded employees for establishing new records. Employees were measured on established productivity instruments. This type of reinforcement and the various forms of feedback caused significant increases in workers' productivity.

The conclusion that should be drawn is that feedback and reinforcement of that feedback can make significant changes not only in the individual but also in the total organizational structure. Finally, there is a skill to receiving and giving feedback and, depending on the skill used, feedback can be destructive or extremely helpful to furthering interpersonal relationships.

LISTENING

We spend more time listening than we do any other communication skill and yet we pay little attention to it. The importance of listening has been stressed by many organizational writers. For instance, one writer says, "Of all the sources of information a manager has to accurately assess the personalities of employees, listening is the more important; no tool rivals skilled and sympathetic listening. They could actually increase substantially—even double—their success by controlling their tongues and really listening. This should be a paramount requirement for managers since listening comprises the largest section of their communication skills."[31]

Research indicates that normal listening results in a 50 percent retention loss immediately after a 10-minute presentation and a decline to only 25 percent retention after a 48-hour period. Consequently, most people experience a 75 percent loss of information due to poor listening habits.[32] One reason is that the mind thinks four times faster than the average person talks (600 to 700 words per minute compared to 125 words per minute). Another reason people don't listen is because there is a personal risk involved.[33] If one truly listens to another, he or she runs the risk of being changed in some way. Change is often threatening, at least initially.

Huseman[34] has identified some of the more typical barriers to listening as follows:

[30]Henry R. Migliore, "Improving Worker Productivity Through Communicating Knowledge of Work Results," *Management of Personnel Quarterly*, 9:26–32, Winter 1970.

[31]Phillip V. Lewis, *Organizational Communication: The Essence of Effective Management*, Grid, Columbus, Ohio., 1975, p. 150.

[32]Ralph G. Nichols, *Are You Listening?* McGraw-Hill, New York, 1957, pp. 1–17.

[33]Carl Weaver, *Human Listening: Processes and Behavior*, Bobbs-Merrill, Indianapolis, Ind., 1972, pp. 30–65.

[34]Richard C. Huseman, James M. Lahiff, and John D. Hatfield, *Interpersonal Communication in Organizations*, Holbrook, Boston, 1976, pp. 107–118.

attending to stimuli that are only relevant to our own goals or objectives, attending to stimuli that serve to satisfy our own needs, not attending to stimuli that do not conform to our own models of the world, and filtering stimuli based on our own frame of reference, our own expectations, our own attitudes and beliefs, and our relationship with the sender of the stimuli.

Thomas Gordon describes a particular type of listening that is particularly effective: *active listening*. Active listening occurs when "the receiver tries to understand what it is the sender is feeling or what his message means. Then he puts his understanding into his own words or code and feeds back only what he feels the sender's message meant—nothing more, nothing less."[35] In this type of listening skill the listener uses phrases like, "What I heard you saying was . . ." or "Sounds like you're feeling . . ." or "What I understood you to say. . . ." First the listener is repeating for the speaker what she heard, in a tentative manner, to give him a chance to rephrase it. This is sometimes referred to as *therapeutic listening*. It is the authors' personal belief that individuals who are particularly good listeners not only provide perhaps one of the greatest kindnesses to others but also improve their own ability to communicate with others as well. Nothing can equal a person's willingness to enter another's world for a few moments and share his experience through intense listening. The word "active" implies that listening is not passive. It requires great mental and emotional involvement with the sender of the message. In order to do this a listener must be willing to clear her desk. This may mean physically turning away from those things in the environment that may distract her (like memos and files on a desk top) as well as clearing her mind in order that the focus can be on this particular person for a time.

CONFLICT RESOLUTION

Bill Pfeiffer, a communication consultant, has provided us with an interesting analogy that explains why conflict so often occurs in an interpersonal relationship:

> In the late afternoon when you observe a sunset, the sun often appears to be a deep red, larger and less intense than it seems at midday. This is due to the phenomenon of refraction, the bending of the light rays as they pass through the earth's atmosphere, and the higher density of dust in the air through which the light passes as the sun goes down. The sun has already moved below the horizon but it is still in sight because its emissions are distorted by the conditions of the medium through which they must travel. In a similar way the messages which we send to each other are often refracted by intrapersonal, interpersonal, and environmental conditions which contribute to the atmosphere in which we are relating. I may distort my message to you by giving out mixed messages verbally and nonverbally, and you may distort what you hear because of your own needs and experiences. The two of us may be located in an environment, physical and

[35] Thomas Gordon, *Parent Effectiveness Training*, Wyden, New York, 1972, p. 53.

psychological, which contributes to the difficulty in clearly sharing what we intend. In an atmosphere of suspicion, for example, we may both become unduly cautious in our communication.[36]

While it is unlikely that total nonrefracted communication is possible, certainly we can improve our chances of meaningful dialogue by keeping in mind some of the principles of conflict management. This becomes particularly important in the organizational setting where individuals often use up large amounts of man-hours attempting to resolve some interpersonal conflict.

There appear to be two types of conflict in the organizational setting: (1) *content conflict*, which is conflict over the goals of the organization, its structure, policies, or networks and (2) *personal conflict*, which takes the form of emotional and personal differences among the individuals within the organization. A conflict over content or issues might revolve around labor negotiations and pay increases while a personal conflict might focus on one group's inability to talk openly with a supervisor because he or she is so dictatorial and unfair.

L. R. Pondy[37] has identified five distinct stages of conflict development: (1) *latent conflict* deals with underlying sources of organizational conflict like competition for scarce resources; (2) *perceived conflict*, which can occur in either the absence or presence of latent conflict. Perceived conflict may cause barriers if the individuals misunderstand each other's positions or such conflict may not be perceived at all because of the desire of the individuals involved to suppress it; (3) *felt conflict* may also be termed the *personalization of conflict* because it is at this stage that conflict actually affects the individual directly; (4) *manifest conflict* is the actual occurrence of conflict, which may range from open aggression to apathy or even extremely rigid adherence to rules; and (5) *conflict aftermath*, which is a function of how well the entire episode or sequence of episodes has been resolved. Perhaps this stage will reveal the basis for a more cooperative relationship, or it might suggest how newly perceived problems might be handled, or it *may* foster more serious difficulties.

Alan Filley[38] has identified some of the causes of conflict in the organization as follows: ambiguous responsibilities, conflict of interests (or competition for scarce resources), communication barriers, need for consensus, dependence of one person on another, suppression of conflict, and personalization of the situation. One of the difficulties in resolving or managing conflicts is that the real cause or issue is often not uncovered but remains hidden behind symptoms. A careful analysis of the real cause is a crucial step toward managing the conflict situation.

At WDTN-TV the chief engineer and the program director may have a conflict over

---

[36]William Pfeiffer, "Conditions Which Hinder Effective Communication," in *The 1973 Annual Handbook for Group Facilitators*, University Associates, La Jolla, Calif., 1973, p. 120.

[37]L. R. Pondy, "Organizational Conflict: Concepts and Models," in John M. Thomas and Warren G. Bennis (eds.), *Management of Change and Conflict*, Penguin, Middlesex, England, 1972, p. 100.

[38]Alan C. Filley, *Interpersonal Conflict Resolution*, Scott, Foresman, Palo Alto, Calif., 1975, pp. 9–12.

a movie scheduled by the program director but aired incorrectly by the chief engineer. The symptom of this conflict may be that the wrong reel of the film was shown first; however, the real cause of the conflict may be that the two individuals involved are engaged in a power struggle. The chief engineer expresses his dissatisfaction over a cut in his staff by means of inefficient operating procedures. Unless a careful analysis of the real cause of the conflict is made, the conflict over the symptom may escalate.

Jay Hall[39] has identified five interpersonal styles, based on the responses of 387 managers, of dealing with conflict. Individuals may use all five styles at one time or another. The *win-lose* style is used when individuals associate winning with status and competence and losing is seen as losing status. The result is an individual who is aggressive, dogmatic, and inflexible. The *yield-lose* style is based on the assumption that human relationships are so fragile that they cannot withstand the process of working through differences. Here the person's need for affection and acceptance is most important and this, in turn, causes submissive behavior on the part of the person. The *lose-leave* style views conflict as hopeless and thus the individual simply tries to protect himself from a punishing experience by withdrawing from the situation entirely. According to the *compromise* style, a little bit of winning and a little bit of losing are better than losing altogether. This strategy attempts to soften the effects of losing by limiting the gains of winning. Often this style results in a climate of suspicion for both individuals since neither individual is completely satisfied with the results. Finally, there is the *synergistic* style, which is the most desirable style. Here major importance is attached to the goals of the participants in the relationship and to the well-being of the relationship at the same time. The confrontation of differences in a problem-solving way and a tolerance for differences are key elements in this style.

In addition to these interpersonal styles that may be useful in resolving conflict, there are definite attitudes that may be helpful in managing conflict, such as: belief in the existence of a mutually acceptable solution, belief in the desirability of such a solution, belief in cooperation rather than competition, belief that the other person is valuable and trustworthy, and belief that the other person can compete but can choose to cooperate.

Phelps and DeWine[40] have enumerated the following ways for individuals to analyze a conflict situation.

Assess immediacy. A relationship in conflict is an emotionally draining experience. One of the first things a person must decide is if this relationship is important enough to him or her to warrant the amount of time and energy it will take to resolve the conflict. Once we are committed to the relationship and realize that it will require our energy and attention, we then seem more willing to try resolution techniques.

How important is the relationship to me?
How willing am I to devote time and energy, and to cope with emotional drain, in resolving the conflict?

---

[39]Jay Hall, *Conflict Management Survey,* Telemetrics International, Couroc, Ten., 1973, p. 3.
[40]Phelps and DeWine, op. cit., pp. 295–300.

*Identify type of conflict. Intra*personal conflict exists within a person and may not involve others (e.g., making a decision between two choices). *Inter*personal conflict exists between two or more people. A relationship is not in conflict unless both persons involved are aware that the conflict exists.

Intrapersonal conflict (within me—for example, a decision I must make)
Interpersonal conflict (between me and one or more other people)

Conflict is either in the open and everyone knows it exists or it is hidden and thus not everyone involved is aware of the conflict.

Decide basic coping strategy. Initially, we must decide whether we can merely control the conflict (not let it get out of hand, cool it down but not really resolve it), or we actually are able to work at resolving the conflict.

Control conflict: (I feel the conflict cannot be resolved at this time; however, I feel I must maintain the relationship so I choose to merely control the conflict, lower the emotional level, have a cooling-off period, etc.)
Resolve conflict: (Conflict can and must be resolved, with all issues out in the open and communication skills in use to resolve conflict.)

Distinguish symptoms from cause. We often waste time trying to resolve symptoms instead of the real underlying cause of the conflict. (For example, when a girl complains about her boyfriend's always being late for a date, it is possible that their disagreement over the time he arrives is only a symptom of a deeper conflict. They may each have different expectations for the relationship—she may want it to be permanent and he looks at her as just someone to date.)

Symptoms of conflict (lets you know a conflict is present)
Causes of conflict (underlying issues)

Identify methods used so far. We must be aware of our basic coping techniques for handling conflict. What have we already tried to do to resolve the conflict (e.g., ignore the problem, hope it will go away, try to win the argument through persuasion, compromise, give in and let the other person win, etc.)?

Identify: Methods used
Success of techniques

Alternatives available. When trying to arrive at solutions to an interpersonal conflict a person must be able to brainstorm ideas. He or she must be willing to list as many ideas as possible without evaluating them, no matter how wild or impossible they may seem. The strategy of brainstorming is that eventually some of these ideas may trigger a possible solution.

Brainstorming: Make a list of other possible actions that might be taken to resolve this interpersonal conflict.

Evaluate outcome of each alternative. Often it is difficult for us to imagine the best possible outcome of a behavior. When a relationship is in conflict, we tend to see only the negative results. It is important that we evaluate each alternative negatively and positively.

Alternative 1:   Worst possible outcome if this alternative is chosen
                   Best possible outcome
Alternative 2:   Worst possible outcome if this alternative is chosen
                   Best possible outcome

Select alternative and communication skills needed to resolve conflict. Finally, we are ready to determine what communication skills are needed to resolve this interpersonal conflict and put into action all of the communication techniques outlined earlier.

What other techniques might I try to resolve this conflict?
Where do I go from here?

The preceding format allows the individual to carefully analyze the conflict situation before entering into a battle. These issues are of prime importance if interpersonal conflicts are to be resolved successfully.

THE HELPING PROCESS

Organizational leaders are often placed in the role of helpers since much of their day is spent solving personal and organizational problems in face-to-face contact with employees. Unless the supervisor is able to deal effectively with another's problem-solving processes, organizational effectiveness will be greatly reduced. The helping process may involve dealing with emotional problems, performance problems, inter- and intrapersonal dynamics, as well as content-oriented issues.

Aubrey Sanford[40] makes an interesting distinction between types of helping processes in the organizational setting. He differentiates between *direct counseling*, which involves finding solutions to problems of others and then persuading and motivating them to accept and implement the solutions, and *nondirective counseling*, which focuses on helping people to understand their own problems and then to develop their own solutions. It is Sanford's belief that many of the situations faced by managers require some combination of the two approaches. The nondirective approach would be more appropriate when employees come to the manager or leader for help and the directive approach would be more appropriate when managers initiate the session to confront employees. We're not sure that we can accept Sanford's classification of the directive approach, as he describes it, as a true type of helping process. Although direct counseling may indeed help solve problems, it is by nature potentially manipulative and if misused may destroy trust.

[41] Aubrey C. Sanford, *Human Relations: The Theory and Practice of Organizational Behavior*, Merrill, Columbus, Ohio, 1977, p. 299.

Lawrence M. Brammer,[42] also writing on the helping process, suggests a formula for the helping process that identifies the key elements.

Personality of helper	+	helping skills	=	growth-facilitating conditions	→	specific outcomes
traits		for understanding		trust		for the person
attitudes		for comfort		respect		for society
values		for action		freedom		

This formula emphasizes the importance of certain personality traits on the part of the helper as well as specific helping skills. The combination of both is necessary to produce the outcomes on the other side of the formula. Egan also emphasizes these initial traits of the helper when he says, "A helper is first of all committed to his own growth—physical, intellectual, social, emotional—for he realizes that he must model the behavior he hopes to help others achieve. He knows that he can help only if, in the root sense of the term, he is a 'potent' human being, a person with the will and the resources to act."[43] At the beginning of this chapter we discussed some of the interpersonal problems in an institute whose role often involved helping others to achieve more effective working relationships. The point is clear in both instances: help starts with your own environment first since modeling is one of the most effective ways of changing behavior.

Consequently, the goals of the helping process include ones for the helper as well as the helpee. Robert Carkhuff[44] has written perhaps one of the most helpful texts on the helping process. He identifies four basic steps to helping: *attending* to the other person physically and emotionally, *responding* to the content of his or her message as well as to the feeling level of the message, *initiating* additional empathy to help the other explore and understand his or her particular situation at deeper levels, and *communicating* your support of healthy behavior and nonsupport of unhealthy behavior. There are simple skills to be learned at each of these steps that will help the process move smoothly.

First, the helper needs to give the other individual some encouragement to continue the conversation. This may simply be direct eye contact, head nods, smiles, and repetition of the last few words said by the other person. Next the helper can begin reflecting feelings with open-ended statements that allow the helpee to decide on the direction of the conversation. "How do you feel about your job?" is an open question that allows the respondent to head in any direction while "Do you like your job?" is a closed question that forces the respondent to make a choice. Once the feeling level has been identified then the helper may want to paraphrase the content of the message to ensure that he or she understands and has interpreted the message correctly. Only after much energy and emotional commitment have been made to the relationship can

---

[42] Lawrence M. Brammer, *The Helping Relationship Process and Skills*, Prentice-Hall, Englewood Cliffs, N.J., 1973, p. 2.

[43] Gerard Egan, *The Skilled Helper: A Model for Systematic Helping and Interpersonal Relating*, Brooks/Cole, Monterey, Calif., 1975, pp. 22–23.

[44] Robert R. Carkhuff, *The Art of Helping*, Human Resource Development Press, Amherst, Mass., 1972, pp. 6–11.

the helper summarize for the helpee what he or she has heard him saying. He can then begin to move the helpee in a more concrete direction. The helper does this by using specific terms rather than general ones, and asking the other individual to speak in the first person rather than "other people" or "they" type phrases and words.

At the same time there appear to be some obvious pitfalls that the helper can and should avoid. Giving advice, always agreeing with the other individual, criticizing, attempting analysis, and preaching are all behaviors that are inappropriate in the helping process. Organizational leaders need a good understanding of the helping process, not so they can become amateur therapists, but so they can improve the flow of communication within the working environment, which will result in increased productivity. This understanding will at least make individuals able to direct others to additional sources for help.

In the final analysis there are some important questions for the helper to ask herself in order to determine her readiness to engage in the helping process. (1) In conversations, do you consistently try to put yourself in the other person's shoes? (2) When someone is making a decision, do you refrain from giving that person the solution but instead allow him to find it for himself? (3) When others are expressing feelings of deep sorrow, are you able to allow them their expression without trying to divert the situation to less-difficult topics? and, finally, (4) When the other person does not really seem to want or need your help, are you able to accept that without feeling hurt or rejected by him?

It is important to remember that the individual in the organizational environment, as in his own home and social interactions, has great opportunities for the development of interpersonal relationships that can be meaningful and productive. Such productiveness is reflected in the outcome of the organization as well as in the development of the individual. In order to achieve such a positive outcome, we must not be afraid to take personal risk. In the words of Hugh Prather:[45]

I want to say something to this person but the fear comes: "I'd better not" (he may misunderstand, he may be in a hurry, ad infinitum). These fears are not based on the present situation, they are based on the past, and I don't have to be governed by what once went wrong. The two of us are standing here in the present. What is the situation now?

[45] Taken from John Stewart, *Bridges not Walls*, Addison-Wesley, Reading, Mass., 1977, p. 178.

Chapter 6

Nonverbal Communication

Six people filed into the WDTN executive conference room on a Monday morning. They positioned themselves around a long rectangular table. Joe chose the chair nearest the head of the table next to the door, while Mike sat at the foot of the table. The remaining four arranged themselves along either side of the table at varying distances from each other. Mike was fidgety, shifting position often and drumming his pencil on the table. Mary, sitting to Mike's left, also appeared uncomfortable; she crossed and uncrossed her legs, quickly glanced around the room, and looked frequently at her wristwatch. At the other end of the table Joe leaned back in his chair and smiled at Sam who was sitting to his right. He reached over and touched Sam's arm to get his attention as he quietly talked with him. Sam smiled in return and moved his chair closer to Joe to hear what he was saying. Jack was sitting along the right side of the table, two chairs away from anyone else, staring at Mary without changing his posture. A slow smile began to emerge on his face as he caught her attention. The sixth person was an observer to the group and sat in the far corner of the room, a nonparticipant in the upcoming meeting. Five minutes later, Gene walked quickly into the room and sat down at the head of the table. After a few seconds of paper shuffling, he said, "I think we should get started. I want to take care of this matter as quickly as possible. First, I'd be interested in knowing your reactions to the memo I sent to each of you concerning this meeting."

Had Gene been in the room previously, he might have already had a good idea of each person's attitude toward the meeting as well as a few of their reactions to others in the room based on their nonverbal cues. It is the intent of this chapter to explore this fascinating and revealing aspect of communication within the organizational context. The goal is not only to improve your ability to note nonverbal cues such as the ones described in this meeting, but also to sharpen your skills at interpreting these cues and their relationship to the total communication message.

Those who write about communication in the organization are focusing more and more on the importance of nonverbal cues to the total understanding of a message. Phillip Lewis says, "Most of us speak at least one oral language, but everyone speaks a nonverbal language. Communication analysts tend to agree that perhaps most of the expression of emotional and motivational states occurs on nonverbal levels and is communicable by facial and paralinguistic cues."[1] Probably more feelings and intentions are communicated nonverbally than through all the verbal methods combined.

Although we use two different mediums to convey messages when we communicate, it is difficult to distinguish our words from our nonverbal cues. Both are intimately woven into our messages and act as complements to one another. Researchers recognize the importance of studying both. Yet, as Knapp[2] has pointed out, nonverbal communication is so inextricably bound up with verbal aspects of the communication process that we can only separate them artificially. In actual practice such separation does not occur. The various areas of nonverbal communication that have been researched are also interwoven. "To leave the impression that you respond to someone's voice, appearance, facial expression, or the distance he stands from you, independently of one another, is to leave you with a distorted impression of the process."[3] The point is that while we may study nonverbal cues separately in the next pages, in actual practice they will all be acting simultaneously to influence the messages we send and receive.

NONVERBAL COMMUNICATION DEFINED

There are any number of ways to look at those aspects of communication specifically covered by nonverbal messages. Porter[4] has defined nonverbal communication in four rather broad ways: *physical*, which covers the personal method, e.g., facial expressions, tone of voice, sense of touch, sense of smell, and body motions; *aesthetic,* which we find in creative expressions such as instrumental music, dance, painting, and sculpture; *signs*, which cover mechanical methods of conveying a message such as signal flags, the twenty-one-gun salute, horns, and sirens; and *symbolic*, including those methods of conveying a message by religious, status, or ego-building symbols.

An equally broad category of cues is included in Lewis's definition of nonverbal

---

[1] Phillip V. Lewis, *Organizational Communications: The Essence of Effective Management*, Grid, Columbus, Ohio, 1975, p. 150.

[2] Mark Knapp, *Nonverbal Communication in Human Interactions*, Holt, Rinehart, and Winston, New York, 1972, pp. 1–25.

[3] Ibid., p. v.

[4] George W. Porter, "Non-Verbal Communications," *Training and Development Journal*, **23**: 3–8, June 1969.

communication. "Nonverbal communication is all messages (or communications) not coded in words."[5] His distinction between verbal and nonverbal communication is that verbal behavior is organized by language systems whereas nonverbal behavior is not. Nonverbal communication has less cognitive content, is used by individuals to act out strong feelings, is received through several sense organs, and is a continuous function of communication.

Harrison has indicated the extremes of a broad interpretation of nonverbal communication by recognizing all aspects that could be included, "everything from the territoriality of animals to the protocol of diplomats, from facial expressions to muscle twitches, from inner but inexpressible feelings to outward public monuments, from the message of massage to the persuasion of a punch, from dance and drama to music and mime, from extrasensory perception to the economic politics of international power blocks, and from fashions and fad to architecture."[6]

Perhaps a consideration of what we will *not* be concerned with in this chapter on nonverbal communication would be more helpful. We are not interested in communication among animals other than the human variety. Nor would it be helpful for the purposes of this text to describe in great depth the detailed research that has been done in specific areas of nonverbal communication such as minute movements of facial muscles. We also do not wish to deal with any area of nonverbal communication that is a discipline in itself (e.g., extrasensory perception). What we *are* concerned with is the use of nonlinguistic symbols in the organizational setting as they enhance and hinder the flow of communication among persons. Thus, we will define nonverbal communication as *the exchange of messages primarily through nonlinguistic means including: kinesics (body language), facial expressions and eye contact, tactile communication, space and territory, environment, paralanguage (vocal but nonlinguistic cues), and the use of silence and time.*

FUNCTIONS OF NONVERBAL COMMUNICATION

Mehrabian[7] has identified three dimensions of human feelings and attitudes often communicated more effectively through nonverbal cues: like-dislike; potency or status (power); and responsiveness. Often by observing posture, facial expressions, and use of the space around them, an observer can develop a fairly accurate interpretation of how comfortable two people are with each other and which person has power over the other. For example, one of the vice presidents of Richdales prided herself on the fact that she treated all employees equally. Yet, when the employees were interviewed, there seemed to be a clear understanding of which staff members were her favorites. The nonverbal cue they were reading was where she located herself in her own office when employees met there. Those individuals she was particularly fond of were consistently invited to sit in a large, comfortable chair near her desk, while all others were asked to sit on a small chair placed nearer the door. This obvious nonverbal use of

[5] Lewis, op. cit., p. 151.
[6] Randall P. Harrison, *Beyond Words: An Introduction to Nonverbal Communication*, Prentice-Hall, Englewood Cliffs, N.J., 1974, p. 6.
[7] A. Mehrabian, *Silent Messages*, Wadsworth, Belmont, Calif., 1971, pp. 1-50.

By observing postures, facial expressions, and the use of space an observer can develop a fairly accurate interpretation of how comfortable two people are with each other.

space sent a clear message to the employees, while the vice president was unaware of the message she sent every time someone stepped into her office.

Delahanty[8] stresses the function of nonverbal communication in a unique context within the organization—that of the interview. It is his belief that nonverbal dimensions of communication play such a major role that they reinforce, contradict, or neutralize the spoken word in the interview. These three effects of nonverbal communication can occur in any setting. Their importance in the interview will be more carefully explored in Chapter 7.

Most writers agree that nonverbal communication can, and usually does, perform the following functions in most communication encounters:

Repeating. The nonverbal cues (pointing to a chair to sit down) actually repeats what the person has just said verbally ("Please take a seat").

Contradicting. If the boss continually looks at his watch during the interview, this gesture will contradict his verbal message ("Take your time").

Substituting. Often the nonverbal message is so clear it substitutes for the use of words (an inexperienced poker player whose unhappy expression reveals he has been dealt a losing card).

Complementing. When the verbal message and the nonverbal message are the same, the nonverbal cue serves as a complement.

[8]David Delahanty, "Three Aspects of Nonverbal Communication in the Interview," *Personnel Journal,* 49:757–759, September 1970.

When a person says he has plenty of time verbally, looking often at his watch may contradict this verbal message, and send quite a different message.

Relating and regulating. Often head nods, eye movement, or shifts in posture become signals to another person that he or she should continue speaking.

All of these functions can work to hinder or facilitate the flow of communication among persons. It is vital that the individual communicator in the organization realizes that his or her messages are always being sent on two levels simultaneously.

VERBAL AND NONVERBAL INTERACTIONS

A fairly large number of research studies have been conducted to determine the influence of nonverbal cues on verbal messages. One researcher[9] asked subjects to evaluate messages that were sent by a speaker who purposely controlled nonverbal cues in order to determine if they were more convincing than the verbal message. Subjects in the study rated the speaker as less sincere than her verbal message would indicate when insincere nonverbal cues were used (e.g., nervous deferential smile, lowered head, nervous eager-to-please speech indicating submissiveness) as opposed to another presentation in which the same speaker used dominant nonverbal cues (e.g., stern, unsmiling facial features, raised head, and a loud dominating tone). The results supported the theory that listeners discriminate between the statement made by a speaker and that same person's intention. When verbal and nonverbal cues are incongruent we

[9]Eva M. McMahan, "Nonverbal Communication as a Function of Attribution in Impression Formation," paper presented at the Speech Communication Association Convention, San Francisco, December 1976.

tend to attribute intentions to the person based on her nonverbal cues that may cause a reinterpretation of the verbal message.

Consequently, even though a manager may speak the right words to represent an openness to differences of opinion among the staff, his real attitude of intolerance for new ideas is more likely to show through in his nonverbal gestures. Evidence suggests that managers who are most encouraging tend to reveal their interest in employees through their listening behavior and emotional support as demonstrated by maintaining eye contact, supportive facial expressions, and effective use of space. Managers who display inhibiting communicative behaviors are uninterested in informal talks with employees and are more likely to express their disapproval in their nonverbal contacts with employees.[10] The result is that whenever there is an incongruity between words and actions, people typically believe the actions. Therefore, it is important that we look more carefully at each of the areas of nonverbal communication mentioned earlier: kinesics, facial expressions, eye contact, personal space, environment, paralanguage, touch, silence, and time.

KINESICS

Kinesics refers to body motion and includes gestures, movements of the body, and posture. Drooped shoulders, a furrowed brow, talking with your hands, and the tilt of your head are all included in the study of kinesics.

[10]Lewis, op. cit.

An emblem is a common gesture which may substitute for the use of words. Emblems may include: shrug, an OK sign, hitchhiking, or waving good-bye.

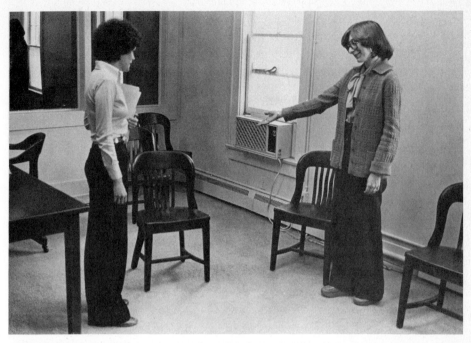

Regulators control verbal interaction and may indicate particular actions other should take.

Pointing at someone may serve to accompany and to complement what someone is saying verbally.

Illustrators serve to accompany and to complement spoken language. They are often used for emphasis.

Two researchers, Paul Ekman and Wallace Friesen,[11] have helped to organize this collection of cues by identifying five types of body expressions: (1) emblems, (2) illustrators, (3) regulators, (4) affect displays, and (5) adaptors.

Emblems refer to common gestures that may substitute for the use of words. They are, in effect, sign language. The conventional wave of the hand indicating good-bye is an example of an emblem. *Illustrators* serve to accompany and to complement spoken language. They are used for emphasis or for directions. A parking lot attendant may be giving verbal directions while pointing with his hand where a car should be parked. When the supervisor holds up three fingers while she explains that there are three jobs that must get priority in the next week, she is making use of an illustrator. *Regulators* control verbal interaction.When you nod your head this is a sign that the person should continue talking. Hand motions in a television station tell the performers to hurry up, slow down, or wait 1 minute. *Affect displays* reveal the emotional state of the communicator. A manager may refrain from chewing out a new employee for bungling a job, but his contorted face, the frown on his forehead, and his clenched fist may indicate his anger more clearly than any words ever could. Last are *adaptors*, which are nonverbal habits unique to the individual. Scratching your nose or wiping your brow would be examples of adaptors.

Ross-Skinner[12] reports that a London-based management consultant named Warren Lamb believes that the best way to assess an executive's managerial potential is not to listen to what he has to say, but to what he does while he is saying it. He has developed what he calls a "new branch of applied behavioral science called *movement analysis.*" Mr. Lamb is retained by large corporations to assist in the promotion and selection of managers. During an interview session Lamb watches for the following movements and their meaning: *side to side movements*—a person who takes up a lot of space while he talks by moving his arms in large circular motions will do much informing and listening and will be best suited to companies that are seeking a sense of direction; *forward and backward movements*—a person who extends her hand straight forward and tends to lean forward during the interview is identified by Lamb as an "operator." This is the kind of manager whose need for action best suits her to companies that need an infusion of energy or a dramatic change of course; *vertical movements*—this individual "draws himself up to his tallest during the handshake. He is characterized as the 'presenter'—a master at selling himself and the company."

Posture/gesture is Lamb's phrase for the relationship between the positioning of the body and the separate movements of limbs and facial expressions. There will always be a certain harmony between posture and gesture, except when a person has rehearsed certain gestures she thinks will impress others and then she will unconsciously tend to separate posture and gesture.

Flow is another of Lamb's terms and it refers to the degree of flexibility with which a person uses his or her body. For instance, some persons begin a movement with considerable force but conclude it with a deceleration of effort. These people are what

---

[11]Paul Ekman and Wallace Friesen, "The Repertorie of Nonverbal Behavior: Categories, Origins, Usage and Coding," *Semiotics*, 1:63–92, 1969.
[12]Jean Ross-Skinner, "Those Telltale Executive Gestures," *Dun's Review*, 95:66–67, March 1970.

The degree of like or dislike can be measured in terms of general body orientation and facial expressions.

Lamb calls the "gentle-touch" type. Their managerial style will contrast with that of the "pressurizer" whose movements push firmly from beginning to end.

We do not know the accuracy of Lamb's analysis or whether it can be generalized to other environments; however, it is significant that corporation executives are so sensitive to the importance of nonverbal messages that they hire consultants to analyze those messages in their own ranks. This alone is certainly proof of the growing importance of this field of study.

Mark Knapp,[13] one of the early leaders in nonverbal research, has focused the study of body movements primarily on the following areas: (1) *attitudes*—the degree of like or dislike can be measured in terms of general body orientation such as noting whether a communicator's shoulders and legs are turned toward rather than away from the person being spoken to in a conversation; (2) *status*—those who assume superior roles more frequently keep their heads raised in a communication encounter while those assuming inferior roles usually lower their heads; (3) *affective states or moods*—high degrees of emotional arousal are associated with large amounts of bodily movement and these movements may vary with a particular mood. The head-face area carries information about anger, joy, etc., while body movements communicate information about the intensity of the emotion; (4) *approval-seeking*—when people are trying to win approval from others they smile, nod their heads, and usually have a higher level of gestural activity; (5) *inclusivness*—based upon positional cues of individuals toward

[13] Knapp, op cit., pp. 97–107.

one another, one may determine how open others are to an intrusion into their conversation; (6) *interaction markers*—certain body movements naturally accompany specific oral language behavior. For example, at the end of a statement a person will generally demonstrate a downward movement of the head, eyelids, and hands. These movements will be upward at the end of questions.

The following is an illustration of how these categories actually function in the organizational setting. The yes-man in the corporation is one example of an individual who typically uses approval-seeking gestures. At WDTN-TV two individuals were next in line for promotion to general sales manager. It was quite obvious that one of the men, George, was trying to win the approval of top-level management. Without hearing any of his words, an outside observer could note his constant smile, and annoying head nod. He had become infected with an illness counselors often get, called, "perpetual head nod." Once again, we must remember that these conclusions about nonverbal cues cannot be generalized to all situations. Each communication exchange is unique and must be analyzed within that context.

One last area of kinesics we want to mention is posture. The posture of an individual often reveals the attitude that person has toward another. Rigid posture usually indicates a dislike or uneasiness in the other person's presence. The more a person leans toward another person, the more he or she feels comfortable with the other, and the more likely he or she will have positive feelings about that person. At the same time, Goffman[14] found that high-status individuals sit in relaxed postures while those of less status sit in more rigid and straight postures. Observation of one executive's office in a radio station revealed that the station manager looked relaxed sitting in an office chair while the secretary sat upright and rigid. Paying close attention to the tension or amount of relaxation present in a person's posture may be an indicator of his emotional state as well as of his relationship to others around him.

One Oakwood policeman discovered what can result from inaccurate interpretation

[14]E. Goffman, *Encounter*, Bobbs-Merrill, Indianapolis, 1961, p. 50.

Figure 6-1 Trying to win someone's approval with a constant smile and head nod can be more annoying than helpful.

of posture cues. Normally Bill stands in a relaxed position when talking to other people by resting his hand on his gun and holster. Since he can't put his hand in his pants pocket, this is a way to do something with his hands while maintaining an informal posture. Others, however, often interpret this as a sign of power and aggression as if Bill were ready to act if necessary. This rather simple nonverbal cue has the potential to communicate a threat when none is intended. It is important that policemen pay attention to all the messages, verbal and nonverbal, that they are sending.

FACIAL EXPRESSIONS

A more specific subject of kinesic research is the face and its expressions. Emotions are generally communicated through facial expressions and we often depend on the face to determine the attitudes of another. The face has a great deal of communicative potential in terms of our ability to interpret emotions. For example, we lift one eyebrow for disbelief, wrinkle our brows and rub our noses for puzzlement, wink our eye for intimacy, and press our lips together tightly for frustration. In an interview with the outstanding trial lawyer, Louis Nizer, the importance of facial expressions in determining a person's honesty was emphasized. "From long experience," Nizer maintains, "we have developed special antennas that tell us when a witness or our own client strays from the truth."[15] A person may hold a hand to his or her mouth while talking or answering a question. Perhaps another person touches his or her face to hide facial expressions. Both of these are telltale signals that they may be lying.

Two researchers who have worked in the area of facial expressions for some time, Paul Ekman and Wallace Friesen,[16] suggest that we humans constantly monitor and control our own facial expressions and at any given moment our faces may convey multiple emotions, rather than a single emotional state. These combinations of several emotions may appear on the face in a number of different ways: (1) one emotion is shown in one facial area while in another area a different emotion is revealed, i.e., lips pressed together in anger and brows raised in surprise; (2) in one part of the face we have two different emotions expressed; or (3) a facial expression is caused by muscle action associated with two emotions but does not contain detailed elements of either.

At present the evidence seems to show that certain facial areas are better at predicting emotional states than others. Researchers have discovered that the best predictors for happiness are the lower face and the eye area. The most revealing predictors for sadness are the eyes. The eye area and the lower face tell us the most about surprise. Anger is identified by the lower face and the brows and forehead. And finally, the mouth conveys a lot of information through a smile. Generally smiles communicate cooperation and friendliness in human relations.[17]

It is important that the organizational communicator be aware of this dimension of nonverbal cues since facial expressions are used for several important purposes in

[15] Theodore Irwin, "Can You Spot a Liar?" *Dayton Daily News*, August 26, 1974, p. 12.

[16] Paul Ekman and Wallace Friesen, "Constants Across Cultures in the Face and Emotion," *Journal of Personality and Social Psychology*, 17:124–129, April 1971.

[17] Ibid., p. 128.

Emotions are generally communicated through facial expressions. We often depend on the face to determine attitudes since research would suggest that facial cues have considerably more force than either verbal or vocal cues.

the communication setting. They can encourage or discourage feedback during communication. They may determine the intimacy of the relationship and, to some extent, control the communication channel.

Tom Brenner, vice president in charge of personnel for Richdales department store, can effectively discourage feedback about dissatisfaction with the results of a new task force primarily through his facial expressions. He is approached by employee Bill Adler who says he wants to complain about this committee. Tom indicates his unwillingness to listen by frowning, lowering his head, slightly turning away, averting his glance to the floor, and tightening his jaw. If Bill is observant he will know that whatever he says at that moment is likely to be unheard. With this knowledge he will know that he needs to communicate his message in a different context, at a different time, or to a different person!

Facial expressions communicate a large portion of a person's message. Based on his research, Mehrabian[18] suggests that facial cues have considerably more force than either verbal or vocal cues. He concludes that verbal cues supply 7 percent of the meaning of the message, vocal cues supply 38 percent of the meaning, and facial

[18]Mehrabian, op. cit., p. 43.

Figure 6-2 The importance of facial expression.

expressions supply 55 percent of the meaning. Thus, as message receivers we often rely on the face to indicate much of the meaning behind the message we hear. Additional research indicates that women are more reliable predictors of emotional interpretation through facial expressions than men are.[19] This may be due in part to a man's inexperience in either displaying *or* interpreting emotions in interpersonal encounters. Our society allows women to deal more frequently in the affective domain while refusing men the same freedom (i.e., "Little boys don't cry"). In any case, the face often tells a complete story.

EYE CONTACT

Of all the parts of the face, the most often discussed and researched is probably the eye. While interest in the eyes has been varied, much of the research has focused on eye contact or mutual glances. Eye contact is one of the most direct and powerful forms of nonverbal communication. Authority relationships as well as sexual encounters are often initiated and maintained through visual communication. For example, in our culture a direct stare is believed to convey openness and candor and theoretically elicits feelings of intimacy and trust. In regard to the meaning of direct mutual eye contact one researcher has concluded the following, "It is part of the occupational folklore of salesmen, trial attorneys, and those in other persuasive professions that a steady, direct gaze increases the probability that the audience will trust the speaker and his message. Insofar as this superstition is accurate, it casts doubt on

[19] Ross Bick, Robert Miller, Virginia Savin, and William Caul, "Communication of Affect Through Facial Expressions in Humans," *Journal of Personality and Social Psychology*, **23**:362–370, September, 1972.

the hypothesis that the stare automatically triggers an urge to escape or combat it."[20] This conclusion reinforces the theme identified at the outset of this chapter, that nonverbal cues must be interpreted within the context of the communication setting. In some instances a long gaze may indicate honesty, directness, and intimacy while in other settings it may prove threatening. Taking visual liberties may suggest prior acquaintance or desire for acquaintance. There are usually variations in the impression an observer may have about the length of time two individuals have had a relationship based on look duration. A brief look usually signals shorter acquaintanceship.[21]

An example of the variety of interpretations that can be given to eye contact is the salesperson working for WDTN-TV who finally lands an account she has been working on for some time. This account will represent a large increase in her commission pay and she feels quite pleased that she was finally able to convince the client to advertise on WDTN. When she takes the ad to the traffic manager she is told that TV time is at present very tight and that the ad might not be worked in for some time. Her prolonged stare at the traffic manager is intended to be a sign of aggression and determination that this ad will get air time; however, the traffic manager interprets her stare as lack of understanding and continues to patiently explain the problem to her. He hasn't gotten the message!

One interesting aspect of eye contact is the difference found between men and women. Nancy Henley[22] has discovered that women have more eye contact than men. She explains this by concluding that the listener in a conversation tends to look at the speaker rather than vice versa. Men tend to talk more than women. Consequently, if women do more listening in a conversation with men, they will also maintain eye contact more frequently. Henley also discusses the status differences within an organization. The superior in the organization will maintain eye contact longer than the subordinate. This seems to be an indication of his or her power over the subordinate.

Finally, Knapp, reporting on a study conducted to determine how we associate various eye movements with emotional expressions, tells us, "Downward glances are associated with modesty, wide eyes may be associated with frankness, wonder, naivete, or terror, generally immobile facial muscles with a rather constant stare are frequently associated with coldness, eyes rolled upward may be associated with fatigue or a suggestion that another's behavior is a bit unusual."[23]

We can usually tell when someone is looking at us. Did you ever feel someone was staring a hole through you? Have you ever been caught staring at someone and felt guilty? Actually, we spend a small amount of our total time interacting with others by engaging in mutual eye contact, and yet this form of communication can have a great effect on our interpersonal relationships.

---

[20] P. Ellsworth and L. Ross, "Intimacy in Response to a Direct Gaze," *Journal of Experimental Social Psychology*, 11:592–613, November 1975.

[21] S. Thayer and W. Schiff, "Observer Judgement of Social Interaction: Eye Contact and Relationship Inferences," *Journal of Personality and Social Psychology*, 30:110–114, January 1974.

[22] Nancy M. Henley, "Power, Sex, and Nonverbal Communication," *Berkeley Journal of Sociology*, 18:1–26, 1973–1974.

[23] Knapp, op. cit., p. 130.

PERSONAL SPACE

One of the most intriguing ways we communicate with one another is through our use of space. Each person's identification of his own personal space as well as his use of the environment in which he is located influences his ability to send and receive messages effectively. How close we stand to one another, where we sit in a room, and how we generally position ourselves in relation to others will certainly affect our own as well as our listener's level of comfort in the conversation.

Burgoon's definition of personal space is "an invisible variable volume of space surrounding an individual which defines that individual's preferred distance from others. The boundary may be based on psychological needs, physiological needs, or a combination of both."[24]

In Burgoon's study, interviews were held between subjects and interviewers to identify how the subject's perception of the interviewer would change dependent on the amount of distance the interviewer placed between him- or herself and the subject. During the interviews the interviewers positioned themselves at either near or far distances from the subjects. Upon completion of the interviews subjects were asked to respond to questionnaires determining how much they learned during the interview, their attraction toward the interviewer, and their assessment of the interviewer's credibility. Results indicated that interviewers who provided positive feedback (in the form of pleasant facial expressions, head nods, positive/warm vocal patterns) were rated higher on attraction and credibility than interviewers who provided negative feedback. No differences were found in the amount of information a subject was able to remember. Interviewers who gave positive feedback were perceived better at closer distances than were interviewers who gave negative feedback. The combined factors of the reward system used by the interviewers and the distance adopted by them were significant determinants of communication outcomes. Consequently, we tend to feel more comfortable at close distances when the person we are talking with exhibits positive reactions to us. We feel less comfortable and less attracted to another individual when we are at close distance and receiving negative feedback.

The results of this study are important for the organizational setting. Persons in leadership positions are often called upon to give feedback to employees. These results suggest when that feedback is negative, the receiver may need more distance or space than usual. When we invade someone's territory we can easily cause him or her to become defensive and hostile. The organizational leader would be wise to consider territoriality when offering negative feedback to employees.

One of the best-known writers in the use and abuse of *territoriality* is Edward Hall. He defines this term as "behavior by which an organism characteristically lays claim to an area and defends it against members of its own species."[25] The word "defends" suggests the protective nature of this nonverbal gesture. One administrator in a hospital maintains his territory by never allowing nurses to enter his office. He requests

[24] Judee K. Burgoon, "Further Explication and an Initial Test of the Theory of Violations of Personal Space Expectations," paper presented at the Speech Communication Association, San Francisco, December 1976.
[25] Edward T. Hall, *The Hidden Dimension,* Doubleday, Garden City, N.Y., 1966, p. 5.

Personal space may be indicated by the positions individuals take at a desk.

Usually persons sitting corner to corner communicate more. Often when individuals are seated across from one another they can maintain their own distance.

We can even maintain personal space while standing side by side by not looking at one another.

Figure 6-3 When we invade someone's territory we can easily cause them to become defensive and hostile.

information by phone from his office and when he needs items from the nurses' station he moves into their territory rather than allowing them to move into his. Many professors defend the territory of their offices by placing their desk across the middle of the room so that the student remains on one side while the professor remains in the other, more protected area.

Hayes[26] emphasizes the importance of maintaining the correct personal and social distance in order to provide an ideal climate for proper interaction in human communication. If one is trying to remove stress from an interaction, one should attempt to adjust to the most mutually comfortable personal and social distances.

Goldhaber[27] has identified three basic principles that summarize the use of personal space in the organization. These principles seem particularly appropriate when one considers the importance of maintaining status within the organization.

Principle 1: *The higher up one is within an organization, the more and better space he or she will have.* In the American corporate structure the president or the chairman of the board of an organization will generally have the largest office, the executive vice president the next largest office, and so on down the hierarchical ladder. Thus, an executive's office may be relatively spacious while a secretary may have a small cubical. Although the amount of space is not an absolute indicator of prestige it is usually a signal of importance. Any administrator who ignores this principle risks causing much dissension. One administrator selected offices for the staff when new facilities became available. An executive was located in an office decidedly inferior in terms of

[26]Merwyn A. Hayes, "Nonverbal Communication: Expression Without Words," in Richard Huseman et al. (eds.), *Readings in Interpersonal and Organizational Communication*, Holbrook, Boston, 1973, pp. 25–39.

[27]Gerald M. Goldhaber, *Organizational Communication*, Brown, Dubuque, Iowa, 1974, p. 150.

space, number of windows, and the general comfort of the environment. At the same time a new female employee was given a larger and more pleasant territory. The message the male executive received, whether intended or not, was that the administrator was trying to appease the new female employee and had given to her the male executive's rightful space. Either the administrator was unaware of the principle of territoriality or he intended to send the message (a put down) the executive received. In another example, a police chief of a small police department confided in one of the authors that he was so concerned about showing favoritism among his three captains that during construction of the new police station he specified to the inch the distance from his office to theirs. In addition, their offices were *exactly* the same size.

Principle 2: *The higher up one is within an organization, the better protected his or her territory is.* As mentioned earlier, important individuals in the organization appear to be sealed away from intruders by protocol, doors, and secretaries. The more important an individual is in the organization, the less visible he or she is. Many executives have public offices and private, less-accessible offices not often seen by the typical visitor.

Principle 3: *The higher up one is within an organization, the easier it is to invade the territory of lower-status personnel.* A manager or supervisor can enter a subordinate's office by telephone or in person whenever he or she wishes. However, it is often unthinkable for the subordinate to interrupt the boss in the same fashion. Similarly, a subordinate can be called to a meeting while the supervisor must be approached through an appointment. In one case the supervisor overextended this principle and

An individual's personal space and the degree to which the environment is protected may be an indication of that person's status within the organization.

Social distance ranges from 4 to 12 feet and is the distance used for most business interactions. Interviews conducted at this range are characterized by formality.

Personal distance ranges from 1½ to 4 feet. This is normally used for interpersonal conversations.

unexpectedly entered subordinates' offices without knocking. Employees grew to resent this nonverbal signal of authority more than any verbal statement he might have made.

The use of space is important to all communicators. An even greater sensitivity to space can be achieved by noting Hall's[28] four types of distances: intimate, personal, social, and public. *Intimate distance* ranges from 0 (touching) to about 18 inches and

[28]Hall, op. cit., pp. 116–125.

is reserved for close personal friends and intimates. Sharp vision is blurred at this range and for this reason individuals often find this distance uncomfortable when they want to maintain eye contact. *Personal distance* ranges from 1½ to 4 feet. At this distance the persons can still grasp one another but there is no occurrence of visual distortion. This is normally used for interpersonal conversations. The amount of space tolerated for conversation will vary from culture to culture. *Social distance* ranges from 4 to 12 feet and is the distance used for most business interactions. Delahanty[29] indicates that the close phase of this zone (4 feet) is where most impersonal business is transacted. The far phase (12 feet) is used for the transaction of even more formal business and social discourse. Interviews conducted at this range are characterized by formality and may emphasize status or position. Subtle shifts within these zones during a conversation will encourage or discourage greater openness and honesty. The final type, *public distance*, ranges from 12 to 15 feet and is outside the distance necessary for personal involvement. Vocal cues are more important here since eye contact is less frequent. If the communicator is unaware of the uses and functions of these zones he or she may unknowingly move into an inappropriate zone for the topic of conversation. One researcher discovered that when an individual invades the space of another he or she may be seen as less credible. In addition, the receiver, once his or her space is invaded, begins to see the sender as an object rather than as a person.[30]

Filley[31] provides us with an interesting example of how space may be used to indicate conflict situations. He observed the interactions that took place in a joint apprenticeship committee that was designed to administer entrance into apprenticeship programs and monitor the progress of apprentices through their educational and training programs. Such committees were composed of both employer and union representatives. At one particular meeting there were several substitute members on both the employer and the union sides, and visitors from the state and federal apprenticeship services were also present. When the group met, the identity of union, employer, and visitor members was not immediately clear. At the beginning of the meeting the spatial arrangement of the participants was that which is depicted in Figure 6-4a.

[29] Delahanty, op. cit., p. 758.
[30] Judee Heston, "Effects of Personal Space Invasion and Anomia on Anxiety, Non-Person Orientation and Source Credibility," *The Central States Speech Journal,* 25:19–27, Spring 1974.
[31] Alan C. Filley, *Interpersonal Conflict Resolution,* Scott, Foresman, Glenview, Ill., 1975, p. 80.

a) at start of meeting   b) at finish of meeting

Figure 6-4 Spatial arrangements of labor (L), management (M), and visitors (V) at joint apprenticeship committee meeting.

By the end of the meeting, the positions of the members and visitors had altered to that which is shown in Figure 6-4b. The opponents had physically grouped themselves into clearly divided positions. Once committee members learned the identity of one another, they moved to different locations around the table. This type of space usage around individuals would help to promote conflict and continue the division between the labor and management committee members. Filley gives an example of a company that has consciously attempted to minimize the use of space to promote conflict:

> In one company ... the potential conflict and divisiveness of space has been re-duced by minimizing physical boundaries, by requiring a sharing of territory, and by providing common problem-solving rooms for everyone's use. The firm has avoided the use of walls and private offices. Instead, desks are grouped in large rooms containing a variety of activities. A potential division between engineering and manufacturing has been minimized by having engineers and production people work together at the production line, running prototypes through the regular pro-duction facilities. When problems do occur, those people who can contribute solu-tions move to one of several meeting rooms. The rooms are common territory and are provided with flip charts and blackboards. The latter focus attention on the problem and, furthermore, minimize the split into fractions or subgroups.[32]

The impact that the use of space or territoriality has on the process of communica-tion is directly related to the environment in which this space is maintained. Conse-quently, it is important to consider the larger area, the environment.

ENVIRONMENT

How we arrange the objects in our environment, such as desks and chairs, as well as the types of buildings we work in, will affect our interpersonal communication patterns. Organizational communication structures are also affected by environment.

Hall[33] has divided *proxemics* (environmental space) into two separate categories, feature-fixed space and semifixed-feature space. *Feature-fixed space* refers to the un-moving and clearly defined space found in buildings and rooms. The design of an office can greatly affect the communication within that office. Most architects and businesspersons now seem to recognize this influence on their communication patterns and pay close attention to the design of their own environments. *Semifixed-feature space* includes the arrangement of movable objects such as tables and chairs. In many organizations it is still an unwritten rule that the supervisor maintain his own environ-mental space by dividing up his office with his desk. One of the authors has carefully divided his office into personal and impersonal areas. His desk faces a lower couch where he seats persons with whom he wishes to maintain some sense of his own domi-nance; however, to the side of his desk is a comfortable black leather chair where he asks individuals to sit with whom he wishes to maintain a sense of equality. Recent research indicates that individuals are more at ease when the desk is removed.[34] The

---

[32]Ibid., p. 82.
[33]Hall, op. cit., pp. 103–112.
[34]Knapp, op. cit., p. 100.

Semifixed-feature space includes the arrangement of movable objects such as tables and chairs. The way in which individuals arrange themselves around a table may determine who is to maintain the leadership position.

desk may be a boundary of a personal space area or a marker used in the design of the environmental space. In either case, the desk often becomes a barrier to communication.

Porter indicates some of the influences of the environment in the business world by stating, "To a great extent business has followed the lead of the military by the appointment of offices and service pins. The type of desk, rug on the floor, the drapes on the windows, the water jug, the number of stars on the pin, all tell the same story as the military symbols."[35] Persons with higher status in an organization usually demand more territory. The pecking order within the organization may be determined by such things as square feet of office space, size of desk, number of windows, and quality of carpet. In one major corporate headquarters the type of painting in an office determines status in the company. Those of lower status have copies of famous pictures framed in plain brown wood while higher-status employees have original oils framed in elaborate ornate frames.

There seems to be little doubt that both personal and environmental space can influence and change levels of comfort and status. They can also serve to facilitate or hinder the flow of communication.

[35]Porter, op. cit., p. 6.

PARALANGUAGE

The old saying, "It's not what you say but how you say it," is being tested as a research question in relation to the effect of paralanguage on messages sent. Often we deliberately manipulate our voice in order to communicate various meanings. When one person briskly says to the other, in a loud stern voice, "Close the door," the meaning is quite different from the same person saying the identical sentence in a soft, drawn-out tone of voice.

Mehrabian and Wiener concluded that when subjects were asked to match attitudes to the tone of voice used by an unknown individual, "When the attitude communicated in the content contradicted the attitude communicated by a negative tone, the total message was judged as communicating a negative attitude."[36] Consequently, as with most nonverbal signals, the verbal content is less believable.

Several studies have been conducted to determine how accurately we can interpret the expression of feelings through content-free speech. *Content-free speech* means that the verbal portion of the speech has no meaning (either through the use of nonsense syllables or the repetition of letters rather than words). Instead, the focus is on the tone, pitch, and quality of the voice, and the rate of presentation. One study concluded that emotions could be accurately judged and identified without verbal meaning through interpreting the paralanguage cues in the message.[37]

Many famous radio, television, and stage personalities are well known for the qualities of their voices. The low, breathy voice is usually identified with the sex goddess, while a low, deep voice with a certain pitch inflection is a requirement for most radio announcers.

Often we manipulate the inflection of our voice to contradict the verbal message. The result of such manipulation is usually sarcasm. The boss may say, "This has been a really terrific day," when his voice indicates, "It's been lousy." A listener's ability to accurately predict these emotions through paralanguage cues depends on the following: (1) the listener's sensitivity to emotions expressed vocally by others and his ability to identify his own vocal expressions of emotions, (2) the listener's ability to make auditory discriminations, (3) the amount of exposure to emotional expressions carried by the voice, and (4) the general intellectual ability of the listener. Studies show great differences in the accuracy of judging emotional vocal expressions depending on the type of emotion expressed. One study found anger identified 63 percent of the time, while pride was only correctly identified 20 percent of the time. Joy and hate were easily recognized but shame and love were more difficult to identify.[38]

Many decisions concerning credibility (or trustworthiness and likableness) are made from word-free presentations of the voice alone. Research indicates that listeners can accurately predict physical characteristics, aptitudes and interests, personality traits,

---

[36] Albert Mehrabian and Morton Wiener, "Decoding of Inconsistent Communications," *Journal of Personality and Social Psychology*, 6:109–114, 1967.

[37] Joel R. Davitz and Lois Jean Davitz, "The Communication of Feelings by Content-Free Speech," *Journal of Communication*, 9:6–13, March 1959.

[38] Knapp, op. cit., p. 161.

ethnic group, education, and dialect region of the speaker based on paralanguage. However, listener comprehension does not seem to be affected by the tone or variation in vocal cues.[39]

In one organization a woman was next in line for a promotion. However, her boss told her that certain personal characteristics kept her from getting the job. Only after asking a colleague for advice did she learn that one of her most annoying personal characteristics was her high-pitched strident voice. Since the new position would require public relations work and representing the company to the public, it was felt the image she would present would be a negative one. The stereotypically high-strung and extremely tense individual is often associated with having a high-pitched voice.

The voice is important, not only as a carrier of a message, but as a complement to that message as well. The communicator needs to be sensitive to its influence on the interpretation of his or her spoken message.

TOUCH

An obvious type of nonverbal language is tactile communication. The touch of a hand, or an arm around someone's shoulder, can create a more vivid and direct message than dozens of words. However, if tactile communication is used inappropriately it can cause barriers and create mistrust. Obviously one could easily invade someone's territory through this type of nonverbal communication.

Jourard and Rubin[40] maintain that each person establishes some type of pattern of touching in most of his or her interpersonal relationships. These two researchers also distinguish between two types of touch avoidance. Some people may avoid being touched while others may avoid touching. Persons may also avoid touching members of one sex but not of the other sex. An individual needs to be sensitive to nonverbal cues that indicate another's discomfort with being touched. One small-town businessman broke off negotiations with a larger corporation for a deal that would have been advantageous to both when the representative from the larger firm put his arm around the small-town businessman as a gesture of accord. The small-town businessman began to suspect that the corporation was trying to manipulate his decision. On the other hand, Delahanty[41] points to the importance of touch where verbal communication is not possible or socially acceptable. He suggests that in an interview between two men a simple pat on the back may convey significant emotional support that cannot be easily communicated verbally by those two men, at least not according to our contemporary cultural mores.

An interesting review of touch literature by Henley reveals, "Women are expected to accept as normal behavior the daily violations of their persons. However, when they reciprocate or especially initiate touch with men they are likely to be interpreted as conveying specific sexual intent."[42] She also discovered that in cases where there was a

---

[39]Goldhaber, op. cit., p. 146.
[40]S. M. Jourard and J. E. Rubin, "Self-Disclosure and Touching: A Study of Two Modes of Interpersonal Encounter and their Interrelation," *Journal of Humanistic Psychology*, 8:39–48, 1968.
[41]Delahanty, op. cit., p. 758.
[42]Henley, op. cit., pp. 192–193.

The traditional handshake is an "acceptable" way to communicate through touch in our society.

Touch is usually reciprocal and indicates solidarity.

difference in some form of status (socioeconomic status, sex, or age) those of higher status (higher socioeconomic status, male, or older) touched those of lower status significantly more often. In the organizational setting the difference in touching and status is most prevalent between the boss and his secretary. A pat on the shoulder is appropriate if the boss initiates the action and quite the reverse if initiated by the secretary. Touch may be the nonverbal equivalent of calling another person by his or her first name. Used reciprocally, it indicates solidarity. When touch is not reciprocal, it tends to indicate status differences.

Ashley Montagu[43] relates a particularly memorable description of the importance of touch when he describes a visit made by an American doctor to the Children's Clinic in Düsseldorf before World War I. Dr. Talbot was shown around the wards by the director of the hospital. The wards were very neat and tidy, but what provoked his curiosity was the sight of a fat old woman who was carrying a very sick baby on her hip. "Who's that?" inquired Dr. Talbot. "Oh that," replied the director, "is Old Anna. When we have done everything we can medically for a baby, and it is still not doing well, we turn it over to Old Anna, and she is very successful." Not until the late 1920s did American pediatricians begin to recognize the importance of tender loving care. At Bellevue Hospital in New York, following the institution of "mothering" on the pediatric wards, the mortality rates for infants in 1 year fell from 30 to 35 percent to less than 10 percent. Doctors had discovered that what a child needs, if it is to prosper, is to be handled, carried, caressed, and cuddled.

It would seem that not only children need to be touched and caressed, but adults as well. Touch, as a means of communication, can be a powerful tool in helping the communicator to convey not only the content of his or her message, but also the emotional impact of that message.

SILENCE AND TIME

Two other areas of nonverbal communication briefly mentioned here are the use of silence and time. Silence can perform a number of highly significant communicative functions. It can serve to provide a link between messages or to sever a relationship. Silence can either heal or wound the emotional state of a relationship. It can create tension and uneasiness. Most often we try to fill in silent periods with pointless verbiage. Silence can also be judgmental by indicating assent or dissent, favor or disfavor.

The use of time can be an indicator of status. The amount of time allotted to an interview often reflects the status accorded the respondent. The length of time a person waits prior to being granted an interview suggests his or her prescribed status and importance along with the urgency of the topic of conversation. The administrator in an organization should be aware of the effect a prolonged waiting period can have on a subordinate. This person may experience much anxiety and tension by having to wait beyond the appointed time.

Another example of the use of time in the organizational setting is the time schedule. A manager may communicate definite values through the maintenance of his time schedule. He can indicate his status by suggesting that his time is more valuable than that of the employee and the employee must arrange his schedule to suit that of the manager. However, both the employee and manager can also use time to communicate to each other their mutual respect.

[43] Ashley Montagu, *Touching: The Human Significance of the Skin*, Harper & Row, New York, 1971, pp. 93–95.

CONCLUSION

In our opening example, six people nonverbally communicated their feelings about their attendance at a particular meeting. Mike was visibly uncomfortable, obviously not looking forward to the upcoming meeting. Mary felt supportive of Mike as indicated by her close proximity to him. Her own nervous behavior (looking at her watch) showed that she also did not look forward to the meeting. Joe and Sam, on the other hand, seemed relaxed and generally in good moods. There appeared to be somewhat of a power struggle between Joe and Mike as they positioned themselves at opposite ends of the table. This was a dramatic demonstration of their different reactions to the situation in which they found themselves on that Monday morning. We could choose any number of explanations for Jack's slow smile as he caught Mary's attention.

As it turned out, Gene, who came late to the meeting, was the president of WDTN television station. He had called the meeting because he had just announced a decision to appoint Joe to a higher-level position in the organization (and Sam would soon be named his assistant). Mike was uncomfortable because this was a position he had expected to receive. Mary's relationship with Mike was friendly, and thus she too felt he should have been appointed. The nonparticipant observer in the corner of the room was present because the president had asked for outside help in reorganizing the structure of communication within the organization. The consultant intended to share her observations of these nonverbal cues with the president. One of the consultant's goals would be to make the president aware of the nonverbal cues being expressed around him.

Throughout this chapter we have emphasized that, regardless of your position in the organizational setting, it is important that you develop a sensitivity to nonverbal messages. We have discovered that individuals gain better cooperation from others if they recognize and respond appropriately to nonverbal cues. By observing posture, facial expressions, gestures, use of personal as well as environmental space, the influence of environmental factors, effects of paralanguage, and tactile communication, the communicator stands a much better chance of reaching others and communicating accurately the intent of his or her message. We have all been somewhat aware of nonverbal cues all of our lives. Perhaps now we can better identify and understand them. In the process we will communicate with each other more effectively.

Chapter 7

Interviewing: Functions and Skills

This chapter on interviewing will discuss what is involved when two people get together for the purpose of interacting. So that we can distinguish interviewing from other forms of one-to-one communication, let us use a definition as a means of establishing the parameters of the interview: *The interview is a form of oral communication involving two parties, at least one of whom has a preconceived and serious purpose, and both of whom speak and listen from time to time.*[1]

When we say that it is *oral communication*, we mean a face-to-face exchange, rather than an exchange that takes place over the telephone or via some closed-circuit television. In other words, both people can hear directly the verbal language and can see clearly the nonverbal cues. These latter cues are important and will be discussed later in the chapter.

The phrase *two parties* refers to the one-to-one idea (a dyad) as distinct from a group meeting of three, four, or some limited number of people. However, this is not to say that more than two people cannot be present or even participate. The word "parties" refers to the idea that the interview is a bipolar interaction. One party may consist of three or four people who conduct the interview with the other party, which may consist of only one person. This often happens in team interviews when several

---

[1] Robert S. Goyer, W. Charles Redding, and John T. Rickey, *Interviewing Principles and Techniques. A Project Text,* Kendall, Hunt, Dubuque, Iowa, 1968, pp. 6–7.

managers are contemplating hiring the same person. Also, it occurs when a panel of news reporters interview one person, which is, for example, the format of the "Meet the Press" television program.

At least one of whom has a preconceived and serious purpose is a phrase used to differentiate the interview from everyday conversation. For an interview to take place, at least one party must be aware of the purpose of the meeting and must have planned (to a greater or lesser extent) what will happen. The word "serious" is used to "suggest that the purpose of the interview goes beyond the enjoyment of each other's company, or beyond trivial and transitory interests."[2] While there may be some social conversation during the interview (especially during the opening moments), it primarily serves as a vehicle for breaking the ice or for acting as a pleasant diversion.

When we say *both of whom speak and listen from time to time*, we are stating that both parties ask questions and both give answers. They speak, listen, and speak again. If one party does most or all (80 to 100 percent) of the talking, then he or she does not participate in an interview, but delivers a public speech to an audience of one. The key to understanding an interview is to perceive it as a dynamic interaction in which both parties are giving and receiving spontaneously. An interview flows sometimes fast, sometimes slow. Its progress is influenced by the participants who can usually control how and what will happen. Even when similar questions are asked, the answers will not be the same. And since an answer can stimulate another question, the interaction that results makes each interview a unique experience.

Since both parties are concerned with the interaction, they must be concerned with feedback. This term refers to verbal and nonverbal answers or responses each party communicates. How you respond to a question, in terms of quickness of response, facial expression, voice quality, etc., can have an impact on how you are perceived. The same is true when asking a question or listening to an answer. As you can see, the interaction is constant, even though one person is speaking and one is listening. Success in interviewing will be influenced by how well you read and give feedback to the other party. Reading the chapter on interpersonal communication will sensitize you to the need of sharing yourself with others. Other chapters can give additional insight; however, you will need practice under an expert's supervision to identify your strengths and weaknesses in using feedback.

STRUCTURE OF AN INTERVIEW

As a structured communication experience, the interview can be analyzed by looking at the logical process of its development. While recognizing the importance of the preinterview stage, we are concerned here with the development of the actual dyadic communication setting. Rather than detail numerous patterns of interview development, it is better for the beginner to look at the interview in a tripartite way: a communication activity that has an opening, a middle, and a closing.

[2]Ibid., p. 6.

The Opening

As the person being interviewed (*interviewee*), your presence in the interview setting is probably a response to an invitation. In other words, you are the guest and the person who is interviewing you (*interviewer*) is the host. It is primarily the responsibility of the interviewer to set the proper tone for the start of the interview. This may involve several interaction activities. First, he will try to establish a rapport with you, to have you lose your feelings of anxiety and to create a positive bond between the two of you. He may ask you a question that deals with a common topic that he feels you can answer easily. "How was your drive into the city today?" "I noticed on your resume that you like to read. What type of books do you like most?" "Your major was accounting. Tell me about some of the courses you took."

The interviewer may make reference to a mutual friend or to a recent news event. It is unlikely that he will start by asking you a question that requires a delicate answer, such as "What is the lowest salary you will accept?" However, if this does happen, the interviewer is testing your mental reflexes more than he is seeking information. He wants some idea of how you handle yourself under unexpected circumstances. If you can handle it, roll with the punch, "That depends on the amount of time and responsibility the job requires." If you are caught off guard, be open about it. "I haven't really given the salary much thought."

A second goal of the interviewer is to establish a bond of understanding between you both. Here he is concerned with making sure you know the purpose or reasons for the interview. If they have been explained fully in a letter or by previous conversation, only a brief restatement will be necessary. If not, he should take time to explain *why* you are there, *what* the interview will cover, and *how* the interview data will be used. You need this information to operate effectively within the framework of the interview. It is your responsibility to ask for the information when it is not volunteered.

The interviewee who is just starting with interviews should follow the lead of the interviewer. Let him set the style of the interaction. When he is jovial, respond in a light, humorous manner. When he wants to talk about trivial matters, respond as intelligently as you can without showing boredom. When you feel he is ready to begin the more substantial part of the interview, move along with him.

The Middle

The middle of the interview is similar to the main course of a meal. It is the largest contributing factor in satisfying your hunger. If it is an employment interview, this is where you make an impression on the employer and where you gather impressions useful in deciding whether or not you want to work for the company. If it is an information interview, this is where you gather the data necessary to meet your objectives.

In most organizational interviews, the interviewer decides on a pattern or style of development that will cover the necessary areas. So that you can understand better how the middle of an interview is developed, we will discuss three styles of interviewing, that is, three different approaches to developing the interaction between the two parties.

Styles of Interviewing   The style of interviewing used to develop the body of the interview can differ. One person may use only general type questions and rely on the respondent's answer from which to develop follow-up questions. The news reporter who asks the city official, "Do you feel the closed council meeting made any progress?" is looking for the respondent to give insights so he or she can ask more specific questions. This style of questioning is referred to as a *nonscheduled interview.* The preparation for the interview usually involves background reading and research rather than the formulation of specific questions. The reason for this is simply that the interviewer's questions depend on the respondent's answers. While this seems like an easy style of interviewing, the skill in handling the unexpected development of questions and answers is outside the ability of most novice interviewers.

In nonscheduled interviews the respondent has significant impact on what topics will be covered. By wording her answers carefully, she can manipulate the interviewer to ask the types of questions she wants asked. Politicians are good at ending an answer with such remarks as, "Of course, there are some hidden factors that contribute to the problem." The average person's response would be, "Oh, what factors are they?" And this is what he wants, because now he can talk about his points as if he is responding to a request for his views. To be effective, the nonscheduled interview style requires experience in handling the give and take of unrehearsed questions and answers.

Some interviewers decide on the major areas that need to be covered and compose a list of questions that relate to the areas. While not all questions are prepared, enough are scheduled in advance to give the interview some structure. This style of questioning is called a *moderately scheduled interview.* Stewart and Cash believe the advantages of this type of interview are that it "forces a higher level of preparation, is easier to replicate and record answers, and is easier for an unskilled interviewer to conduct."[3]

News journalists frequently make use of the moderately scheduled interview as well as the nonscheduled interview. At a news conference or when conducting a private interview, the reporter will be seeking information about specific areas and will have developed carefully worded questions with which to probe the topic area. Again, background research and reading are necessary to the formulation of valid, germane questions. Frequent users of the nonscheduled and moderately scheduled interviews are police officers. When they are dispatched by the police department to respond to a citizen's call, they usually have only cursory information on which to carry out an interview. In this situation, the officers are forced to use a nonscheduled interview, relying on their experience and the responses of the citizens to develop the interview strategy. However, if the officers are involved in a follow-up interview, they will have knowledge of specific subject areas and will have formulated specific questions to use. In this situation a moderately scheduled interview would seem most appropriate. One final user of the moderately scheduled interview is personnel people employed to carry out employment interviewing. When interviewing prospective employees, a personnel interviewer will have identified areas of interest about which she desires information.

[3]Charles J. Stewart and William B. Cash, *Interviewing: Principles and Practices*, Brown, Dubuque, Iowa, 1974, p. 81.

To investigate an area, she will ask specific questions, but she will use the answer to formulate further questions or probes.

The last type of interaction is called a *highly scheduled interview*. To use it the interviewer prepares *all* the questions in advance. The interviewer asks only the questions prepared. It is most frequently used by public opinion pollsters, social science researchers, and by marketing research companies. The following is a comparison of the advantages and disadvantages. "Highly-scheduled interviews are easier to replicate, easier for unskilled interviewers to conduct, and take less time.... They have the disadvantage of no probing into answers and no flexibility in adapting to different respondents."[4]

While the structure of the interview dictates the amount and to some extent the types of questions to ask, it does not tell us how to arrange them, that is, what sequence they should have. One frequently used ordering of questions is known as the *funnel sequence*. Here one moves from the general to the specific, moving from a broad question to more and more narrow ones. An example would be a supervisor seeking to determine a prospective employee's views about drugs.

First Q: Do you feel drugs are a problem in America?
Second Q: Do you feel the drug problem is affecting young people?
Third Q: Are young people aware of the consequences of drug use?
Fourth Q: What do you feel we should do with young drug users?
Fifth Q: What has been your experience with drugs?

By starting with a general question, allow the interviewee to establish his frame of reference. Using the information given, the interviewer can ask a more restrictive question, the answer to which can be used to narrow the topic even more. By the time she gets to the last question, the interviewer has provided a complete picture of the respondent's views. Usually the funnel sequence begins with a generally oriented question and moves toward specifically oriented questions. Besides providing information, the funnel sequence provides a good method for developing full communication. It allows the respondent to do most of the talking, and provides an easy way for the interviewee to develop his thoughts.

The Closing

Frequently the conclusion of an interview comes as a natural process of the communication interaction. The two parties have made the statements they felt were important and the questions they had were answered. At other times, the interview continues because one or both parties feel they want more information or they are not sure how to end the interaction.

The interviewer has primary responsibility for ending the interview. One easy procedure is to have a summary of the major points he has derived from the interview. Then he asks the person to clarify or add to the summary statement. This use of a summary helps each person to clarify what he or she felt the other person said. If one party feels he has been misinterpreted or his views omitted, then he can make the correction before the interaction ends. This is an important part of the employment

[4]Ibid., p. 82.

interview. If the applicant is not clear as to what happens next, he should seek the information from the employer. Such questions as "Will there be another interview?" "When will the decision be made?" "What do I need to do now?" need to be answered if the information has been omitted.

If the interviewer is the one who asks for the interview to take place, then he should make every effort to be a gracious host and end the discussion by expressing his appreciation of the time and energy spent by the interviewee.

Finally, there is an increasing awareness of the role that nonverbal actions play in the process of leave-taking at the end of an interview. Often the interviewer will give physical cues to people, consciously or unconsciously, about his intention of ending the interaction. Such actions as leaning forward toward the other party, increasing head nodding, breaking eye contact, and making a major change in sitting position are usually viewed as signals to the other party that the interviewer seeks to end the interview.[5]

ROLE OF THE PARTICIPANTS IN THE INTERVIEW[6]

In the majority of interviews that occur in business and industry, in the criminal justice area and with the mass media, there are two participants, each of whom accept a role. The role is either as the interviewer or the interviewee. Both parties share responsibility for the successful outcome of the interview, and both parties must participate in the interaction. While they do have some similar responsibilities, there are other obligations that are assumed by each separately.

Responsibilities of the Interviewer

The interviewer is the person who initiates the interaction. Consequently, she is considered the person in charge, who often assumes the leadership role in an interview. Among her responsibilities are the following:

Establishing the Time and Setting for the Interview It is fair to say that in most interviews the interviewer calls for the interview. She may be stimulated by someone else requesting an interview, but she decides whether it will take place or not. The employer sets up the meeting with the employee, or the counselor arranges the meeting with the counselee. Usually the interviewee goes to the interviewer's location for the interview. There are some exceptions for this as when the news reporter or policeman (interviewer) goes to the building of the businessman (interviewee), who has been robbed.

Establishing the Purpose of the Interview The interviewer decides on the goals or outcome of the interview. The news reporter wants information for a story, the police

[5]For further information on the implication of nonverbal actions when ending an interview, see Mark L. Knapp, R. P. Hart, G. W. Friedrich, and Gary Shulman, "The Rhetoric of Goodbye: Verbal and Nonverbal Correlates of Human Leave Taking," *Speech Monographs*, **40**:182–198, August 1973.

[6]This material has been adapted from Goyer et al., Unit 2, in James M. Black (ed.), *How to Get Results from Interviewing,* McGraw-Hill, New York, 1970, chap. 2; John W. Keltner, *Interpersonal Speech Communication: Elements and Structures,* Wadsworth, Belmont, Calif., 1970, chap. 12.

officer wants information for the crime report, the manager wants to know why the employee is so often late to work, and so forth. It is important for him or her to make the purpose clear to the interviewee, so they both start out working toward the same goal. Knowing that the employer wants to congratulate you and not to reprimand you will have a big influence on how you interact with him.

Establishing the Level of Psychological Proximity with the Interviewee The question here is how involved, on a personal level, should the interviewer become with the interviewee? Sometimes we need to relate on an interpersonal level to allow the interviewee to respond openly. What psychological distance is best needs to be decided before the interview. If the interviewer sees it is not working to facilitate communication, then she must change the proximity. As Keltner states:

> We cannot say that the interviewer should always maintain a certain objective psychological distance from his informant. Sometimes a high level of interpersonal involvement is essential to reaching the necessary levels of acceptance that will allow the respondent to speak freely. No two informants have the same acceptance level to any one interviewer. In short, the interpersonal relationship for each interview is different—even when it involves the same person at different times.[7]

Control and Focus the Direction of the Communication Usually it is the responsibility of the interviewer to see that the interview begins on time, covers specific areas, and ends when appropriate. To do this, she must manipulate the interaction to keep the interview moving toward its goals. If, for example, the conversation moves away from the topic and into a discussion of something that is irrelevant, then she should maneuver the interaction back to a relevant area. Much of this is done through questions and answers, the use of which will be covered in this chapter. On the other hand, the interviewer does not want to dominate the interview, or to suppress the flow of information through her control. The best strategy to use is to start with specific topics to get the interview going, and then to allow the interviewee to participate in the style and to the degree he desires.

Help the Interviewee Perceive his Functions "Why did you want to see me? Oh, I thought you were going to...." If this conversation takes place in the middle of the interview, the interviewer has not helped the interviewee correctly perceive his function. It is important that the interviewer communicate why she has called for the interview, and what she expects the interviewee to contribute toward its success. If possible, this should take place prior to the meeting.

Responsibilities of the Interviewee

As an equal partner in the dyadic interaction, the interviewee must contribute to its successful outcome. While his responsibilities are not as many as the interviewer's, he nevertheless has definite obligations.

---

[7]Keltner, op. cit., p. 277.

Provide the Information Needed Sometimes the interviewee feels he should give as little information as possible, thereby minimizing the risk of revealing some flaw or of putting his foot in his mouth. Being prudent with what one says is usually a wise decision. However, to withhold information that is needed for a valid discussion or to stay silent out of fear usually results in a decision that does not reflect a common reality between the two parties. Many novice interviewees are alarmed when they are asked question after question on the same subject. The interviewees feel as if they were being scrutinized by an inquisitor. It is not that they want to withhold or distort information, but rather they are not sure what information the interviewer is seeking.

Holm discusses this ambiguity and suggests some appropriate strategies:

> If you are in doubt, either about the purpose of the question or about what you should say in reply . . . take your time, observing the questioner to see if you can fathom the motive or the attitude behind the question; thereby gauging the nature of the appropriate response. Repeating the question will assure that you have heard it correctly and will give you a bit of added time to consider your answer. Do not bluff; but if you feel that you must qualify your answer, do not withold your qualification.[8]

If you feel you don't understand the question or the reason for the information requested, *ask* the interviewer for a clarification of what he wants. If he is left with only his assumptions, then he can very possibly misjudge you.

Avoid Irrelevant Answers Don't allow your own special interest to override the discussion of relevant topics. Even when it shows you in a good light, your information must be germane; if not, it does little to help the interviewer understand you in relationship to the goals of the interview. However, if you feel your elaboration of an answer is relevant, then ask the interviewer if he believes the information would help in the decision-making process. If the answer is affirmative, provide him with the information.

Have Clear and Specific Answers Be specific when you reply. Make sure your responses are directly connected to the question asked. A good rule of thumb is to include parts of the question in the first few sentences. Question: "How do you think your past work experience will aid you in performing this new job?" Answer: "My past work experience involved handling ledgers, petty cash, and financial records. With this new job, my responsibilities will involve. . . ." Also, try to use supporting material (examples, illustrations, analogies, etc.) that are specific and helpful in understanding the topic.

Correct Misunderstandings and Ask for Feedback Often your role is to share your feelings, attitudes, and information with the interviewer. If it happens that what he receives is not an accurate picture of what you sent, then you need to assist in the corrections. If you feel he has not fully understood, then try to clarify the topic in his

---

[8]James N. Holm, *Productive Speaking for Business and the Profession*, Allyn and Bacon, Boston, 1967, p. 241.

mind. Usually this means not a restatement of the same words, but a new choice of words to explain the same topic. Ask the interviewer to explain how he views the information, attitudes, or feelings you have discussed during the interaction. Use this feedback as a way of assessing the congruity that exists between your ideas in your mind and your ideas in his mind. But the fact that both parties participate in the interaction is a *constant given* element found in all interviews. How we go about participating in this interaction will be discussed in the next section on the use of questions and answers in the interview.

THE USE OF QUESTIONS AND ANSWERS

As we stressed in the early part of this chapter, the interview is a dyadic process involving the interchangeable roles of listener and speaker. For a fuller understanding of this concept, it is important to examine the primary mechanism of this dynamic process, the use of questions and answers.

The quality and quantity of a response is directly linked to the question asked. The proper use of questions can allow the interviewer to guide the nature of the responses to insure information that is clear, valid, and relevant to the subject being discussed. Also, good questions give the interviewee a direction in which to develop his or her responses and some idea of the amount of information the questioner desires.

Use of Questions

In the interview both parties speak and listen. That is, both have the opportunity to seek responses by asking questions and to give responses by answering questions. We shall separate the act of asking questions from the act of giving answers. First, we will focus on several types of questions that can be used during the communication interaction.

Open Questions This type of question allows the respondent to open his mind and to give as much information as he desires. The question is worded in general terms to identify only a topic or a direction for the respondent to follow. When the employer asks, "Would you please describe your last job?" he is asking an open question. What the job applicant wants to say about his past work experience is left to his discretion. The police telephone operator is using an open question when she asks, "Would you please tell me what happened?" as is the sales clerk who is trying to help the gift purchaser make a selection by saying, "Well, tell me something about her." The decision on what information to give is left to the respondent. While it seems like an easy question to handle, there are advantages and disadvantages to its use. Stewart and Cash identify several:

Advantages
  1 Open questions may reveal what the respondent thinks is important, and he or she may volunteer information the interviewer might not think to ask.
  2 They may reveal a respondent's lack of information or misunderstanding of words or concepts, and they may show the respondent's intensity of feelings to an issue.

3 In addition, lengthy answers to open questions may bring out the respondent's frame of reference, prejudices, or stereotypes.

Disadvantages

1 Open questions may consume a great amount of time if the respondent does not judiciously choose his or her words.

2 If they do use too much time, they can limit the amount of progress an interview can make toward reaching its goal.

3 Often fewer topics are covered with open questions than with questions that seek a specific response.[9]

The open-ended question can be qualified and still give the respondent freedom to choose an answer. When a car salesman asks a customer, "What kind of safety features are you looking for on a new car?" he is narrowing the topic area, but still is allowing the respondent a choice in selecting an answer.

Often the open-ended question will provide information on which further clarification is necessary. To obtain this clarification, the next kind of question is used.

Closed Question With this question you are limiting the freedom of choice of the respondent. The question suggests, to the respondent, guidelines to follow in giving a response. These guidelines can limit the response to a simple yes-no answer, "Will you work overtime today?" or they can offer a multiplicity of answers from which the respondent chooses one, "Will you take your vacation in June, July, or August?" Sometimes the closed question implies a number of responses from which a person must select the one that best describes his or her beliefs or attitudes, "Which of the new car models is your favorite?" When one is seeking to tap the respondent's attitudes, beliefs, or knowledge about a specific topic, then the closed question is appropriate. Closed questions usually result in shorter answers than open questions do.

Again, Stewart and Cash have identified several advantages and disadvantages to using closed questions.

Advantages

1 More questions can be asked, in more areas and in less time.

2 The interviewer can more closely regulate the direction and intensity of the interview.

3 For the respondent, closed questions require less effort and can be less threatening than some open questions.

Disadvantages

1 Closed questions may give the questioner only a limited amount of information.

2 They may close off other information from the respondent that could be potentially valuable.[10]

Most interviews will use both types of questions with the open kind more at the beginning and the closed variety more toward the middle or when specific responses

---

[9] Stewart and Cash, op. cit., p. 48.
[10] Ibid., p. 50.

are desired. The key to using the open and closed questions is this: If you want the respondent to choose what is important and put it into his answer, then use an *open question*. If you want to present him with alternatives and have him select one, then use a *closed question*.

Bias Questions   There are two types of questions that should be avoided because they can bias the answer of the other party. They are the leading question and the loaded question.

You must be careful not to lead the respondent to think you desire one alternative over another. The host who asks his dinner guest, "Don't you think this wine is excellent?" is leading the respondent toward only one response. The employer who says to the job applicant, "You can type, can't you?" is asking a *leading question* that implies if you want the job, you had better answer in the affirmative. Also, avoid the use of leading questions that force people into socially acceptable answers. "You don't use drugs, do you?" or "Of course, most of you don't drink." These questions are worded in order to force the respondent into a socially agreeable answer.

In addition to asking leading questions, avoid questions that make the respondent feel threatened. "Did you exercise your patriotic right to vote in the last election?" is the kind of question known as a *loaded question*. It is loaded in one direction, for if you say you did not vote, you are also inferring that you are not patriotic. Some questions are loaded so that any answer is a threatening one. If you answer, "Have you stopped smoking dope?" in the affirmative, then you imply you did smoke dope. If you have never smoked marijuana, then how can you answer this question? Again, avoid loading your questions so that the response threatens the respondent.

Follow-Up Questions   Finally, there are two types of questions that are frequently used to follow up on answers given by the respondent. If the answer is not clear, does not give enough detail, or is somehow incomplete, then you can use the mirror question or the probe question.

With the *mirror question* you are reflecting or playing back the response. You do this so the interviewee can elaborate on an answer that was either incomplete or lacked enough detail. When you do reflect or restate the response, make sure you use his or her language. If the official in a news interview stated, "The city revenue will be spent on a priority basis," a mirror question could be, "What projects are top priority?" Another example would be the police officer who asks the victim of a burglary about home security and she replies, "I always keep my house locked up tight." A mirror question would be, "When you say 'locked up tight,' what does that include?"

Another type of question that is based upon the respondent's answer is the *probe question*. But rather than reflect the answer, the probe uses the nondirective method to encourage the respondent to say more. Such natural phrases as "I see," "Uh-huh," "Go on," "Why is that?" "Tell me more," "Will you give me an example of that?" are used when you wish the respondent to say more about the subject. Frequently probe questions are used while the respondent is speaking as a means of giving him or her feedback, in order to ensure that the respondent is on the right track and will remain so. Probes may be viewed as a form of encouragement, the success of which depends on the respondent's attitude toward the interviewer. Richardson et al. see these encouragements and attitudes as tied to the respondent's level of participation.

> If the respondent is initially well disposed toward the interviewer and is comfortable with the subject matter of the interview, it seems likely that encouragements will increase his level of participation; but they may not be necessary for this purpose, since participation may already be high. If the respondent feels neutral toward the interviewer and the subject matter, encouragements may increase his level of participation. But, if he feels hostile toward the interviewer or uncomfortable about the subject matter, he may well interpret an "Uh-huh" as a criticism of his response. And, if he cannot respond at length without guidance or if he tends to express himself succinctly, encouragements may make him generally uncomfortable and thus reduce his level of participation.[11]

Both parties in the interview can prepare questions that they feel will help accomplish their goals. But mirror and probe questions must arise from the interaction. The successful use of these questions is a skill that comes from experiencing many interactions and by studying one's successes or failures in applying them. Usually the degree of success one has in using these questions is a valid indication of how alert the interviewer is during the interaction.

Use of Answers

Earlier in the chapter we said that both parties speak and listen from time to time. Up to now we have concentrated on the speaking part as the act of asking a question. Now we will shift to the other side and discuss speaking as the answering of questions.

First, let us analyze the general categories by which inadequate answers can be classified. *Ototherverbalized answers* are inadequate because they usually go beyond the intent of the question and give useless or irrelevant information.

The opposite response to the previous category of answer would be *no answer*. If the respondent refuses to answer the question, then you must decide whether to follow up with a reworded question or to drop the matter. As you can imagine, too many no answers and the interview will grind to a halt.

Another inadequate answer is the *inaccurate answer*. Here the respondent exaggerates, misspeaks himself, or simply lies. Often the best way to validate an inaccurate answer is to reword it and ask it later. The consistency of the responses should help judge the accuracy of the answer. According to some police detectives, this method of validating an answer through the consistency of the responses is the best way to determine if a suspect's story is an accurate picture of reality.

A fourth unacceptable answer is the *partial answer*. If this occurs, the interviewer may follow up by asking directly for that part of the question not answered. By

---

[11] Stephen A. Richardson, Barbara S. Dohrenwend, and David Klein, *Interviewing: Its Forms and Functions*, Basic, New York, 1965, p. 203.

staying alert, we can avoid accepting partial answers as a full response to our inquiry. It is the lazy or incompetent interviewer who accepts partial answers when what is needed is full disclosure. Remember how vigilant your mother was when she found the package of cookies empty and asked how many you had eaten, and your reply was a partial answer of, "Just a few." She wanted to know how many was "just a few" and followed up with another question. If you feel the answer is not complete, then use follow-up questions until you are satisfied.

Style is another aspect of answering questions that should concern us. A competent interview participant needs to be concerned with the way in which he or she responds to queries.

First, answer the question the way it was asked. Use the same sequence of ideas, give as much information as requested, and observe the questioner to determine the reason or attitudes behind the question. If you have any doubts about the intent of the question, ask for clarification before you answer. But make the answer specific and substantial enough to answer the question.

Second, if a follow-up question is used, try to determine whether the questioner is seeking more details, clarification of a point, or is narrowing your response to a specific point on which he desires more information. If you are not sure, ask the questioner to repeat or rephrase his question so that you can better understand his needs. In the employment interview, when the manager asked the applicant for more information about his work experience, the applicant responded, "Well, let's see, I . . . eh . . . worked there a long time . . . and did several different things." The applicant was more concerned about remembering his past job than with the interaction taking place at present. If the applicant had asked, "What, specifically, would you like to know?" he would have been open, and giving a definite response to the manager's question.[12]

Third, what if you feel the question asks for information that is confidential, or for information that you have no knowledge of or insight into. Usually you have the option of not answering such questions. However, it is best to offer some explanation for declining to answer. While your explanation need not be elaborate, it should be substantial and, most important, it should come across as being an honest, straightforward answer. Many people will feel the reason for not answering is more important than the answer itself.

Fourth, and last, is the style you use when handling resistance to an answer. This can occur when the questioner disagrees with a statement or is suspicious of your attitude and motives. Your best strategy is to work toward creating a common meaning. That is, try to see it from his point of view, and to bring his point of view closer to your point of view. Accentuate the similarities rather than the differences. Explain the reasoning behind your answer. Try to have the questioner talk about his feelings. Above all, don't meet resistance with stronger resistance. This will stop interaction rather than facilitate it.

---

[12]Holm, op. cit., p. 241, notes a survey of employment interviewers that reported an indefinite or vague response was deemed to reflect unfavorably on the interviewee.

TYPES OF INTERVIEWS

There are numerous types of interviewing situations that occur between two parties. While we cannot investigate them all, we do feel some are more important than others in understanding organizational communication. Table 7-1 lists and describes the interviews most frequently used in an organization.

We have chosen two types of interviews for indepth analysis. The information-getting interview and the employment interview are ones in which you are most likely to participate during your student years and when you begin to look for a job. Since both parties share in the successful outcome, we will discuss the roles and responsibilities of the interviewer and the interviewee. However, so that we can aid you better in using these principles and practices, the approach will be from the role you are most likely to play. In the information-getting interview you are the interviewer or person seeking the information, and in the employment interview, you are the applicant.

The Information-Getting Interview

If you were to inventory your attitudes, beliefs, and knowledge and to decide how much of this awareness was formulated primarily through firsthand experience and how much through others or secondhand experience, what would you find? Among the vast majority of people, awareness received from others would be predominant. The growth of the electronic media of radio-television has had a great impact on our awareness. But even without TV and radio, we would still need to depend on others to help us understand and to influence our attitudes and beliefs. This is why the information-getting interview is so widely used today. For news reporters, police, and personnel directors, as well as for many others, it is a necessary part of the communication process.

As the party seeking information, it is your responsibility to plan the strategy for the interview. To insure that you receive valid and useful information, follow the steps identified in Figure 7-1. If possible, every step should be developed in depth. However, we recognize that circumstances do not always allow for systematic development. The

Table 7-1 Types of Interviews

Category	Purpose
Information-getting interview	The interviewer is seeking information from the interviewee, e.g., reporter at a news conference or public officer interviewing crime victims.
Appraisal interview	The manager and the subordinate share their feelings about the subordinate's work situation, e.g., police captain holds 6-month probational appraisal interview with new police officer.
Persuasive interview	Interviewer attempts to change the interviewee's attitudes or behavior concerning a specific subject, e.g., salesperson for ski equipment company interviews sports department manager.
Employment interview	The employer and the applicant exchange information for the purpose of reaching a decision about the applicant's employment with the organization.

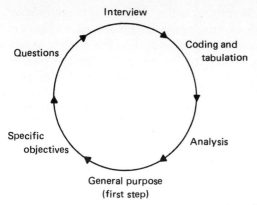

Figure 7-1 (From Robert L. Kahn and Charles F. Cannell, *The Dynamics of Interviewing: Theory, Techniques and Cases*, Wiley, New York, 1957, p. 103.)

reporter who covers the twenty-car accident on the freeway will not have time to develop his questions before he begins interviewing. But by investigating each step, we can be prepared to use the information when time and other factors permit.

General Purposes   The first step is to identify the purpose or reason for holding the interview. Be as specific as possible. Write down a statement that clearly defines the goal you want to accomplish as a result of the interaction. "Why did the candidate choose not to run for reelection?" "Why are the young people in this neighborhood hostile to the police?" "To determine if years in college influence income." These statements allow us to set the parameters of our purpose so that we know if we have been able to fulfill our goals. In addition, they give us direction in working toward meeting the specific objectives, which is the second step.

GENERAL PURPOSE

To assess the impact a crime
prevention program had on
home owners.

Developing Specific Objectives   "What is it I want to know?" is the question, and the answer can give you a way of identifying your objectives. The objectives are the statements we use to define the area of interest. They identify topics that should be investigated to achieve our purpose. "These objectives are links between the general purpose or the problem that is to be solved and the specific questions which must be asked in the interview."[13]

Each objective should identify only one topic. Often each topic has subobjectives that help define what specific information the topic seeks. As you will see, these

[13]Robert L. Kahn and Charles F. Cannell, *The Dynamics of Interviewing: Theory, Techniques and Cases*, Wiley, New York, 1957, p. 98.

objective statements are very useful in identifying and writing out the interview questions. We know it is easier *said* than *done*, but perhaps the following guidelines can help you formulate objectives. First, search through sources of reading material including books, magazines, pamphlets, lecture notes, etc. Second, talk to people who have knowledge of or experience with the purpose of your interview. Third, play your hunches. Speculate about the purpose and about what objectives are needed to carry it out. We are not speaking of unstructured brainstorming, but rather of good reflective, critical thinking.

GENERAL PURPOSE

> To assess the impact a crime prevention program had on home owners.

SPECIFIC OBJECTIVES

A. How did citizens become aware of program?
  1. From mass media
  2. From neighbors
  3. From police officers
B. What actions have citizens taken?
  1. Increase home security
  2. Develop neighborhood watch program
  3. Have valuables marked with identification numbers
C. What has changed since the program started?
  1. Change in pattern and number of burglaries
  2. Citizens' feeling of safety in their homes
  3. Citizens' feeling of safety in their neighborhood
D. Has the crime rate increased or decreased?

Remember, the more preplanning for the interview, the more likely it is that the data received will fulfill your needs.

Questions We have finished two steps in the information interview. Now we need to take the objectives that tell us what we want to know and formulate questions that will tell us how to get the information from the interviewee. As with any type of interview, we are concerned with how well the questions fit the respondent. We are seeking information so the questions should concern the person's knowledge or experience and motivate him or her to respond.

Information-interviewing questions can be either open or closed. If you want to know the specific ways the citizen has changed his or her home security, then ask a closed question "Would you list the ways in which you have modified your house to make it more secure from burglars?" On the other hand, a citizen's feelings about his or her neighborhood are better analyzed with an open question. "Tell me how you feel about the safety of your neighborhood." If the answer is not complete enough, phrase follow-up questions to gather more information. It is important that the open question allow the respondent to answer in reference to his concept of what is important and what is not. If you close the question by narrowing down the possible responses, then you are forcing your priorities on his awareness.

The needs of the objectives should influence the type of question used. If you seek to know the respondent's participation in an anticrime neighborhood watch program, then don't close the question by listing activities in which he could have participated. It would be better to open with a simple, "Are you familiar with any type of anticrime program in your neighborhood?" If he answers no, then save his time and yours by going on to the next question. If he says yes, then follow up with a moderately closed question. "Could you tell me of any participation you have had with this program?" If you desire to know how he felt about the program's success, ask a closed question. "Do you feel the program has been successful?" Remember, in order to know more about the answer given, use probe and mirror questions to help extend or focus the respondent's answers.

Conducting the Information Interview If one were to compare interviewing with playing football, then the preceding three areas would be the days spent preparing for the next game. You decided what game plan to use (general purpose) and developed this plan with strategies for the defensive and offensive (specific purpose); then you decided when and how your players would carry out the strategies (questions). Now, it is time for the game (interview). If you have properly prepared, you should be successful.

The football analogy can help us understand the need for preparation; but when we become involved in the interaction of an interview, the analogy breaks down. The reason for this is simple. Football is a win-lose situation: information interviewing is a win-win situation. A successful interview occurs when both parties receive enough information to make a rational decision. As the questioner, you want the respondent to understand what you are looking for so his answer can meet your needs. If you try to fake him out, then the respondent is confused. Also, if he senses you are not being honest with him, he is more likely to protect his ego than openly answer your questions.

As a beginner, you will make mistakes. Stewart and Cash, in a study of information interviews, have drawn up a list of guidelines for novice interviewers. Here is a portion of that list:

Communication skills
　　Relax and smile.
　　Maintain eye contact.
　　Speak louder and clearer.
　　Keep the pace of the interview slow.
　　Avoid "you know," "like," and other overworked expressions.

Figure 7-2 "No, sir, I'm not a robber. I would like to ask you some questions about how safe you feel in your home."

Respondent attitudes
 Take the interview seriously, don't joke about it.
 Be more positive.
 Don't apologize for the interview.
 Show sincere interest in the answers; don't act as if you regard it as just an exercise in asking questions.

Questioning skills
 Know your questions.
 Avoid biased questions.
 Don't suggest answers if the respondent hesitates.
 Don't mention how others answered.
 Don't cut people off in their answers.
 Probe more; don't take just any answer given.[14]

These comments are meant to serve as general interviewing guidelines. They represent approaches and mistakes that are common among beginning interviewers. We hope being aware of them can help to improve your first few interviews.

As you take notes during the interview, try to be as inconspicuous as possible. Don't allow your writing to interfere with the interaction. Remember, you usually don't have to write down every word that is said. After you have finished, go back to your notes and fill in a more complete picture. Of course, the longer you wait, the less complete the picture will be due to your forgetting some material. Some interviewers like to use tape recorders. If so, then be sure to ask permission. The respondent may

[14] Stewart and Cash, op. cit., pp. 93-94.

feel that the information you want is too confidential to be recorded live on tape. He can always say later that you misquoted him; but with the tape recorder, he can be held to his exact words.

Also, make sure that the overall structure of your interview is clear and direct, that it flows from one point to another in a logical sequence. Let the respondent know when you leave one area and proceed to another. One way to do this is to use an initial summary in which you outline subjects to be covered.

Finally, be sure the interview ends in a mutually satisfying manner. Ask the respondent if there is any additional information that he feels is important. If possible, praise the respondent for his clarity, wit, depth of understanding, language, etc.; try to find something positive to say about his participation in the interview. Before leaving, thank the respondent for his time and effort.

Coding, Tabulation, and Analysis If the interviewer is concerned with the information from only one respondent, then her coding of the results is fairly simple. She gathers her notes and tries to reconstruct the interview. If she remembers information she failed to write down, then she revises her notes. After she has established what was said, she then refers to the specific objectives she established prior to the interview. The information is analyzed in terms of those specific objectives. The results of her analysis are then written out in an informal manner for personal reference, or are prepared in a final report to another person.

If there have been several interviews, then the interviewer must decide how to handle the coding and tabulation of the information. Coding and tabulating closed-end questions are easy. One merely lists the alternatives presented to the respondent and counts the number of times each alternative was selected. Reporting what was said is usually done in raw numbers or percentages. Open-ended questions are more difficult to work with. Since each respondent answered in his or her own words, we cannot always compare one answer to another. The best procedure is to view all responses to one question. Look for similarities in language and in ideas. Place similar answers into separate categories. For example, when the citizens are asked, "How effective do you feel the anticrime program has been?" there could be four general categories of responses: nothing has changed, crime has been reduced, people feel safer now, and citizens are involved in working together. Try to avoid overlapping between categories, and if there are a few answers that are not similar to other answers, add a final category—*other*.

The categories become the information analyzed in terms of the specific objectives. This will determine how you have achieved the specific objectives and, ultimately, the purpose of the interviews.

Summary The information interview seeks to tap the awareness possessed by other people. The interviewer must be sure his language, appearance, and attitudes make the respondent feel at ease and that he can trust the interviewer. In the information interview, we need to consider the following: (1) the identification and statement of a general purpose; (2) the definition of the purpose in terms of specific objectives, worded to identify the specific kinds of information desired; (3) the formulation of questions to allow the interviewer to know how to get the information; (4) the participation in the interview; and (5) the coding and tabulation of answers so that the information can be used to satisfy the objectives.

Employment Interview

Each year millions of people are hired for a new job. Unless they are the president's son, they will have participated in an employment interview. While the goal of the employment interview—the exchange of information for the purpose of making a decision—is the same, there are numerous methods and materials used. For some, the employment interview consists of filling out an application, waiting several weeks or months, being called in to sign the appropriate papers, and then being shown where to work. Little or no dyadic interaction takes place. But other job seekers have to complete an application, present a resume, go through three separate interviews, have a physical, sign papers, and then show up for work.

To assist you in participating in the employment interview, we shall detail those methods and procedures most frequently used in employment interviews in business and industry. We will analyze the duties of both parties, but we will lay heavy emphasis on the role you will most likely play—that of the applicant.

Preparing for the Interview We feel it will help you to identify two stages of preparation for the employment interview. The first stage takes a long view of your life (career planning), and the other stage a short view (the specific job interview).

Decide on career goals as early in life as possible, preferably before looking for your first job. Now, while you are in school, is the best time for planning a career. To do this involves a good deal of analysis, on your part, of your past, present, and future

Figure 7-3 Berry's World. (Reprinted by permission of Newspaper Enterprise Association.)

personal life. One major consideration is how a career matches your interests and aptitudes. The job area that you select should make a neat fit with what you want to do and what is physically and mentally within your range of accomplishment. Before making this fit, you need to draw up an inventory of your major interests and skills (e.g., things you like and do well). Using the list, analyze each possible career area as to how what you have and what you want fit with what the job requires.

Another major consideration is your desired future lifestyle. This involves the role money, social position, family, etc., will play in your later life. How much money do you want to make? Is it of prime importance? The answer to these two questions can help narrow your career possibilities. For instance, most of the professions that earn higher incomes require college and professional school education. If you want this type of profession, then postpone immediate monetary and social rewards. If you want more immediate gratification, then choose a career area where your drive and aptitude can be rewarded sooner, such as sales work on a commission basis. Another way of looking at lifestyle considerations is to discover what makes you content and happy. Do you prefer to work with people or alone? Do you want to make most decisions or would you rather implement decisions? Do you need a lot of creative self-satisfaction, or can you be satisfied with a job well done? The answers to these questions can help determine what careers are best suited to your present and future lifestyle.

When you have decided on your career goals, then develop methods for gaining admission to your chosen field. In other words, *get a job*. Remember that the job market is similar to any other market—there are people buying and people selling. The job market is subject to the restraints of the law of supply and demand. For example, in the 1970s broadcasting has shown a strong growth, especially in the areas of local station news and programming. But the supply or number of applicants for jobs has grown ten times as fast. For every one job, there are ten interested applicants.

There is a similar situation in police service careers, as well as in some career areas of retailing. To get the job, you must sell your product—*yourself.* You must convince others to buy your services. Where does this selling take place?—in the employment interview.

After having decided on a career field and specific job area, you are ready to move into the second stage of preparation for the employment interview, *the specific job interview.* Here is where you sell yourself.

It is difficult to sell yourself unless you are sure of your own facts and figures, which can be summarized on a personal fact sheet or resume. Figure 7-4 presents an example of an employment resume.

The resume must be neatly typed on bond paper and all copies should be reproduced to look like the original. It should not exceed two pages, and one page is preferable.

Another area of importance in preparing for the employment interview is that of researching the company. Find out what the organization manufactures, sells, or what kind of service it offers. Then, seek out written material (books, magazines, pamphlets) that describe the particular area of industry or service in which the organization is found. For example, if you are applying for an assistant buyer's position with Richdales, you would research department store retailing in general, and what is

```
                       EMPLOYMENT RESUME

Name and residence:                    Home address:
  Carol Downing                          630 Stewart Street
  2126 S. Main Street                    Chicago, Illinois 63945
  Oakwood, Ohio 45400                    314-669-2700
  517-229-3645

Personal data:
  Date of birth:             April 18, 1957 (21 years old)
  Height and weight:         5'9"; 120 lbs.
  Health:                    Excellent
  Marital status:            Single

Education:
  High school:        Alter High School, Chicago, Illinois
  College:            University of Dayton, Dayton, Ohio
  Major:              Business Administration (4.0 scale--3.25)
  Minor:              Speech Communication (4.0 scale--2.80)
  Date of graduation: June, 1978

Extracurricular activities:
  Member Alpha Kappa Psi, business administration honorary fraternity
  (2 years); member Sigma Society (3 years); chairman of the inter-
  mural council (1 year).

Professional goal:
  To obtain a job in retail personnel training and to work toward
  becoming a director of executive training.

Work experience:
  Summer 1974--Clerk in Stiff's Shoe Store, Chicago, Illinois
  Summer 1975--Receptionist for Animal Hospital, Chicago, Ill.
  Summer 1976 to present--Full and part time work as clerk in Rike's
                     Department Store, Dayton, Ohio.

References:
  Dr. Steve Bell               Mr. Charles Smith
  Municipal Animal Hospital    Manager, Rike's Department Store
  Chicago, Illinois 63940      Dayton, Ohio 45450

  Dr. Peter McGraw
  Business College
  University of Dayton
  Dayton, Ohio 45469
```

Figure 7-4 Employment resume.

involved in the job of department store buyer specifically. It is a common practice for the interviewer to ask, "How did you hear of our company?" or "What do you know about our company?" Your response tells the employer that you are concerned about where you will work and that you have spent time researching his or her company. In addition, your research can help you decide if the company is right for you. If you don't want to sell, then don't waste time with a company for which all entry-level positions are in sales. If the company has plants in many areas, but you want to stay in your home town, then find out where the position will be located and the chances of being transferred.

Before an interview many people write a company and ask for material about jobs and working conditions. Others seek information from the library's reference areas. Another way is to talk to people who are working for the company. Whatever avenue of research you take, it behooves you to learn as much as possible about the company offering employment.

The last step in preparing for the employment interview is to decide on where you want to go in your personal and occupational life with the company. (The work done in analyzing career interests and lifestyle can help you here.) Firm up your life and professional goals. This is especially true if you are young, under 25. Employers will ask if you plan to marry, where you want to live, what kind of community involvement you will seek, etc. In addition, they will want to know why you have chosen their company and a particular job area. "What do you hope to achieve with this job?" is a reasonable question to ask a prospective employee. Think about these things before the interview, and your response will show forethought, an asset for any employee.

Participating in the Interview While it seems unlikely that you will participate as the interviewer in an employment interview, at least in the near future, it can be beneficial for you to know what the interviewer hopes to accomplish in the interview. One important goal is to secure information about you, the applicant. This information is needed to decide if you fit the job. In a recent article, David Austin identified three basic levels of information gathered in an employment interview:[15]

Level one contains the most concrete data. It deals with the applicant's personal and work histories. These data allow the interviewer to make assumptions regarding the applicant's level of ability. Austin describes *level two* as the observable responses of the applicant's verbal and nonverbal responses given during the interview. We can try to relate these responses to how well he or she might behave on the job. *Level three* concerns the inferential data gained from careful observation of how the applicant handles certain issues and the information he or she tends to omit. These data can be used to make assumptions about the applicant's values, fears, motivations, and strengths.

The first and second levels deal with what an employer can know from your past and from your physical behavior during the interview. The third level is the guesses he makes about you. You can't do much about your past, but you can influence his perception of you from the observable responses and the inferential knowledge he tries to gain.

In other words, how you handle yourself during this interview will greatly influence his perception of you. Here is a checklist to use in planning your interaction with the interviewer:

Be honest and frank. Let him get to know you as a person with strengths and weaknesses. If he wants to fit you to the job, he needs all the correct information you can give him. But beware not to shoot from the hip; give your answers some thought before explaining.

Be ready for a surprise question. Some interviewers want to see how you react to the unexpected. Stay cool and give your reply some thought.

[15] Stewart and Cash, op. cit., p. 143.

Let the interviewer take the lead. He knows how much time he has and what is important to the job. If he has not covered an area you feel is important, wait for a break, and ask him if you can supply the information.

Make personal observations objective. Don't speak of yourself in glowing terms. Use natural or factual language. Be direct, complete, and proud when talking about yourself, but don't brag.

Sell yourself. If you don't, no one else will. Point out your qualifications to handle the job. Come across as a confident person who can and will do a job well. Especially sell yourself for the job you are being interviewed for.

Leave salary questions for the end. If possible, let the interviewer bring up the subject. Usually, companies have a salary range for people that relates to education and experience. Don't leave until you have some idea of the salary range.[16]

So far we have discussed what kinds of information the employer is seeking and some guidelines on how you present this information. There is one other area that affects how you are perceived during the interaction. This is the area of nonverbal communication.

Nonverbal communication refers to *how* you say it: your vocal characteristics, your gestures, your dress, your eye contact, and so forth. We will divide these nonverbal communications into two areas: vocal and physical.

Vocal characteristics are especially important for jobs in the retail, mass media, and social services agencies. In these occupation areas, much time is spent talking to customers or clients. If your rate of speech is so fast that the average person loses some of the ideas, or so slow that he or she becomes impatient for the end, the employer may view this in a negative manner. The same is true of pitch and volume. When these do

---

[16]For more detail and additional items, see "Making the Most of Your Job Interview," New York Life Insurance Company pamphlet.

Figure 7-5   Your nonverbal cues can influence the interviewer's judgment about you.

not vary and stay on the same level, you probably are speaking in a monotone. The best way to break a monotone is to become interested in or even excited about a topic. This will emphasize words, increase pitch for one phrase and lower it for another. Finally, watch your articulation. It makes a difference what words a person hears. If you substitute one sound for another, drop the last syllable, or slur a sound, the listener may be confused. Also, this shows a lack of awareness of how you come across. And in organizations that stress human interaction, this can make a difference in who is hired. It takes just as long to say, "Pleased to meet you" as it takes to say, "Pleased to meetcha"; to say "just" takes the same effort as saying "jist."

The second area of nonverbal communication behavior concerns what you wear and how you handle your body movements. The basic point to remember is *you cannot stop communicating*. What you wear presents cues to the interviewer to which he will attach meaning. That is, before you say a word, you have communicated to him about yourself. What you say and what you do will be viewed and interpreted by the interviewer, who will use these data in making a judgment about you. To help influence his judgment in a positive manner, consider the following guidelines:

A recent study of 100 personnel interviewers reported that women wearing jeans, shorts, or sandals created "a mildly to strongly negative impression." Also, men who wore suits created a stronger positive impression than men wearing sports coats and ties. To either male or female, our advice is wear your best, conservative clothes.[17]

Maintain strong eye contact. This establishes a visual bond between the two parties that can aid the free flow of communication. Also, some people view a lack of eye contact as an indication of insecurity or falsehoods. Neither one is a benefit to you.

Don't smoke.

Don't tense up. Try to lean toward the interviewer in a relaxed manner.

Try to show a range of emotions without being extreme. That is, smile sometimes, frown on occasion; look very interested sometimes, and interested most of the time. Like your voice, a visual monotone can be deadly dull.

Don't come on too strong, physically or vocally. In the study cited earlier, "strong positive ratings were given if the [applicant] seemed relaxed, balanced, and professional."

Try to project an image that fits the job. For instance, if you want to go into selling, have neat clothing, trimmed hair, and give a strong, firm handshake.

Remember, verbal and nonverbal cues can have a strong influence on the judgments an interviewer makes about your character and motivation. You can influence these judgments; try to make them positive ones.

Summary

It is likely that employment interviews will have more impact on your life than other types of interviews. You can influence the interviewer's decision by carefully preparing for your role in the employment interview. In the preparation stage, make sure

[17]*Parade Magazine*, November 9, 1975, p. 12.

(1) you have made some decision about professional and personal goals; (2) the resume reflects accurately your past and present life; (3) you know something about the company and why you want to work for it.

Concerning your participation in the interaction, you should be concerned with the following: (1) that some decision will be made based on how you handle yourself during the interview; (2) that you follow the interviewer's lead by keeping comments relevant and honest, emphasizing your strengths and selling yourself; (3) that your verbal and nonverbal behaviors communicate to the interviewer, so make these messages positive.

Chapter 8

Small Group Behavior

Most of the life of an "organization man" is spent in groups. Information exchange, problem solving, decision making, and the development of interpersonal relationships are all functions of organizational groups. In fact, some organizations are "over-grouped." This occurs when individuals are assigned to groups that have little function or power, or are assigned to several groups simultaneously, which then makes their effective participation impossible.

Bureaucrats tend to form committees in order to avoid problems they do not wish to deal with themselves. We have all had the experience of being a member of a committee and of feeling our time has been wasted due to poor planning: the student senate housing committee whose function is to rubber stamp the housing director's decisions, the sorority ethics committee formed by the president who wants to avoid dealing with a touchy ethical question, or the student representatives group that sits in the faculty senate but has *no* voice *or* vote.

The problem of overgrouping is partly due to the move toward *participatory management*. This type of management, in contrast to the one-man decision approach, includes individuals in the decision-making process who will later administer or enforce the decisions. In this way, support for the decision is gained through participation. Unfortunately, many managers have misunderstood the underlying principles of this concept. Not *all* decisions can be reached through participatory management. Some

Figure 8-1 The Monday morning board meeting: the problem of being "overgrouped" means trying to handle every decision by forming a group.

decisions are more effectively made by a few or even one individual. For example, one nationally known food chain operation needed to make a decision about the color of the uniforms of its employees. Top-ranking executives of the company had recently returned from a management training seminar. They felt since the employees would have to wear the uniforms, they should *all* take part in the decision-making process. Because they didn't want decision by majority but instead hoped the employees would reach *consensus* (a general agreement without voting), what followed were months of deliberations and negotiations. This decision could have been made more effectively at the executive level. The attempt to use participatory management principles with such a large group on a rather insignificant issue was doomed to failure.

The result was the opposite in another company where the use of group decision making was very appropriate. This was a manufacturing firm that was family-owned, its president being the company's original founder. When the firm grew to a size requiring separate directors for each of the company's service areas, the founder-president had a difficult time relinquishing his control and power over decision making. Through a consultant intervention, participatory management and decision by consensus were instituted within the company. The directors began to participate in decisions requiring their support for implementation.

The key is to know the appropriate uses of group decision making. The purpose of this chapter is to identify the functions of groups within an organization, and the effective and ineffective outcomes of such groups. An analysis of the uses of groups, the developmental stages experienced by groups, the decision-making processes, and the individual member behaviors, will help you function more effectively as a group member.

OVERVIEW OF GROUPS

Definition of Organizational Groups

Groups exist in the organizational setting when they meet the following criteria: *three or more individuals who meet in a face-to-face setting for a reasonable length of time to work toward a common goal* such as organizational problem solving, information exchange, or development of interpersonal relationships within the organizational structure. Groups can be *formal or informal. Each participant normally has a stake in the outcome, has an opportunity to develop relationships, and takes on a role that will either implement or impede group process.*

Let's analyze the parts of this definition closely. A group is defined as *three or more individuals* since two individuals constitute a dyad, and their relationship is different than the relationship among members of a group. As Wilmot has pointed out, "A collection of three or more individuals constitutes a small group. And while the dyad is obviously the . . . material of small groups, it is qualitatively different from them. When a group numbers three or more, the basic properties of all larger groups begin to emerge like: leadership functions, communication networks, and coalitions and subsystems."[1]

Face-to-face limits our discussion primarily to verbal and nonverbal interaction and eliminates analyzing the writings of various individuals who might correspond with one another.

Reasonable length of time means that the group endures for longer than a few minutes, and that its members recognize themselves as a group. The *common goal* is what brings the group together. The members have this goal whether they have chosen to be a member or have been assigned to the group. The goal may vary or change while the group is functioning. However, the group will only exist as long as some type of goal is maintained.

Stake in the outcome means that each individual is affected in some way by the actions of the group. Consequently, the success or failure of the group's actions will influence individual members either positively or negatively.

Formally organized groups are those whose members have been assigned to permanent or temporary task groups to achieve some specific organizational goal. There are also informal groups that naturally form within the organization.

Two researchers, Massie and Douglas,[2] have reached the following conclusions concerning the existence of informal groups within the organization: (1) all organizations have informal work groups; (2) managers in formal leadership positions cannot possibly satisfy all the needs of individuals, thus informal groups emerge to meet these needs; (3) an organization with strong informal groups will be more effective than an organization with weak informal groups; (4) needs not met by formal and informal groups will create frustration and disrupt organizational objectives; (5) strong informal groups frequently handle vital information faster than the formal channels

[1]William Wilmot, *Dyadic Communication: A Transactional Perspective,* Addison-Wesley, Reading, Mass., 1975, p. 18.
[2]Joseph L. Massie and John Douglas, *Managing: A Contemporary Introduction*, Prentice-Hall, Englewood Cliffs, N.J., 1973, pp. 97–98.

of communication; and (6) the manager influences both formal and informal groups. These conclusions clearly show that informal groups can often fulfill as many useful management functions as formal groups. However, it is a mistake to assume that these two types of groups have separate existences.

Edgar Schein,[3] a specialist in organizational psychology, has pointed out that a common finding in organizational groups is that most of these groups have both formal and informal functions. Usually groups meet individual as well as organizational needs. For example, a formal work crew in the organization provides psychological support for individual members while the group is completing a task.

Importance of Organizational Groups

Much criticism has been made against the use of small groups in organizations yet they continue to be one of the most prevalent forms of communication networks within the organizational structure. In one study of 1,200 respondents, 94 percent of firms with more than 10,000 employees and 64 percent of those with less than 250 employees reported having formal committees.[4] In another survey of organization practices in 620 Ohio manufacturing firms, a similar relationship between committee use and plant size was discovered.[5] While these studies made no attempt to identify the informal groups existing in these organizations, the findings at least indicate the high-level use of small groups, and the significant role they play in the organizational setting.

Advantages and Disadvantages of Groups

To insure that the most appropriate communication channel is chosen for sending messages within the organization, individuals need to be aware of the drawbacks as well as the advantages of using small groups. The *advantages* of small groups often include the following:

Decisions are usually better received. Participation implies a degree of individual responsibility for decisions reached by the group. The more people involved in the decision-making process, the more people there are who have accepted the decision and are willing to enforce it. Usually group decisions are more faithfully carried out than decisions handed down by one administrator.

Greater occurrence of attitude change. Often the group provides a support system for beliefs that can cause the attitudes of individual members to move in the direction of the group's majority. The small group setting is conducive not only to attitude change, but also to improved thinking as well. The small group can become a testing ground for new ideas, a place to try out concepts and refine individual thinking as members get immediate feedback on the validity of their thoughts. Many feel this type of intellectual exchange leads to more effective decision making.

---

[3] Edgar H. Schein, *Organizational Psychology,* Prentice-Hall, Englewood Cliffs, N.J., 1970, pp. 82–84.

[4] Rollie Tillman, Jr., "Problems in Review: Committees on Trial," *Harvard Business Review,* 38:6–12, May–June 1960.

[5] A. C. Filley, "Committee Management: Guidelines from Social Science Research," in Richard C. Huseman, Cal M. Logue, and Dwight I. Freshley (eds.), *Readings in Interpersonal and Organizational Communication,* Holbrook, Boston, 1973, p. 430.

Decisions may be superior. The common belief, "Four heads are better than one," is often proven true in the small group setting. The decision reached by the group may be superior in terms of *inclusiveness* (the more people involved, the more aspects of the problem that are explored); *practicality* (people who implement the solution have been involved in its formulation so the procedure adopted is usually simpler and easier to carry out); and *flexibility* (since a group usually raises more issues than an individual alone would, the members are more aware of changes that may have to be made later during implementation).

These advantage statements have a number of levels of support. Yet some would say that the *disadvantages* of small groups are more readily validated. Disadvantages might include:

Domination by a few. Small group communication can result in domination of the group by a few powerful individuals. This could mean that the group decision does not represent the views of the entire group, but views expressed by the most vocal or highest-status individuals in the group. How to control this type of individual within the group is the problem raised most frequently by participants in group dynamics workshops.

Wasting time. Individual decisions can be made quickly. In groups time can be wasted on matters not central to the decision. The interpersonal dynamics of group formation must be dealt with before effective group decision making can take place. If there is a need for a fast decision, spending time on developing interpersonal relationships in the group may seem like a waste of time.

Different levels of ability and motivation. Individual members vary in their ability to solve problems. Some members simply lack the capacity to gain an overview of the situation and cannot understand the complexity of a problem. Other members may want to make a quick decision before all aspects of the problem have been considered. These are usually members who have been assigned to the group, are not motivated to participate, and want to arrive at the decision as soon as possible. For these reasons the group may not be task-oriented and may have a tendency to reach a decision just to get it over with.[6]

It is clear that the organizational leader must be aware of the dynamics of a particular situation and choose the most appropriate channel of communication. The small group is not always the most effective or desirable channel. Considerations of the time available, need for equal participation, task importance vs. relationship importance, implementation of decision, level of motivation, as well as the ability of group members to complete the task, all influence the organizational leader's decision on whether to utilize a small task group.

As well as determining if the group is the most appropriate decision maker, the organizational leader must also decide what form the group will take. Some groups are given more power than others to make and implement decisions. The type of meeting the leader designs indicates the type of communication that will take place in

---

[6] Adapted from Richard C. Huseman, "The Role of the Nominal Group in Small Group Communication," in Richard C. Huseman, Cal M. Logue, and Dwight I. Freshley (eds.), *Readings in Interpersonal and Organizational Communication,* Holbrook, Boston, 1973, pp. 412–413.

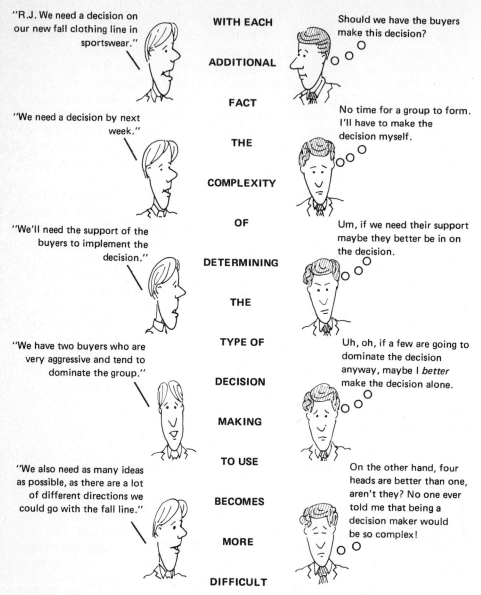

Figure 8-2 When a decision must be made, which is better: an individual or group decision?

the group. Bormann and his colleagues[7] have identified different levels of usefulness for group meetings: (1) the *ritual* meeting, which serves to maintain traditional procedures for the group (a "state of the organization" address by the president or a weekly organizational meeting of department heads); (2) the *briefing* meeting, which is used

[7]Ernest G. Bormann, William S. Howell, Ralph G. Nichols, and George L. Shapiro, *Interpersonal Communication in the Modern Organization*, Prentice-Hall, Englewood Cliffs, N.J., 1969, pp. 111–113.

to provide members of the organization with information needed to carry out a program and thus is crucial to the organization's task efficiency; (3) the *instructional* meeting, which is designed to provide employees with additional training, making them more proficient in their jobs; (4) the *creative* meeting, which is set up to brainstorm for ideas, techniques, or procedures and that serves as a stimulus to the creativity of the members; (5) the *decision-making* meeting, which is designed to make plans and decisions; and finally, (6) the *consultation* meeting, which is where the group is merely asked to offer advice and suggestions to the authority who will make the final decision.

Any one task group may be involved in all six types of exchanges as each serves to increase the group's effectiveness. The ritual meeting gives unity to the group; the briefing meeting brings information to the group; the instructional meeting increases expertise, the creative meeting taps the resources of the members; the decision-making meeting promotes action; and the consultation meeting asks for expert input.

It is important that the members of the group fully understand the function and the purpose of their meeting. Too often groups overestimate the power they will have over decisions. For example, if the Oakwood police chief asks new members of the force to have an informal meeting to air gripes they have about departmental organization, he had better make it clear that they have no decision-making function, if he sees their function as one of consultation rather than one of decision making. This means that the chief wants their input but does not intend to allow them in any way to actually make decisions about department policy. He will simply take their suggestions "under advisement." It is easier to work when the limitations of the group's power are known than to operate under the illusion that the group can itself make changes.

GROUP DEVELOPMENT

It is important to be able to monitor and influence the developmental stages of organizational groups. Group members and organizational leaders both need a high level of awareness of the stages of growth that any group may experience. Determining the stages of development increases behavioral options for everyone involved in, or influenced by, the group. A group development model will be useful as the group attempts to diagnose interaction problems, identify resources available to it, and determine its progress toward problem solving.

Here is an example that demonstrates how important it is to be aware of group-process stages. Let's assume that a task force has been formed at Richdales department store to determine the desirability of organizing a grievance committee for employees. The function of this committee is to provide a direct like between the sales personnel and the top executives so that dissatisfaction with working conditions can be expressed without fear that the individual's job might be affected. The purpose of the task force is to determine if there is a need for such a committee at Richdales and to determine how it would be structured if the need proves to be real. The task committee consists of Tom Brenner, appointed chairman of the committee by the president of the company and vice president in charge of personnel relations; Bill Adler, head sales clerk in sporting goods; Joe Johnson, a buyer for home furnishings; Alice Meyer, floor manager for the bargain basement store; George Benson, vice president in charge of distribution; and Joan Alderton, department manager of training and development. At the beginning of the first meeting, Tom introduces the group members and explains the goals of the group as he understands them. He then begins the discussion by asking the group members how they personally feel about the establishment of a grievance committee. Tom allows the members of the group time to explore their own feelings in relation to serving on this committee and to clarify exactly what this group will and will not be able to decide. He feels very positive about the members since they seem to have no major problems communicating and everyone is polite with each other. About an hour into the meeting, the group's focus has shifted. The members appear to be engaged in a bitter deadlock. Tom observes the following conversation with growing uneasiness:

Bill: It is obvious to me that several of you in management positions feel threatened by a grievance committee and are going to block any actions to form one.

George: Hold on there Bill, I think that's an unfair accusation and I personally resent your implication. I think we all came here in good faith and I don't think we'll get anywhere if we start attacking each other.

Alice: Frankly, I'm fed up with all this bickering. Why don't we get back to our agenda.

Joe: I'm with you Alice. This is ridiculous.

Joan: Wait a minute. I don't think we can go on until we get some of the issues Bill and George are raising resolved.

Should Tom become discouraged at the apparent failure of the group to discuss the issues rationally? Would an understanding of the normal development stages of any group be helpful in aiding his leadership role? As we discuss the stages of a group experience, see if you can identify which stage best characterizes this group.

There are many theoretical approaches to the stages of growth commonly experienced by groups. However, most seem to be some variation of the five stages represented in Table 8-1.

Basically, any model of group development involves two elements: how the task is accomplished and how interpersonal relationships are formed during the process. There is always some kind of balance that has to be achieved between getting the job done and maintaining strong human relations. This balance is often achieved through trade-offs (e.g., "We'll take time for a coffee break during the meeting so people can relax with each other and then we'll expect them to work harder when they return") or compromise (e.g., "We'll only try to get through half of the agenda items today and finish the rest at a later meeting. I think we need some time just to get to know each other better").

In Table 8-1 these two dynamics are represented as "interpersonal structure" and "task activity." The *interpersonal structure* refers to the patterns of interpersonal relationships that can be defined as how people feel about each other, how they expect others to behave, their commitments to each other, and the general problems they encounter as they move from a collection of individuals to a cooperative team. *Task activity*, on the other hand, concerns the content of the group as its members

Table 8-1 Developmental Stages of Group Process

Stages	Interpersonal structure	Task activity
1 Polite	Testing and dependence	Orientation to task
2 Goal orientation	Trial behavior	Information sharing
3 Bid for power	Intragroup conflict	Emotional reaction to task demands
4 Constructive	Development of group cohesion	Open exchange of relevant interpretations
5 Synergistic collaboration	Interdependence and group commitment	Emergence of solutions and action steps

Source: Adapted from Burce W. Tuckman, "Developmental Sequence in Small Groups," in *Groups and Organizations: Integrated Readings in the Analysis of Social Behavior,* Bernard L. Hinton and H. Joseph Reity (eds.), Wadsworth, Belmont, Ca., 1971, pp. 74–75; and George O. Charrier, "Cog's Ladder: A Model of Group Development," in John E. Jones and William Pfeiffer (eds.), *Annual Handbook for Group Facilitators—1974,* University Associates, La Jolla, Calif., 1974.

work on the task or goal of the group—what information the group shares and receives as it relates to its particular task as well as its attempts at problem solving. Both interpersonal structure and task activity are affected differently at various stages of the group's progress. These stages have been identified as the polite stage, goal-orientation stage, bid for power stage, constructive stage, and synergistic collaboration stage. An examination of each of these stages will aid our understanding of the changes that occur in the two major activities of the group.

The *polite stage* is the period of initial contact group members make with each other that allows them to get to know each other informally. This stage is very important since individuals need to feel comfortable within the group before attempting to work together as a task team. The conversation centers around less personal information: communicating names, jobs, positions, and other preliminary data. Each member needs to feel accepted and included in this initial stage. William Schutz has identified this as the first interpersonal need expressed by individuals. The term he uses for this group dynamic is *inclusion.*[8] Members need to feel included in the group's process. Important issues revolve around identifying boundaries for developing relationships, building trust, determining who is or is not a member, and maintaining individuality while simultaneously being a group member. A group leader who ignores or allows little time for this stage to develop runs the risk of having to resolve such issues much later in the group's development, thus delaying the problem-solving process.

During the polite stage the interpersonal structure centers around a testing process. Nonverbalized issues are raised such as, "Who is going to be a dominant member of this group?" and "Who will be friendly to and supportive of my suggestions?" The

[8] William Schutz, *The Interpersonal Underworld,* Science and Behavior Books, Palo Alto, Calif., 1966, pp. 18–28.

interpersonal structure during the polite stage is also used to discover which interpersonal behaviors will be acceptable. Dependency issues are resolved such as, "Can we depend on our leader to provide all the ground rules and agenda items?" The corresponding task activity centers on identification of relevant dimensions of the task and the manner in which group members will tackle it. There must be a common understanding at this stage of what the group has been asked to do. Consequently, group members are establishing the initial interpersonal relationships while identifying what task has called them together. Some groups do not move beyond this stage. The secretaries who occasionally eat lunch together constitute a group without any task goal and one in which the members remain polite while exchanging technical information. If we return to our task force for Richdales department store we find that Tom Brenner, the group leader, established a climate for participating in the polite stage when he introduced group members, explained the task, and opened the discussion by asking members how they personally felt about the group's task. What followed was a testing period, which Tom's group seemed to move through. From his perspective anyway, the group completed this initial stage of group development.

Stage 2, *goal orientation*, usually emerges when the group is ready to move beyond the polite stage in order to answer the question, "What are our goals and objectives?" Some groups may demand a formal agenda or procedural outline while others prefer more freedom in generating an order for proceeding. There is no set time at which a group will move to this stage and no definite limit on the amount of time the group will spend discussing these issues. How long a group stays at this stage is partially determined by how clearly the task was identified for it prior to the first group meeting. Groups who received vague instructions will spend most of their time attempting to identify the limits of their own activity, while others may omit this stage altogether. The interpersonal structure during this phase consists of trial behavior by individual members as risk taking increases. The group begins to sense individual motivations as it tries to verbalize group objectives. The task activity focuses on information sharing. Early in the group's development the leader usually has more information than other group members and often most additional input comes from that source. Information generally relates to the group's purpose.

During stage 3 group members often make a *bid for power* in order to determine which members will be leaders and dominate group decisions. It is at this point that the interpersonal structure often reveals open conflict among group members. Members become hostile as a means of expressing individuality. At the same time the task activity focuses on emotional reactions to the demands of the task. This reaction may be a form of resistance to these demands. This is the stage the task force for Richdales department store has reached. With Tom's knowledge of the developmental stages of group process, he realizes that Bill and George are making bids for power in the group and the other group members are aligning themselves with one or the other. The group will need to resolve this power issue before moving on to task considerations. The presence of this conflict does not mean the group is failing. On the contrary, the group is dealing with some important issues in its interpersonal structure. Too often the group leader looks at conflict negatively and tries to smooth over issues instead of letting the group work them through.

The fourth stage in group development is the *constructive* stage. Once the group has been able to resolve power conflicts, they are more likely to move from attempts to actively control, to attempts to actively listen. In this stage members are more willing to change their preconceived ideas or opinions on the basis of facts presented by other members. A team spirit begins to build. This does not mean that conflict will not occur, but that the group will deal with conflict issues as a natural part of the process rather than as a win-lose battle. The interpersonal structure is characterized by the development of group cohesion and the task activity by an open exchange of relevant interpretations. Group leaders are most effective during this stage as clarifiers and summarizers in an attempt to be tolerant of group members' widely varying abilities.

The final stage of group development is not often reached by many groups, as it suggests the highest level of group morale and intense loyalty to the group. Both individuality and creativity are high. Cliques are absent since the group accepts each member and respects their differences. Members participate as equally as they ever will. The term used to describe this stage, *synergistic collaboration*, implies a total group effort to work together as a team. The interpersonal structure is characterized by interdependence and group commitment. The task activity revolves around the emergence of solutions and action steps.

Not all of these stages are experienced by every group and their sequence may vary. For example, two researchers, Bennis and Shepard,[9] suggest that groups typically deal first with issues of power and authority, and then deal with more personal issues among group members. Bales and Strodtbeck[10] believe group development occurs in the opposite direction. Groups first deal with problems of orientation, then problems of evaluation, and finally problems concerned with control. The group process is in constant motion and groups often move backward to issues discussed previously.

Change occurs naturally in a group and individual members respond differently to changes as they occur. An understanding of some of the basic processes they might experience makes the members of the group more sensitive to issues they may want to deal with more openly. In our example of the task force at Richdales department store, the leader's knowledge of the group process should help him avoid becoming discouraged by the conflict exhibited by his group, and instead should help him recognize it as one of the many changes the group will go through as it develops. His skill at helping the group manage its own conflict issues will be reflected in the group's ability to move on to yet another stage in its development.

GROUP DECISION MAKING

Types of Decisions

The authors have served as consultants to many small groups within the organizational setting. In these groups we have observed four major types of decision-making

[9]W. G. Bennis and H. A. Shepard, "A Theory of Group Development," *Human Relations*, 9: 415–437, 1956.
[10]R. F. Bales and F. L. Strodtbeck, "Phases in Group Problem-Solving," *Journal of Abnormal Social Psychology*, 46:485–495, October 1951.

behaviors. Groups tend to either fight fires, decide by procedure, use a synergistic approach to decision making, or ignore the problem in hopes that it will go away and thus decide to make no decision. When a group *fights fires* it tends to only make decisions when forced to by the desperateness of the situation. Often the decision should have been made earlier to *prevent* the fire and the group finds itself putting Band-aids on problems that may require major surgery.

The executive negotiation committee for a medium-sized midwestern company exhibited the fight fire characteristic. The function of the committee was to represent the management side in labor disputes. The group had not established any effective ways for dealing with problems and for making decisions quickly and efficiently. Consequently, it often found itself in the middle of a heated dispute before it recognized any problem existed. When this happened it would usually develop a short-term solution (or would use a Band-aid to cover a small wound), when what was needed were long-range solutions that would establish a precedent for handling these types of encounters in the future.

Groups that *decide by procedure* are at the opposite end of the structured-unstructured continuum. A group may be so governed by the way in which decisions have been made in the past that it is unable or unwilling to adapt to a new situation. One of the authors participated in one small group (about ten people) whose role often included determining how small amounts of funds would be distributed. Several members of the group had belonged to this committee for some time, and felt a need to continue making decisions using a procedure normally used with a much larger group—decision by majority. While this type of decision making may be the foundation of a democratic society, it often becomes a barrier to group process when used improperly. It effectively cuts off discussion and, in a group this size, can inhibit individual responsiveness. The group became so tied to one procedure that it could not effectively deal with and adapt to a new situation and different problem-solving techniques. Groups such as this become incapable of resolving serious issues.

We have termed the third type of decision-making behavior *synergistic resolution*. The term synergistic is used frequently in the literature on group process to denote a totally cooperative group effort. The philosophy underlying this behavior is that the collective efforts of a group of people can be more productive than the sum total of individual efforts made by all group members. In other words, the whole is greater than the sum of its parts. Since groups often move from one type of behavior to another, rarely is a group exhibiting synergistic behavior over long periods of time. Usually groups have periods of synergistic interaction.

The final type of decision making is making *no decision*. Here the group hopes the problem will straighten itself out; thus making no decision *is* a decision. Another interesting way to look at the types of decision-making behaviors is to observe groups making decisions during times of crisis. Mike DeWine[11] has designed a model of group decision making that contrasts groups that normally function under a "crisis-motivating act" with those that are more stabilized and use carefully devised procedural processes. The three graphs in Figure 8-4 represent three types of group decision making in crisis

[11] Mike DeWine, as presented in a seminar given for Kentucky Manpower, Lexington, Kentucky, 1976.

Fire fighting

"If we agree to a 5-cent pay increase, maybe they won't bring up overtime and we won't have to make a decision on that now."

Temporary decision making

Procedural tactics

"We've always taken a survey of employees before when making a decision, so we should do so now."

Unyielding decision making

Synergistic resolution

"Let's put our heads together and plan ahead so this issue will not come up again."

On-going, flexible, and responsive

Figure 8-3 Types of decision-making behavior.

situations. When a crisis occurs a group will either make decisions according to predetermined procedures for such events, make decisions as a reaction to the crisis event, or follow general guidelines determined previously and adapt to the precipitating event. It is DeWine's theory that the more a group makes decisions either as a response to a crisis situation with no prior procedural planning, or makes decisions under crisis that follow procedures without regard to the context in which the crisis is occurring, the less effective those decisions will be (see Figure 8-4). He feels that a group must have outlined, prior to the crisis, the steps to be taken, and that it must have a built-in flexibility that allows the group to adapt its decisions to the uniqueness of the

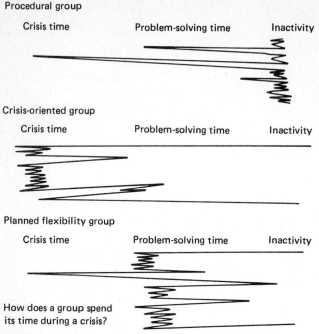

Procedural group

Crisis time   Problem-solving time   Inactivity

Crisis-oriented group

Crisis time   Problem-solving time   Inactivity

Planned flexibility group

Crisis time   Problem-solving time   Inactivity

How does a group spend
its time during a crisis?

Figure 8-4   Decision making under crisis.

situation. The specific effects of the three types of groups on time and decision effectiveness are summarized in Table 8-2.

Another approach to analyzing the types of decision-making processes is to look at where a group begins. Does the group start by defining the problem, and then select ways to solve it? Or does the group identify ways of dealing with problems and then apply its technique to a particular problem?

Ivor Davies,[12] a specialist in curriculum design, provides an interesting concept that can easily be applied to group problem solving. He identifies two types of planning. The first type of planning or problem solving is labeled *path X—systematic planning*. Here the group defines the ends or objectives to be achieved and then selects the means or procedures necessary for realizing them. This approach assumes that you have a very clear idea of the future you wish to command. Frequently, ends are seen as unchanging once they are defined. All too often the path X approach appears to argue for a static rather than a dynamic view of the world.

Path Y is another approach to problem solving, but it is characterized by *expedient planning*. Here the group first defines the means or procedures to be used, and then determines those objectives or ends that will best accommodate the limitations they have imposed upon themselves. This path is closer to the normal way of operating within the organizational setting. Often the limits set by the organizational situation and budgetary demands dictated by the economic situation make the path Y approach desirable.

Finally, there are seven common terms applied to the method in which a decision

[12] Ivor K. Davies, *Objectives in Curriculum Design*, McGraw-Hill, 1976, pp. 6–11.

Table 8-2   Group Decision Making in Crisis Situations

	Crisis-oriented group	Procedural group	Planned flexibility group
Majority of time spent in:	Crises	Planning periods	Mostly planning, some crises
Amount of time spent resolving crisis	Large	Small	Average
Range of decisions is:	Short term	Long term	Short and long term
Recurrence of problems	Frequent	Frequent	Normal
Alternatives considered	Limited	Limited	Extensive
Decision-making effectiveness	Weak	Weak	Strong

has been made. A *self-authorized decision* is made by one group member who assumes authority from the group to make the decision. Group commitment to this type of decision is usually low and decreases if this type of decision is repeated often. *Handclasping* is a decision made by two members of the group who join forces. Often such a decision emerges suddenly and catches the group off guard. Again, group commitment is usually low.

Cliques can form to determine the decision for the group. This method is very similar to handclasping except for the number of group members involved. Often these decisions are made outside the regular group meeting and are acted upon at a subsequent meeting. This indicates a low level of trust in the total group and tends to further divide the group into competing factions. *Baiting* is a form of decision making used by individuals as a type of threat of future conflict. Such statements as, "Does anybody disagree with that?" or "We all agree don't we?" are typical of this type of decision making. Often groups want to remain objective and thus use a form of voting like *majority rule* to finalize decisions. Yet vote taking tends to solidify opposing forces and may polarize the group. *Unanimity* is a decision apparently made with 100 percent agreement of the group membership. It is viewed as an ideal situation. However, if pressure to conform is not strong enough and the group feels unanimous decisions are a must, group decisions become impossible to reach. Finally, *consensus* decision making is achieved after all aspects of the issue and all possible solutions are heard and dealt with by the group. While the decision may not be his or her first choice, each member must feel that the group's choice is the most operable under the circumstances. Decisions made by consensus tend to have higher group commitment than other decisions.

Try observing the members of a group in action. Note the type of decision-making process they typically use. Are there a few individuals who usually join forces to push some decision on the rest of the group? Does the group as a whole own the decision, either through some form of voting procedure or consensus reaching? How groups make decisions will say much about their typical patterns of communication.

Steps in Decision Making

Most discussions of decision-making steps begin with identifying the problem. However, Bassett[13] suggests that unless the group has developed a "feedback loop" it may never *find* the problem. The group needs a way of finding out how messages are being understood. Bassett emphasizes the importance of business organizations having direct, open, two-way communication that allows for immediate feedback. Once open lines of communication are established, the typical steps of decision making include *problem definition, goal setting, problem diagnosis, idea production, evaluation of alternatives, deciding on a solution, planning how to carry it out,* and *action steps.*[14] This type of decision making is very similar to a management technique called *management by objectives,* developed by theorists like Peter Drucker and George Odiorne.[15] These men believed that the process by which an organization defines its objectives gives it a sense of direction and determines the amount of growth the organization may experience. Similarly, a group within the organization needs to define its objectives early in the decision-making process in order to give itself a sense of direction.

Table 8-3 indicates individual member behavior needed at each step of the problem-solving sequence outlined above, along with the potential blocks that could stop the process. One way to look at these steps is to analyze behavior that would either assist or hinder the group's decision making.

Let's assume that a group has been formed at the WDTN television station to promote an increase in advertising. The group is composed of the promotion manager, one community services director, one program director, one disc jockey, and the general sales manager of the company. The vice president and general manager appointed these individuals to the group for the purpose of generating suggestions for increasing sales to advertisers. As the members of the group begin to discuss how they should go about their task, the issue of how much power the general manager has actually given them begins to emerge (block: ambiguity). The general sales manager says that according to the information the general manager gave him, the group would not have final say on what decisions would be implemented. They would only serve as an idea-generating force (member role clarification). The community services director suggests that they need a larger sales force to adequately cover the community. Immediately the program director says that would mean diverting funds from programing to pay additional salaries, which would severely limit the effectiveness of program design (too early evaluation of solutions). The disc jockey suggests they brainstorm all the ideas they can think of without first evaluating them, so as to generate as much creative thinking as possible (member role harmonizing).

As the group moves through the rest of the problem-solving steps, individual members will either carry out roles that lead to effective decision making and/or present blocks that temporarily stop the process. It is important that all participants are aware

---

[13] Glenn A. Bassett, *The New Face of Communication*, American Management Association, New York, 1968, p. 211.

[14] *Reading Book on Educational Systems and Organization Development*, National Training Laboratories, Washington, D.C., 1973, p. 27.

[15] Glenn H. Varney, *Management by Objectives*, Dartnell, Chicago, 1971, p. 3.

Table 8-3 Problem-solving Design

Problem-solving steps	Critical member roles	Blocks
1 Problem definition	Clarification	Ambiguity
2 Goal setting	Summarizing	Overgenerality
3 Problem diagnosis	Testing—asking questions	Overrigorous definition
4 Idea production	Informing Giving ideas	Too early evaluation Status threat Size of group
5 Evaluation of alternatives	Reality testing Searching out resources Clarification Summarizing Harmonizing	Lack of experience Too hasty decision Straw voting Evaluating the person instead of the ideas
6 Deciding on solutions	Developing criteria for decision making Testing for consensus	Polarizing Failure to take conditional try Mixing policy and action groups
7 Planning how to carry it out	Initiating	Failure to pin down responsibility
8 Action steps	Informing	Lack of involvement Lack of specification of mechanics

Source: Adapted from *Reading Book on Educational Systems and Organization Development,* National Training Laboratories, Washington, D.C., 1973, p. 27.

of the blocks as well as the motivating forces they will be generating as they make group decisions.

TECHNIQUES OF GROUP DECISION MAKING

One of the authors was asked to design and direct a communication workshop for top-level executives and middle management of a medium-sized manufacturing firm. The vice president of training helped design the training objectives and was instrumental in convincing the firm's president to invest in such a venture. In a planning meeting held 2 days before the first group session, the vice president and training directors decided that decision-making skills needed to be developed early in the training. Two days later at the beginning of the group session, the president of the company made an astounding announcement, "As of yesterday, Jim Roberts (the vice president of training) is no longer with our company." He sat down with no explanation or indication of how this change would affect the company. This was the background for the first session—a session dealing with the importance of maintaining open channels of communication in an organization, and with gaining practice in various decision-making techniques. Unfortunately, the president did not stay for the training session.

The range of an organization's problems is matched by the availability of methods to solve those problems. In the above example the president limited his decision-making process unnecessarily. Poor or hasty decisions usually result from a lack of knowledge concerning the various options open to decision makers. Of the techniques available, four seem to offer the most practical approaches to group decision making.

Kurt Lewin's[16] *force field analysis* is a fairly simple yet effective way of analyzing the positive and negative forces affecting a problem. It is Lewin's theory that there are restraining forces that keep individuals from moving in a particular direction and motivating forces that continue to help support movement in the original direction.

In Figure 8-5 the arrows pushing downward represent the restraining forces that keep the system from moving toward some change. The arrows pushing upward represent those factors in the system that support the change, and that act as barriers to the group's movement *backward*. This combination of forces is known as a *force field*. The length of the arrows in the force field describes the relative strength of the forces. The longer the arrow the stronger the force. It is Lewin's belief that if the group decides to *increase motivating forces*, tension will increase and restraining forces may become more resistant. If instead the *restraining forces* are *reduced* or eliminated, a lower degree of tension will result. Once the group has identified all the forces, the next step is to attach priority to them, so the most important restraining forces can be dealt with first. Identifying actions that will eliminate or reduce the critical restraining forces is the final step in this decision-making process.

To demonstrate how this technique might be used, let's look again at the opening example. The president of the firm was concerned that he was not in close contact with the company's area directors. Instead of looking for all the possible factors causing this problem, he saw only one factor—the vice president. Since the vice president had become a mediator between the president and the other executives, the president thought that by eliminating his position, the other top-level managers would be forced to report directly to him. For the sake of discussion, let's say that instead of making this decision alone, the president called a meeting between himself, the vice president (Jim Roberts), and the eight division executives. He opened the meeting by saying, "I am concerned that I no longer have direct contact with any of you. I get all your

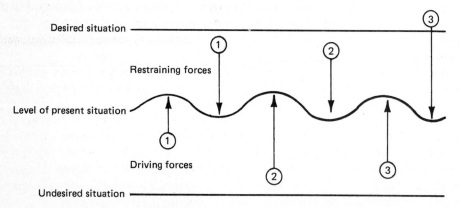

Figure 8-5   Force field analysis decision making.

[16] Kurt Lewin, *Field Theory in Social Science*, Harper & Row, New York, 1951, pp. 30–59.

reports through Jim Roberts and I would rather be talking with each of you directly. I would like for us to decide on a change in our organization that will result in more direct communication." He then asks the group to identify all the factors that prevent them from reporting directly to him. They mention Jim Robert's mediation role and their assumption that the president preferred that they report through him. However, in *addition* to this restraining force, they report that they stopped trying to see the president directly when it became extremely difficult to get an appointment with him, since he was often out of the office. His secretary made it clear that unless it was an emergency the president was too busy for conferences about normal operating procedures. They also raised some issues about the required monthly written report. They felt it was a waste of time. It forced them to gloss over problems they might be having, since a written report would be a permanent indicator of how their group was progressing. A final restraining force was their fear of personal interviews. The president also conducted annual evaluation interviews with each executive to judge the effectiveness of his or her program. The executives felt these two types of interviews would need to be clearly separate from each other.

On the positive side, the motivating forces they mentioned included the president's willingness and openness in discussing this issue with them and allowing them to participate in the decision-making process, the fact that interviews would take less time for the executives than written reports, and finally that Jim Roberts was willing to change his role description so that he could spend more time in developing training programs instead of being a mediator. It is interesting that the group and the president both identified Jim Roberts's mediation role as a restraining force. However, the group saw other forces as *more important*. As the length of the arrows in Figure 8-6 indicates, the group saw the president's inaccessibility as the strongest restraining force. Consequently, the group would work on resolving that issue rather than on one of lesser importance. Force field analysis is an excellent method for analyzing a problem before attempting to solve it. Once the removal of a powerful restraining force has

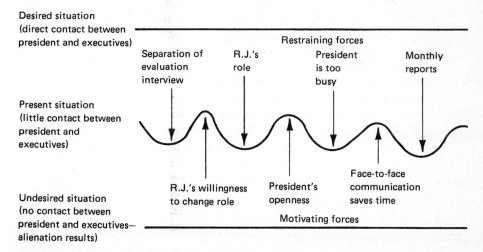

Figure 8-6 Force field analysis for company "X."

been accomplished (inaccessibility of the president), this same force can then become an additional, strong driving force (frequent face-to-face interaction with the president) in the direction of change.

A second method of group problem solving involves specific planning procedures. Its title is *PERT* (Program Evaluation and Review Technique) or "Now that we've agreed on where we want to go, how do we get there?" Greene points out that PERT is "a technique which gained acceptability in government and industry after meeting with unusual success in the Polaris ballistic missile program. In such a program innumerable parts must be brought together at the right time to produce an extremely complex product. PERT is an ideal tool for scheduling such activities."[17] PERT is also an ideal tool to aid organizational groups in carrying out solutions to problems. As an example of its usage, let's look at the writing of this book.

The authors of this book decided to write a text on organizational communication in August 1976. One of the first decisions that had to be made was about a publication date. We wanted the book to have an early 1978 publication date so we had to figure backwards to determine due dates. The publisher told us that once the final manuscript had been delivered it would take 6 to 8 months for the book to be published. That meant a completion date of June 1977. Based on comments from the publishing company we figured on 3 months for editing and rewriting, and thus determined that by March 1977 all chapters should be in final form. We were each responsible for at least three chapters and felt we might need a month after the completion of each chapter for rewrites based on suggestions from the coauthors. Thus, our first chapter would need to be completed by the end of November or early December 1976. Consequently, our first authors' meeting to review initial chapters took place in November 1976.

Figure 8-7 is a visual representation of this process. PERT is basically a reverse sequence where the group begins by identifying the final activity, and works backward to set up time lines. The originators of PERT[18] have developed a formula to determine

---

[17]James Greene, *Operations Planning and Control*, Irwin, Homewood, Ill., 1967, p. 89.
[18]*PERT Summary Report, Phase 1*, Department of the Navy, Bureau of Naval Weapons Special Projects Office, U.S. Government Printing Office, Washington, D.C., 1961, pp. 1–25.

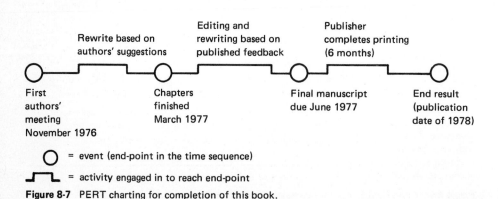

Figure 8-7 PERT charting for completion of this book.

how long it will take to finish a project. You first estimate three times: t_o—optimistic time or shortest amount of time activity could be accomplished; t_p—pessimistic time or the greatest amount of time a project could take; t_m—the best guess of the time needed. For example, the best estimate of the amount of time needed to finish this chapter is 8 to 10 hours. If things really go quickly, it may be finished in 5 hours and if things go slowly it may take as many as 15 hours to finish. Thus, $t_o = 5$, $t_p = 15$, and $t_m = 10$. These figures are plugged into the following formula:

$$t_e \text{ (or expected time)} = \frac{t_o + 4t_m + t_p}{6} = 10 \text{ hours.}$$

Thus, 10 hours is the best estimated time it will take to complete this chapter. PERT is a tool of communication that allows for revision of the plan when a snag develops in the original plan. Plans rarely are perfect. For example, the author may get involved in a television show tonight and not finish as much work as planned on this chapter. However, the *planning process* is indispensable. People carry with them an overall timed sequence of events that will govern their completion of the task and while they may deviate from the plan they now have a clock in their head controlling their actions.

Another decision-making technique widely used in organizations is known as the *Kepner-Tregoe* problem-solving approach.[19] According to the authors, problem solving is a process that follows a logical sequence: identification of the problem, analysis to find the cause, and decision making. The authors define a problem as a *deviation from a standard of performance*. Decision making involves: establishing the objectives of a decision, classifying objectives as to importance (listing the "must" requirements and the "wants" or what you would like to have), developing alternative actions, evaluating alternatives against established objectives, choosing the best alternative to achieve all objectives, exploring a tentative decision for future possible adverse consequences, taking actions to prevent possible adverse consequences from becoming problems, and making sure actions that have been decided are carried out. One interesting feature of this decision-making sequence is its method of potential problem analysis. It is a way to anticipate problems and involves seven questions; (1) What could go wrong? (2) What specifically is each problem? (3) How risky is each problem? (4) What are the possible causes of each problem? (5) Can each cause be proved? (6) How can a cause be prevented or its effects minimized? (7) How can the most serious potential problems be handled?[20]

A fourth tool that can be used by decision-making groups is brainstorming and/or the nominal group technique. *Brainstorming* is a technique used to generate as many ideas about the problem to be solved as possible. The *nominal group* is used to control for individual dominance and social pressure for conformity, behavior often found in brainstorming sessions. Although the two methods have opposite approaches, they can be used together to effectively generate the best ideas from a group. The rules for

---

[19]Charles Kepner and Benjamin Tregoe, *The Rational Manager,* McGraw-Hill, New York, 1965, pp. 1–50.

[20]An excellent comparison of different problem-solving techniques is found in J. H. McPherson, *The People, the Problems and the Problem Solving Methods,* Pendell, Midland, Mich., 1967, pp. 1–25.

brainstorming are simple: (1) evaluation and criticism by group members are forbidden, (2) all contributions are to be encouraged, (3) an attempt is made to create the greatest quantity of ideas, and (4) a combination of ideas and solutions is sought.[21] Eliminating all criticism initially allows group members freedom to offer suggestions, no matter how wild, without fear that the group will reject their ideas. Brainstorming does not guarantee successful results as group members must process the ideas to be drawn out in a brainstorming session. The nominal group, unlike the brainstorming session, directs individuals to work in the presence of others but does not allow verbal interaction in the initial stages. Written output is generated by all members and is sequentially shared and listed for all members to see. The facilitator presents the problem to the group and asks each member to respond by defining the critical elements of the problem *without discussion*. Each group member then reads aloud his ideas without comment from the other group members, and his ideas are listed on newsprint for the entire group to read. The group recorder leads the group in a discussion of the recorded ideas for the purpose of clarification, elaboration, and evaluation. Each item is discussed sequentially. Then each participant is asked to rank order the ten most important items on the list without interacting with other group members. A group decision is made, based on the average of the members' individual votes. The nominal group seems to be most effective when fact finding or idea generating is the purpose while the brainstorming group is more effective for sharing and evaluating information.[22]

The use of these four decision-making techniques, force field analysis, PERT charting, Kepner-Tregoe, and brainstorming/nominal groups, depends on the type of decision to be made and the dynamics of the group making it. At the beginning of this section, we implied that decision makers often make ineffective decisions due to a lack of knowledge about the various options open to them for arriving at decisions. Perhaps one of the most valuable characteristics that group members can have is the flexibility to adapt to the situation and use the most appropriate strategy.

GROUP LEADERSHIP

The impact of leadership style on how the group communicates is great. In Chapter 4 the authors examined the appropriate use of various leadership styles within the organization; consequently, our concern here is with a few additional aspects of the effect of leaders on small group behavior.

Likert[23] has conducted extensive field studies within organizations of various types including government agencies and industrial organizations. He has concluded that leadership characteristics differ markedly between productive and unproductive groups.

---

[21]Ronald L. Applbaum, Edward M. Bodaken, Kenneth K. Sereno, and Karl W. E. Anatol, *The Process of Group Communication*, Science Research Association, Chicago, 1974, pp. 276–277.

[22]Daniel L. Ford and Paul M. Nemiroff, "Applied Group Problem-Solving: The Nominal Group Technique," in John Jones and William Pfeiffer (eds.), *The 1975 Annual Handbook for Group Facilitators*, University Associates, La Jolla, Ca., 1975, pp. 179–182.

[23]R. Likert, *New Patterns of Management*, Harper & Row, New York, 1960, pp. 222–236.

Contrary to what one might expect, the leaders or supervisors of highly productive units do not appear to devote their greatest time and efforts to technical or job-oriented functions with their subordinates. Rather, the leaders whose subordinates show the best performance records focus their primary attention on the human aspects of their relationships and attempt to build work groups with high-performance goals. They tend to spend more time than their low-production counterparts in motivating their subordinates, providing them with structure, keeping them informed about what is going on, getting their ideas and suggestions on important matters before going ahead, training them for more responsibilities, trying out new ideas with them and, in general, showing consideration for the follower and his needs. The low production leader, on the other hand, frequently demands more from his subordinates than they can do, criticizes them in front of others, treats them without respect for their feelings, rides them, and refuses to accept their ideas and suggestions or even explain the actions he has taken.[24]

It would appear that the human relations aspects of the group are affected by the leadership that takes place within a group. One of the authors has been interested in the role of the leader during the actual group process. It would appear that during group interaction six distinct types of leader behaviors are exhibited with varying results.[25] Figure 8-8 identifies these roles and their various outcomes. *Structurer*: the role of structurer involves leader behavior that carefully outlines acceptable roles to be played by other group members, establishes well-defined patterns of organization and channels of communication within the group, and places considerable emphasis on goal achievement. The leader interventions often include goal clarity activities, outlining or "mapping" procedures, and decisions by objectives. The group outcome is best exhibited by increased productivity and a high efficiency level. The leader assumes this role when his or her focus is attainment of specific group goals. *Energizer*: the role of energizer emphasizes revealing feelings, challenging, confronting, and participating often as a member of the group. The leader interventions include emotional stimulations and trainer-centered activities. The most common outcomes for the group from the leader role include a high level of satisfaction among individual members concerning the group, and a desire to encourage others to become members of the group. A leader would be more likely to adopt this role when he or she views member satisfaction as a high priority. *Nonleader/Observer*: this is a leader who adopts the stance of non-involvement, particularly in the initial stages of a group. He or she would avoid making suggestions for discussion content and avoid participating at the content level. His or her role is essentially that of an observer who occasionally makes observations and interpretations of the group process. His or her interventions focus on nondirected group exchanges. Leader interventions decrease as participant contributions increase. This role is effectively used when group independence is viewed as a desired outcome. *Modeler*: when the group leader displays modeling behavior, particularly in the case of self-disclosure, this increases the degree of self-disclosure of the participants. The

---

[24]Bobby R. Patton and Kim Giffin, *Problem-Solving Group Interaction*, Harper & Row, New York, 1973, pp. 73–74.
[25]See Sue DeWine, "The Role of the Trainer/Facilitator During Group Process," *Organizational Renewal Newsletter*, 5(6):p. 1, September–October 1975.

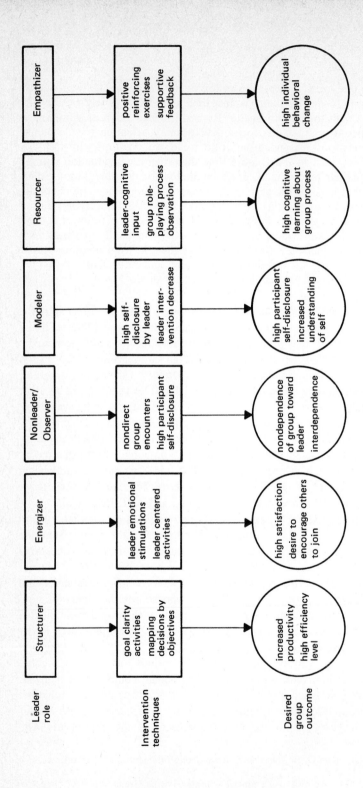

Figure 8-8 The leader-role effects flowchart. (*Source:* Adopted from Sue DeWine, "The Role of the Trainer/Facilitator During Group Process," *Organization Renewal Newsletter*, **5**(6):1, September–October 1975.)

Leader role	Structurer	Energizer	Nonleader/Observer	Modeler	Resourcer	Empathizer
Intervention techniques	goal clarity activities, mapping decisions by objectives	leader emotional stimulations, leader centered activities	nondirect group encounters, high participant self-disclosure	high self-disclosure by leader, leader intervention decrease	leader-cognitive input, group role-playing process observation	positive reinforcing exercises, supportive feedback
Desired group outcome	increased productivity, high efficiency level	high satisfaction, desire to encourage others to join	nondependence of group toward leader, interdependence	high participant self-disclosure, increased understanding of self	high cognitive learning about group process	high individual behavioral change

Table 8-4 Leadership Requirements for Superleaders

The performance factors	Far exceed requirements	Exceeds requirements	Meets requirements	Needs some improvement	Does not meet minimum requirements
Quality	Leaps tall buildings with a single bound	Must take running start to leap over tall buildings	Can leap over short buildings only	Crashes into buildings when attempting to jump over them	Cannot recognize building at all
Timeliness	Is faster than a speeding bullet	Is as fast as a speeding bullet	Not quite as fast as a speeding bullet	Would you believe a slow bullet	Wounds himself with bullets when attempting to shoot
Initiative	Is stronger than a locomotive	Is stronger than a bull elephant	Is stronger than a bull	Shoots the bull	Smells like a bull
Communications	Talks to VIPs	Talks to the assistants to VIPs	Talks to self	Argues with self	Loses those arguments

modeler provides a mirroring effect by expressing his or her own feelings and attitudes, and showing how it's done. Intervention techniques typically include the use of personal experience and self-disclosure. Early establishment of this role is associated with the understanding of self as a desired outcome for the group. *Resourcer*: the participants expect the leader to provide them with information about their own behavior and the task before them. Often participants retain more of the cognitive understanding of group process when leaders adopt a role indicating a high desire to give knowledge and experience. This is in contrast to the trainer role, which indicates a high desire to receive knowledge and experiences from participants. *Empathizer*: a leader role that focuses on behaviors of protecting, offering friendship, affection, and frequent supportive reactions to other members' comments. This role is characterized by the establishment of personal relationships between the leader and group members.

Leadership roles, of necessity, will shift from one to another, or combine in various ways to ensure the desired group outcomes.

Often a leader is expected to be superhuman (see Table 8-4). One has to realize that a leader makes as many mistakes as the rest of the group members but often has to assume more of the responsibility for those mistakes.

INDIVIDUAL MEMBER BEHAVIORS IN GROUPS

It is natural for organizational group members to focus on human behavior within the group because it is available for all to view. Members can profit from observing a person's behavior as an explanation of intergroup dynamics.

The *intent* behind our behavior within a group is very different from the *impact* of that same behavior. Although our intentions may be worthwhile, our impact may serve to disrupt the group process. For example, in one group whose task was to plan a conference, one member, Shirley, is anxious to get her group moving and keep it on the task. She interrupts while Jim is talking to say, "I think we'd better get going and decide on a date for the conference we'll be hosting." Her intent is to motivate the whole group to deal with the task. But Jim hears antagonism in her voice, sees a frown on her face, and concludes that since she was looking directly at him, she's criticizing his previous comment. Consequently, the impact of her comment is to cause resentment in Jim. He withdraws from the group, thinking, "Well, if she thinks that I don't have anything worthwhile to say I just won't say anything at all." Explaining her intent will not change the impact. It may add additional information, but it cannot *erase* the impact. Therefore, it is important for group members to ask for feedback about the impact of their actions to discover if they have any communication habits that cause others to misinterpret their behavior. We tend to explain away public behavior by talking about our intentions. As we examine various member behaviors in the group, remember that we are concerned about the impact these behaviors have on the group.

Some of the initial behaviors of group members focus on *entry* questions. When an individual first enters a new group an orientation process occurs as he or she resolves these dilemmas: (1) *Individual identity*: Who and what am I to be in this group? (2) *Control, power, and influence*: How much power and influence will I have over other individual members and on the group outcome? (3) *Individual needs and group needs*: Will my needs and goals be incorporated into the group? (4) *Acceptance and intimacy*: Will I be accepted and how close and intimate will I have to be? Many of the entry dilemmas revolve around the process of group selection. Did group members voluntarily join the group or was their participation a mandatory decision made by a superior? An early behavior that often disrupts the group, referred to as *hidden agenda*, may be caused by the different motivations of each group member in joining the group.

Often the organization has made the task clear for the participants. They should discuss possible ways of increasing production, establish a grievance committee for future personnel problems, or form an entertainment committee for the annual Christmas party. This public purpose is the *agenda* for the group. This is their stated purpose for meeting. However, we are all familiar with groups whose meetings break down when warring factions develop. Sometimes they argue over issues that did not initially seem relevant to their publicly proclaimed task. Part of the reason for such breakdowns is what Bradford has called hidden agenda. According to him:

> Unlabelled, private and covered, but deeply felt and very much the concern of the group, is another level. Here are all of the conflicting motives, desires, aspirations, and emotional reactions held by the group members, sub-groups, or the group as a whole that cannot be fitted legitimately into the accepted group task. Here are all of the problems which, for a variety of reasons, cannot be laid on top of the table.[26]

The following is an example of hidden agenda. Charlie has been placed on the committee to discuss ways of increasing advertising sales at WDTN-TV. But since he is up for a raise and needs all the brownie points he can get, his personal goal is to establish himself as the leader of the group. Consequently, he tries to dominate the group by overriding suggestions made by others when privately he might support them. A personally hidden goal does not *necessarily* impede group progress. Charlie might make an excellent leader even though his motive is his own personal advancement.

The group itself may have a hidden agenda that will impede the progress of the group. The group that has a task of setting up a grievance committee may have a hidden agenda to slow down on this task, since everyone knows that serving on such a committee may place them in the middle of conflicts between labor and management. The longer they prolong taking definite action, the longer they have avoided potential risks. It is important that each member realize that either a personal hidden agenda or a group hidden motive may be the cause of unproductiveness or divisiveness within the group. Some hidden agendas should be brought to the surface of the entire group's awareness in order that they may be dealt with openly. Others are best left ignored. A sensitivity on the part of group members will help in determining what issues need to be dealt with openly.

[26] L. P. Bradford, "The Case of the Hidden Agenda," in *Group Development*, Selected Readings Series One, National Training Laboratories and National Education Association, Washington, D.C., 1961, p. 60.

One of the most productive observations to make of a group is the distinctions between task behavior and maintenance behavior. Members who exhibit *task* behavior tend to facilitate and coordinate the collective effort to get the group task accomplished. Members who exhibit *maintenance* behavior are oriented toward the functioning of the group as a group, with a focus on the building of interpersonal relationships in the group setting. Both types of behavior are needed in a group. Your awareness of the effects of such behaviors will help you contribute to the interaction process. Benne and Sheats[27] have identified several types of behavior exhibited by members of both categories:

Task Roles
Initiating (proposing tasks or goals)
Seeking information or opinions (asking for facts and feelings)
Giving information or opinion (stating a belief, giving suggestions)
Clarifying and elaborating (interpreting ideas, clearing up confusions)
Summarizing (pulling together related ideas)
Consensus testing (asking group if it is near a decision)

Maintenance Roles
Harmonizing (reducing tensions)
Gate keeping (helping to keep communication channels open, facilitating participation)
Encouraging (being friendly, warm, and responsive)
Compromising (admitting error, modifying in the interest of the group)
Standard setting Identifying norms that guide group behavior)

Every group needs both kinds of behavior and it is best to work out a *balance* of task and maintenance activities. In addition to these two major types of member roles, there also exist disruptive individual roles such as: the *aggressor*, who often attacks the group and the problem it is working on; the *blocker*, who tends to be negative, stubbornly resistant, and disagreeable; the *recognition-seeker*, who calls attention to himself through boasting, reporting on personal achievements, or acting in unusual ways; the *self-confessor*, who uses the group to express personal nongroup-oriented feelings or insights; the *playboy*, who makes a display of his lack of involvement in the group's process through cynicism, nonchalance, or horse play; the *dominator*, who tries to assert authority or superiority by manipulating the group with flattery, assuming a superior status, or giving directions authoritatively; and finally, the *help-seeker*, who attempts to call forth a "sympathy" response from other group members through expressions of insecurity, personal confusion, or deprecation of himself beyond reason.

SUMMARY

At the beginning of this chapter we stated that most of the life of an "organization man" is spent in groups, and that this activity is just as often unsuccessful as it is

[27]K. D. Benne and P. Sheats, "Functional Roles of Group members," in *Group Development,* Selected Reading Series I, National Training Laboratories, Washington, D.C., 1961, pp. 63–64.

successful. Our definition of groups indicated that each member has a stake in the outcome of the group as each is affected by its results. We identified the typical group developmental stages in terms of *interpersonal structure* and *task activity*. Decision making was analyzed through the types of decisions made in an organizational group, the decision-making steps, and four techniques for decision making (force field analysis, PERT charting, Kepner-Tregoe problem-solving approach, and brainstorming/nominal groups). Leadership during group process was analyzed. Finally, individual member behaviors in the group were emphasized, including impact and intent of behaviors, hidden agendas, and task vs. maintenance roles.

A key to the success of a group is for its members to develop the ability to maintain flexibility in the types of roles and behaviors that they exhibit within the group setting. The group member who is able to adapt to the uniqueness of the situation will provide the greatest assistance to the group.

Chapter 9

Public Communication

The role of public speaking in our history cannot be overemphasized. It has been used by politicians, ministers, reformers, employers, and employees as a means of informing and persuading a group of people. Nevertheless, with the growth of literacy and the mass media, public speaking became a secondary means of communication. Newspapers, radio, and television were used when it was necessary to communicate with more than a few people.

Since the 1960s, however, there has been an increased awareness of the need for a more personal, nonmedia approach to communication. Managers have been told that they are in the people business and that person-to-person communication can accomplish as much as or more than mass media communication in an organization.

This chapter will introduce you to the principles and practices of effective public speaking. It will explain how and where to gather material useful in a speech, and how to put this material into an organized message with a beginning, a middle, and an end. The chapter will discuss the use of voice and body when speaking to an audience. Finally, it will identify and examine some of the more frequent occasions on which public speaking is used.

Since this book describes communication within the organization, public speaking will be analyzed as a channel of communication utilized within an organizational setting. However, many of the principles and practices described are applicable to public speaking, whether within or outside an organization.

GATHERING MATERIAL FOR YOUR SPEECH

It has been the experience of the authors that for every minute a speaker spends talking to an audience, he or she spends 50 to 60 minutes preparing. How the speaker uses this preparation time will have an impact on the effectiveness of the speech. For many speakers the majority of preparation time is spent finding material that could be useful in developing the main points and subpoints of the speech. In fact, most speakers, when their research is finished, have more material than they can use. As with other decisions concerning speaking one must make, what material is used and what is left out depends on the objectives of the speech and on the type of audience.

After selecting the specific topic, identifying the audience, and setting objectives, one then starts searching for useful materials. To help in the research, this section will discuss where to locate sources of ideas for main points and the types of information that can be used to explain and support these main points.

Sources of Information

First, the speaker needs to explore his own knowledge and observations. After inventorying his personal awareness, he can turn to other sources, including printed materials and interviews.

Knowledge and Observations   The speaker is his own best source of information. After all, he has been storing up impressions of the world all his life. To make use of this storehouse of knowledge, he needs to make a systematic search of his memory. Take, for example, an organization to which you belong now. As a student member of your college or university, you are aware of student social activities, as well as of types of students who attend class and their attitudes toward the usefulness of the education they are receiving. You have impressions about the quality of instruction that takes place and the fairness with which you are graded. Your firsthand knowledge of the organization is a valuable source of information. It can add unique insights that would not be found in a speech by a person who had only printed and other secondary sources of information. The best approach is to outline your knowledge, separating it into categories. This will reveal what and how much you know about the school. This same procedure is useful in the preparation of any speech topic.

When relying on your memory, be cautious when assessing its accuracy. Time tends to wash out the details and distort what is remembered. Also, perception is colored by attitudes and expectations; this can affect *what* one remembers and its importance in one's thinking.

What you see and hear on a daily basis can provide information for a speech. By focusing attention on matters that pertain to the speech topic, you can make surprisingly keen observations. For instance, if you work at a television station and your superior tells you to explain television commercials to a group of high school students, how could focused observation help in gathering material? Would observing the interaction between the salesperson and a potential time buyer be helpful? Would observing the film crew recording the video portion of a commercial provide information for your talk? Not only can observation provide new material for the speech, but it also can help validate what you think you already know. That is, observation can help you know if your memory is accurate.

Once you have explored your knowledge and have made focused observations, the next step is to move outside yourself and to explore other sources of information.

Printed Sources This refers to materials that have been publicly or privately published. If the speech concerns a broad topic (the influence of juvenile delinquency on crime) then publicly published sources such as magazines, books, newspaper articles, etc., should be investigated. However, if the speech primarily concerns the internal workings of your organization (profit sharing for all employees), then printed materials produced by the organization, such as memos, reports, directives, operating manuals, etc., can be used in gathering information.

Periodical Indexes The most commonly used index is the *Reader's Guide to Periodical Literature*, which presents a monthly index of articles published in more than a hundred popular periodicals. There are indexes for published articles in business, science, education, behavioral sciences, and humanities, as well as in public affairs. Most of the indexes list their articles by subject heading. If you want to read about the hospitalization coverage used in retailing companies, consult the business index and look under the subject heading, "Fringe benefits."

Newspapers These are especially useful in researching local issues or occurrences. Many daily newspapers maintain a library and index stories that are printed. Most public and college libraries keep microfilm copies of newspapers.

Pamphlets Government agencies publish thousands of pamphlets in a year's time, covering a myriad of topics. To find them, check the library's vertical file. In addition to federal government pamphlets, state and local agencies also disseminate information through pamphlets. Finally, business and industrial firms print and distribute information pamphlets that describe their purpose, activities, and financial status. Often your company library will have copies, or you may write directly to the organization, usually in care of the public affairs or public relations offices.

Organizational Files For speeches on topics of an internal nature, as mentioned earlier, printed materials produced by your own organization could be the primary source of information. An example would be if you, as president of the student body, were asked to speak to a group of freshmen on the topic of student social life on campus. Printed sources of information could be: (1) the student guide or handbook, (2) the annual report of the interfraternity/sorority organizations, (3) the list of university-approved student social functions held on campus, (4) the report of the sports intermural organization. These sources of information and others have been produced by and for the organization and could prove valuable in your research.

Interviews Most of us have gathered information about a topic by talking to another person; relatives, friends, and associates have shared ideas with us. However, to use the interview as a source of information, purposely select a person who possesses knowledge and insights about the topic. The best place to start looking is among people in your own organization. The credit manager can explain how interest is computed on a charge account, department buyers can inform you of new clothing trends, and so forth. For some topics, it may be necessary to look outside of the organization. If you are seeking information about the power of police to arrest people in your town, then select a municipal judge or common pleas judge to interview. If you want information on property taxes in your town, then make an appointment with the local tax assessor or one of his assistants.

For a detailed description of the steps involved in gathering interview data, refer to the chapter on interviewing, especially the section on the information-getting interview.

Types of Information

As you search yourself and other sources for information, you will collect a sizeable amount of material. This material should be analyzed on two levels. One level will identify the main points to make in the body of the speech. The second level of analysis will identify the materials that can be used to amplify or prove the main points. This second-level material is used to develop subpoints. The following is a detailed list of specific types of information useful in developing data for the subpoints.

Comparisons This involves a process of clarifying an idea or subject by comparing it to another. This is often done in normal conversation when we say a Chevy is not as good as a Ford, or that laws setting driving age are similar to laws setting drinking age. Comparisons are used to help explain an idea. The most common form of comparison is the *analogy*. Here similarities are emphasized between concepts, ideas, people, experiences, etc. Based upon these similarities one can make some inference or draw a conclusion.

Often an analogy is used to explain something unfamiliar to an audience, or to compare it to something its members already know. For instance, one could explain the game of Rugby by comparing it to American football, or explain the flow of money in banking by comparing it to the human circulatory system.

When using an analogy, make sure the comparison is relevant to the main point and that the audience can observe the similarities clearly. In addition, remember that a comparison cannot prove a point, but it can help explain one.

Examples and Illustrations An *example* is a description of a specific instance, while an *illustration* is an example in greater detail. An example picks one specific instance out of many. If someone asks for an example of how government regulates business, you would have hundreds of examples from which to choose. Usually it is not hard to think of one example, but it does take time and concentration to find an example that is directly related to the main point and that can be readily grasped by the audience. The same is true when details are added to the example to make it into an illustration.

Examples/illustrations can be classified as real or hypothetical. The *real* or *factual* example details events that have taken place. It deals with the reality of the past. A factual example of how supplies of energy can affect the economy would be the winter of 1977, during which natural gas shortages resulted in the closing of factories and businesses. A factual example of the high cost of living would be to trace the rise in the cost of automobiles. Examples that deal with what happened are an excellent means of explaining or clarifying a main point. If the factual example is verifiable, then it could be used to prove a main point. *Hypothetical* examples can never be used to prove a point. Since they deal only with what would be, the real value of hypothetical examples is in focusing the attention of the audience on something that could affect them personally and emotionally. "What if gasoline were rationed? How would you drive to work, to the store, to the market, to visit a friend, to recreational facilities? How would you go *anywhere* outside of a few blocks from your home?" Hypothetical examples are used to clarify or support a main point; as with the factual examples, make certain they relate directly to the idea and are easily understood by the audience.

Testimony/Quotation   In a trial the factual statements of a person can be used as evidence to prove one side of a case. In our private conversations we often ask people to identify the source of the information they gave us. In both instances, we are concerned with who said what. Acceptance of the testimony depends on the expertness of the source and the relevance of the information to the main point. In other words, when an expert in a field makes a statement, it is of little value unless it specifically proves or supports your main point. If you use the testimony of an expert or authority, make sure the audience is aware of his or her stature. If necessary, list some of the important credentials of the source.

When using testimony, remember to (1) cite the complete source (who said it and where you found the information); (2) make the quotation as brief as possible; and (3) indicate the beginning and end of the quotation, to differentiate the expert's ideas from your own.

Statistics   These are facts presented in a numerical fashion. Statistics can be simple numbers like 147 votes per precinct, percentages like 45 percent, proportions like two out of every three arrests end in conviction, or even a fraction like $\frac{7}{10}$ of 1 percent. Statistics can be used to prove or to explain a main point. When using statistics, the following rules should be observed.

1   Use the most recent statistics. Dated statistics can give a false representation of reality. What was true in 1974 probably is not true this year. However, you can present statistics from this year and compare them to those of previous years.

2   Don't present too many statistics. The use of too many numbers can confuse the listener. Presenting a few numbers in an understandable manner is more beneficial to your case.

3   Make sure the statistics relate directly to the main points they support. In addition, you should reveal the source of the numbers.

4 Check on the accuracy of the statistics. Search for other sources of statistics that corroborate what you have already found. Be careful with statistics from special interest groups that might distort numbers in their support or attack of some concept.

All the types of information (comparison, example/illustration, testimony/quotation, and statistics) can be used as subpoints to support main points. If you do adequate research, you will have more material than you can use. Trying to incorporate all the information will overcrowd and lengthen, unnecessarily, your speech. Be judicious. Select only those types of information that help clarify the message and help the audience understand your point of view.

ORGANIZING THE SPEECH MATERIAL

If you have ever listened to a speech, whether in a formal or informal setting, and have said to a friend afterward, "I couldn't follow what he was saying" or "Did you understand what he was driving at?" then probably you have listened to a poorly organized speech. Reflect on your experience with this speaker. It wasn't his words that bothered you; his use of examples and illustrations were appropriate, and he spoke loudly enough. The problem was in following his ideas. One of the biggest mistakes a beginning speaker can make is to deceive himself into thinking that because he has thought about his message and has put his ideas down on paper, his speech is ready to deliver. Well-developed ideas are lost on an audience unless they are organized in a manner that creates clarity, specificity, and completeness.

Developing the Topic

For some public speaking occasions, the speech topic has already been determined. When your boss tells you to prepare a brief talk about the new inventory forms, she is identifying your topic. If the school counselor asks the police department for someone to talk about the impact of the new state drug laws, the police officer has no choice in his topic. However, there are occasions when you have only a general idea and need to develop a more narrow topic. In these instances, write a *key idea statement* that clearly specifies your topic. To test the key idea statement, use two guidelines:

1 Is the key idea one that can be covered in the amount of time provided? It should not be just a cursory examination, but one that adds to the understanding of the audience. Example: "How the 6 O'clock News Is Produced" cannot be covered in 6 to 8 minutes.
2 Is the wording such that the topic area is clearly and specifically identified? Watch use of technical jargon, but do be descriptive.

Developing the topic area into a specific key idea statement is important in writing your speech because it helps you to organize the ideas. In addition, it helps the audience identify the goal and content of your message.

Key idea: When selecting a multispeed bicycle, you need to consider the cost, where you will travel, and how often it will be ridden.

This key idea statement identifies the goal of the speech (the purchase of a bike) and the main points considered in developing the key idea.

Developing Main Points

The body of a speech consists of main points. These main points contain the ideas, concepts, thoughts, assertions, statements, etc., that you wish to make about the key idea. Sometimes the main points are easy to identify. If you wish to tell your audience about the two changes in the new inventory procedures, then the two changes become the main points. However, there are some occasions when you must analyze the material first to decide what main points should be covered in the speech. Samovar and Mills[1] have developed a set of guidelines to use in selecting and phrasing main points.

1. Each main point must grow out of the key idea statement. Here we are concerned that there be a kinship between the key idea statement and the main points to be expressed. That is, the main points must relate directly to the topic area as presented in the key idea. For example:

Key idea: Cigarette smoking is harmful to your health.

  Main point 1.   It contains substances identified as cancerous agents.

  Main point 2.   It is highly related to incidence of heart attack.

Key idea: Today's television shows are different from those of 20 years ago.

  Main point 1.   Today movies are made solely for showing on television.

  Main point 2.   Today situation comedy shows star characters from racial and ethnic minorities.

  Main point 3.   Today live broadcasts are infrequent.

2. Each main point must be separate from other main points. While all main points are related to the key idea, they should each constitute a separate part. This separateness will help you organize the main points and will make it easier for the audience to follow the message.

Key idea: When buying a house, make a complete inspection.

  Main point 1.   Inspect the land surrounding the house.

  Main point 2.   Inspect the exterior of the house.

  Main point 3.   Inspect the interior of the house.

3. Your main points should adequately develop the key idea. Be sure to use main points that cover the material necessary for the audience to understand the key idea. Put yourself in the listener's shoes. What points must you cover so that he or she will fully understand your topic? If you wanted to brief new employees on the operation of the standard cash register used in the store, you should be concerned with explaining the *purpose*, the *parts*, and the *procedures* for operating the machine.

Main points cannot stand alone. They need to have material that supports the idea being expressed. You need to fill in the details to have a complete main point. Supporting materials that are used in this way are referred to as *subpoints*. Most, but not all, main points have one or more subpoints. Earlier in this chapter we discussed the

---

[1]Larry A. Samovar and Jack Mills, *Oral Communication: Message and Response*, Brown, Dubuque, Io., 1972, pp. 97–100.

types of information used in developing subpoints (comparison, example/illustration, testimony/quotation, and statistics). We feel the guidelines used in selecting and phrasing your main points are also applicable to the subpoints. That is, subpoints should be directly related to the main point; each subpoint must contain a separate form of supporting material; and subpoints must adequately explain and support the main point.

Arranging the Main Points

After you have decided on the main points, place them in some pattern or arrangement. The pattern you choose depends on the purpose of your speech. Here are several organizational patterns that might be useful. Also included are examples of speech topics relevant to an organizational setting.

Time Pattern   This is used when main points are developed in a chronological manner. This pattern is especially useful when discussing the idea of progress or evolution of some idea, institution, or group. Also, it can be useful in explaining the process (steps) in making a substance or performing a task.

In a training program for police recruits the instructor developed his presentation on police forensic science by using a time pattern:

Key idea: There have been three major developments in the evaluation of forensic science.

Main point 1.   Fingerprinting as a means of identification

Main point 2.   Ballistics tests for guns

Main point 3.   Polygraph tests for measuring the truthfulness of a person's statements

Spatial Pattern   This pattern is used to arrange main points in a space order. To describe a building from the bottom to the top, floor by floor, would be an example of using the spatial pattern. It can be used to explain the layout of a retail store by going from front to back. It may also be used to measure geographical areas, such as from east to west.

The research and development director of Richdales used a spatial pattern in developing his oral report to members of the board of directors concerning the layout of a new store.

Key idea: Each wing of the new department store has a special purpose.

Main point 1.   The right wing houses the administrative offices and storage area.

Main point 2.   The center wing features all the retail departments.

Main point 3.   The left wing contains dining and recreation facilities.

Topical Pattern   This pattern is used to break the topic into natural divisions or component parts. Here the speaker would be concerned with explaining the *parts* of an engine, the *criteria* for selecting a new suit, the different *roles* of a police officer, the different *features* of a new typewriter, and so on.

In a speech to the Optimists Club, WDTN's program director used a topical pattern to arrange the main points that described local news programs.

Key idea: Most local television news programs have three main features.
Main point 1. Hard and soft news stories
Main point 2. Sports results and stories
Main point 3. National and local weather reports

Problem-Solution Patterns This is a common method for arranging main points when the speaker wants to change or sustain a point of view. Simply stated, the speaker describes the problem and its consequences; then he or she develops a solution and supports its implementation.

In a speech presented to department managers, the director of training for Richdales used a problem-solution pattern to explain her proposal for a new training program.

Key idea: All retail clerks should have training in interpersonal communication.

(Problem)	1.	Ineffective handling of people who are rude, disorganized, or undecided can create problems in a store.
(Consequences)	2.	Problems result in wasted time and dissatisfied customers.
(Solution)	3.	Training in methods for communicating with people on an interpersonal level can help eliminate the problem.
(Support)	4.	The disadvantages of costs of the training and employee time away from the store would be outweighed by the advantages of improved customer satisfaction and increased sales.

All of the above organizational patterns can help you arrange the main points of the message. The decision about which one to select should be based on the type of topic chosen and on the goal of the speech.

Introducing and Concluding the Speech

Now that you have selected and narrowed a topic, decided how you will develop the topic (main points), and organized your thoughts, you are ready to prepare the beginning and end of the speech. This task should not be taken lightly. These parts are not two ends attached to hold the middle together. The material used to start and end the speech will have an impact on the audience's acceptance of the topic.

Preparing the Introduction There is a substantial amount of evidence to show that the first impression people have of an individual influences their perception of that individual's credibility. The introduction of your speech will be a part of the first impression the audience has of you as a speaker. Use the introduction to let the members of the audience see you as a concerned person wanting to share ideas with them.

In addition to establishing personal rapport, the introduction should catch the attention of the audience. Several techniques that could be used are:

Startling Statement This technique is similar to a splash of cold water in the face. It cuts through the listener's present thoughts and quickly focuses his or her attention on the topic. As an employee, would you give your attention to a speaker who began by saying, "If the company eliminates all fringe benefits, your spendable salary will drop by 35 percent."?

Quotation   You can catch the listener's attention by using a quotation that has a definite relationship to the topic being presented. A thought-provoking quotation from the Bible, a famous speech or document, a phrase associated with an organization or person, a quote from a book or poem—all can be used when they are relevant to the topic and are presented in a concise manner. On the occasions when there is more than one speech being presented, you can make references to something that was said previously.

Illustration or Story   This can be an effective method of opening a speech. The key to its use is to have a short narrative and one that can be related to the topic. Also, make sure you can tell it well.

Reference to Audience or Occasion   When a speaker uses this technique, he is suggesting a connection between his topic and the listener or between his topic and the occasion that brought the speaker and audience together. Making reference to members of the audience includes them in the speech. This can result in more attention for the topic. Notice how the police officer makes a connection between himself and the student audience on the topic of drugs:

> You and I know that the short-range effects of marijuana are almost negligible. We both know that you cannot burn out on pot, and that the next day's craving is not primarily dependent on the previous day's consumption. But, how much do you know about the long-term impact of marijuana, such as chromosome damage, psychological dependency, and sex hormone secretion? Let me help you understand these side effects by sharing with you the results of recent research.

The speaker's choice of attention-getting techniques depends on the interest of the audience and on his or her topic. There are other techniques for catching attention that could grow out of the topic or the speaker's imagination. The important point is to plan your introduction so you won't have trouble starting.

Preparing the Conclusion   Many beginning speakers don't plan their conclusions. They think that a speaker need only come to his or her last point, finish it, and sit down. The problem with this approach is that the audience is caught by surprise and is confused. To be effect, a conclusion should (1) finish the speech by directing the audience's attention to what you have said and (2) give the receiver a sense of completeness. Some methods used to end a speech include:

Summary   Make a brief restatement of the main points of the speech. Don't make the summary too long, or it becomes a repeat of the same speech. Instead of repeating the main points, some speakers paraphrase them. The summary is especially useful when the speaker wishes to include another method in the conclusion.

Quotation   The same guidelines for using a quotation in the introduction apply to its use in the conclusion; it should be concise and relevant to the topic. On some occasions the speaker may find it appropriate to use the same quote for the introduction and for the conclusion. This can give the speech a sense of wholeness.

Appeal or Challenge   The appeal is used to suggest that the audience turn the speaker's ideas into beliefs or actions. To be effective, the body of the speech must have explained *why* the audience should adopt the belief or behavior suggested.

Frequently the appeal is presented in emotional terms to arouse the sympathy of the audience. The following is a good example of how a well-known business leader related himself to the audience by using a patriotic appeal.

Are we willing to protect our free enterprise system? From what I've said here today, it should be obvious that we haven't been doing a very good job of it—regardless of our desire to do so. Fortunately, however, the game isn't over yet. We are still a nation with a representative government. You and I and other Americans can still express our opinions . . . communicate with our representatives in government . . . speak up and speak out on how we want our government to operate, and serve the best interests of our companies and our society.[2]

Personal Reference In this conclusion the speaker relates his personal interest to the topic and then relates both his interest and the topic to the audience. The personal reference made should be direct and nonflattering in nature. This type of conclusion was used by General Douglas MacArthur in the "Farewell to the Cadets" speech delivered at West Point in 1962.

In my dreams I hear again the crash of guns, the rattle of musketry, the strong, mournful mutter of the battlefield. But in the evening of my memory always I come back to West Point. Always there echoes and reechoes: duty, honor, country.
    Today marks my final roll call with you. But I want you to know that when I cross the river, my last conscious thoughts will be of the corps, and the corps, and the corps.[3]

There are two key factors to consider when selecting a conclusion. (1) The conclusion should seem to be an extension of the key idea and main points. The conclusion should have a direct relationship to some element of the topic. (2) The speaker should select a conclusion that best fits the audience. In a police officer's speech, on the need for law and order, presented to a group of college students, it would be better to conclude with a quote from John F. Kennedy than one from Richard Nixon. Also, it is unwise to introduce new material into the conclusion. The end of the speech is a time for drawing together the essential thoughts, not for adding new ones.
    Remember to make the final moments before the group positive and conclusive. When it is time to stop, do so, and avoid trailing off to an inconclusive finish.

Outlining the Speech

"An outline contributes both to simplification and order: it simplifies because it reduces the content of the speech to its essentials; it provides order because it necessitates arranging materials logically and systematically."[4]
    The process of putting the different parts of your speech into an orderly and

[2] Edgar Speer, "Winter's Chill—And the Cold Hand of Government," *Vital Speeches,* 43(11): 306, March 15, 1977.
    [3] Robert C. Jeffrey and Owen Peterson, *Speech: A Basic Text,* Harper & Row, New York, 1976, p. 182.
    [4] Ibid., p. 205.

manageable sequence is termed *outlining*. An outline benefits the speaker because it allows her to observe the different ideas she is considering and the relationships among these ideas. These observations are useful when the speaker decides which main points are best suited to the topic and the audience. Also, an outline will reveal the relationship between a main point and its supporting material. This can help the speaker identify main points that need more, fewer, or different forms of support. In addition, an outline can help the speaker to remember her material and to estimate the amount of time each part and the sum of the parts will use.

For the listener, the outline also can prove beneficial. A clearly organized message will help the listener follow the speaker's train of thought from beginning to end. In addition, there is some evidence to show that people retain more information from an organized speech than from a disorganized one.

An outline can be used to prepare the material for speaking and in the actual delivery of the speech. When speaking from an outline, the speaker writes only 15 to 25 percent of the actual message; the rest is delivered extemporaneously. That is, she uses one sentence to identify each main point, and one sentence to identify each subpoint or sub-subpoint. The information used to elaborate on the main points or subpoints is stored in the speaker's mind. An exception to this is the use of quotations, statistics, or other material that needs to be repeated verbatim. An alternative to this method of delivery is the memorized speech, which is written word-for-word, committed to memory, and delivered to an audience. A second method is to write the speech word-for-word as a manuscript, and deliver the speech, reading the manuscript. If you choose either alternative method, then you need expand only your outline to include all the words you would use in the speech. Your authors do not recommend using a memorized speech, due to the high risk of forgetting or confusing the material you wish to present. A rule of thumb is that shorter speeches (5 to 15 minutes) can be handled by use of an outline; longer speeches need more developed outlines or manuscripts.

To help you in understanding the outline process, we suggest several guidelines:

Use a Set of Symbols You use symbols to identify your ideas in a hierarchy form. Major divisions of the speech are indicated by Roman numerals: **I** Introduction; **II** Key idea; **III** Body; **IV** Conclusion. Main points are labeled with capital letters (**A, B, C**); supporting material or subpoints are identified by Arabic numerals (**1, 2, 3**). If further subdivision is needed, small letters are used (**a, b, c**).

Each Main Point or Subpoint Should Contain Only One Idea This keeps the ideas separate and helps to identify excessive overlap between main points.

Use Proper Subordination Subpoints should relate to main points. As stated earlier, main points are the ideas, statements, assumptions, concepts, and thoughts that develop your topic. Subpoints are used to support or prove the main points. Don't put supporting material under a main point heading.

To explain the guidelines, we have included the outline of a speech delivered by a police communication commander to a group of police recruits:

I Introduction
  A Short history of police telecommunication from telegraph to computers.
  B Police officers need reliable communication systems.
II Key idea
III Body
  A The telephone is primary link between citizens and police.
    1 A citizen calls for assistance.
    2 A citizen calls to give information.
    3 Police call citizens for follow-up investigation.
  B Computer and telex systems serve as links between police agencies.
    1 NCIC (National Criminal Information Center) links local police to national criminal information system.
    2 LEADS (Law Enforcement Automated Data System) links local police with state agencies.
  C Radio communication serves local law enforcement needs.
    1 The radio is used by the command staff to communicate with field officers.
    2 The radio is used to communicate messages between adjacent police departments.
    3 The radio is used by police to communicate with emergency services.
IV Conclusions
  A Summary of main points in the body
    1 Telephone link between citizens and police
    2 Electronic communication between local police and federal or state agencies
    3 Use of radio with internal and external police communication needs
  B Knowledge of the communication system can allow the police officer to act more efficiently and quickly.

Summary

Often the beginning speaker feels that he can set his ideas on paper and then be ready to speak. Effective speaking requires time to organize your thoughts. Good organization makes it easier for you to deliver, and for the audience to listen to, your speech.

Your speech should address a specific topic, one the audience can quickly grasp. To accomplish this, you need a clearly worded key idea statement and main points that fully develop your key idea. These main points are to be arranged in a pattern that fits the topic and the goal of your speech.

The introduction is used to catch the audience's attention in a way that prepares its members for the key idea and motivates them to want to listen. Several attention techniques include startling statement, quotation, illustration or story, and reference to the audience or occasion. The conclusion should bring a sense of completeness to your message. In addition, you want to leave the members of the audience with orderly arranged material that can enhance their understanding and impact upon their opinions or actions.

DELIVERY—USE OF YOUR VOICE AND BODY

When speaking to an audience, you communicate through more than one channel. This idea was stated earlier, but it is important enough to be amplified further. The words selected and the sequence in which they are placed constitute the *primary message*. You give meaning to the ideas and supporting material by choosing words that will reflect accurately your thoughts in the minds of the listeners. As a manager, your selection of words to describe how the clerks in your department are to fill out the new inventory forms is important. If you choose to use words for which there are several meanings, then your primary message may not be accurately received. We are speaking here of *what* you say when speaking to an audience.

However, there are *secondary channels* through which you communicate with an audience. Now we are referring to *how* you present the primary message, that is, the use of your voice and body to deliver the ideas/supporting material. These secondary channels contribute much to successful communication. For instance, when you are explaining the new inventory forms, if your rate of speech is too fast, some clerks may not have enough thinking time to decode and process the information in order to understand how the inventory form is to be used. The words (primary message) are understandable, but the speed of delivery (secondary message) is creating a barrier to successful communication. The same consequence could occur if the volume of your voice is too low to be heard. The impact of poor vocal delivery is compounded when accompanied by ineffective use of the body. Remember how your mind screamed for relief when you had to sit through a lecture in which the teacher read from notes in a monotone voice. It was not his words that bored you, but rather his lack of eye contact and lack of variety in his vocal delivery. We can get by with weak or ineffective use of the voice and body in one-on-one/one-on-few communication situations, due to the directness of the interaction; however, when that few become ten, twenty-five, fifty, or more people, then we must rely more on effective use of the secondary channels to come across in a personal, direct manner.

Vocal Delivery

The way you use your voice may add to your speaking success, or it can contribute to your poor performance in front of a group. So that you may have better control over your voice, we shall analyze three variables that greatly affect vocal delivery: volume, rate, and pitch.

Volume Here we are referring to the loudness or softness of your voice. Because most people speak in public so infrequently, they feel embarrassed to speak above a conversational level. They feel as if they were shouting. However, remember that if

Figure 9-1 The Wizard of Id. (Reprinted by permission of Johnny Hart and Field Enterprises, Inc.)

the farthest member of the audience is more than 10 feet away, you will need to increase your volume to be heard. It only sounds loud to you because it is so near to your ear. But, it is *their* ears you need to reach.

The key to the successful use of volume is to adjust it to fit the speech location and the material you present. The larger the room and the more people there are, the louder you should speak. People cough, cross their legs, move their feet, scoot their chairs, etc. In other words, they produce sounds that compete with your voice. Adjust your voice to overcome these extraneous sounds. In addition, use your volume as one way to emphasize some idea or phrase. Raising or lowering the volume will draw more attention to what is being said. If used sparingly and with other vocal delivery elements, volume can control the attention of your audience for short periods of time.

Rate   Here we are concerned with the speed at which you speak. Beginning speakers often use too rapid a rate of speech. A fast rate of speech impacts upon the audience's interest and understanding. If you speak too fast, the audience is likely to lose some of the meaning you intended and, consequently, lose interest in your speech. Except for dramatic effect, a speaker should avoid using a machine-gun rate of vocal delivery.

A rapid rate of speech is usually caused by (1) nervousness and (2) lack of understanding of the factors that influence our rate of speech. Everyone is nervous *before* he or she speaks to a new audience. Nervousness only becomes a problem when it extends into the speech itself. The best way to combat it is to be familiar with your ideas/supporting material and to work on convincing your listeners that what you have to say is important to them. Concentrating on the audience, not on yourself, will help reduce the level of nervousness. There are two factors that influence your rate of speech—duration of the sound and pause. The *duration* of sound refers to the amount of time you spend saying the vowels and consonants that are pronounced in a word. For instance, you can spend 1 second uttering the word "operator," or you can spend 3 seconds saying the word "o-per-ra-tor." The difference is caused by the amount of time you spend in pronouncing the vowel and consonant sounds. By spending more time uttering the sounds, you slow the rate of speech. *Pause* is the amount of time spent between speech sounds, syllables, and words. Pauses can serve as vocalized periods, commas, or question marks to slow the rate and provide the listener with a signal that a thought has ended or that you wish to emphasize an idea or concept. Some beginning speakers have a problem with spoken pauses rather than with silent ones. They feel every second must be filled with sound and say their pauses, such as "uh," "er," "mm," or extend them beyond their normal pronunciation pattern, such as "Noooow," "aaaannnd," "buuut."

Pitch   Soprano, tenor, or base describes a singer's normal pitch range; and the terms *loudness* or *softness* are used to describe the pitch range of a public speaker. Each person has a normal pitch range, some naturally higher and some naturally lower. Problems occur when a person will not vary his or her normal pitch range to match the intensity of the primary message. Changing the pitch to reflect the meaning of the words used coordinates the primary and secondary messages. When this does not happen and there is little or no change in pitch level, a monotone occurs.

Figure 9-2 Avoid a singsong pattern.

Monotone pitch patterns can be the result of anxiety, with the speaker primarily concerned with rushing through the message and not with using the pitch level to emphasize phrases or ideas; or they can result from the speaker's using the same vocal pattern throughout the speech. The pitch level changes but in a predictable, repeated manner referred to as a "sing-song" pattern. It can put people to sleep just as fast as a one-pitch-level monotone.

When practicing your message aloud, vary your pitch level to match your phrases or ideas. Mark your outline or notes with arrows to show where you want to raise ⌝ or lower ⌟ the pitch. Also, use a tape recorder in your practice sessions. When you listen to your recorded voice, notice the amount and quality of vocal variety. Especially listen for changes in your pitch level, which are usually more subtle than changes in rate and volume. Finally, to demonstrate to yourself the difference in meaning that can be projected through vocal inflections (pitch change), say the word "no" to express the following meanings:

1 No. (I didn't know that.)
2 No? (Are you sure?)
3 No (Maybe.)
4 No (Definite.)
5 No (I think I have a better idea.)

One "no," five different meanings, all of which are caused by a change in the pitch level.

Physical Delivery

The speaker's bodily actions contribute to the secondary message being sent to an audience. What we have said about the need for coordination between the words and vocal delivery is also true about physical delivery. Your facial expression, gestures, and posture all contribute to *how you say it.*

Facial Expression We probably express more nonverbal messages through our facial muscles and eyes than through any other part of our body. People express their feelings and awareness through their facial expressions. Your face can say, "I agree or I disagree," "I like it or I don't like it," "It will work or it won't work," without your uttering one sound. People look you in the eye to determine the truth of your words. The sadness or joy of a face can express more than any words you choose.

Your facial expression produces a secondary message that can reinforce the ideas you express. This coordination between the nonverbal and verbal signals you send out help the listeners to understand your meaning. In addition, it tells the listeners that you want to communicate with them and that you are concerned that they understand what you have said. Many of us have sorrowfully experienced the speaker who reads his message to us, seldom looking at the audience. Is he more concerned with including every word on the manuscript than with sharing his ideas and feelings with us, the audience? Consistent eye contact can help hold the audience's attention. If you look at me, I feel you are talking to me, and I want to return the courtesy by giving you my attention.

Some beginning speakers feel that they will reveal their stage fright by looking at the audience. If we were in a football huddle, perhaps you could see the anxiety in my eyes, but in public speaking situations where the audience is 10 to 1,000 feet away, the whites of your eyes cannot be discerned. Look at the members of your audience as if you were conversing with them. Keep your eyes moving around your audience, but don't use repetitious sweeping back and forth patterns. Establish eye contact with various individuals in your audience. Watch their facial expressions or body actions in order to gather information on how well they seem to understand your message. In other words, you look at your audience to facilitate understanding of your message, but you also search for feedback as to how well the message is coming across. If you feel your listeners do not understand, then rephrase or repeat material that may have confused them.

Body Movement Here we are concerned with how you approach the platform, your movement at the platform, and your use of gestures.

The audience forms a first impression of your dynamism as a communicator when you approach the speaker's platform or podium. If you hesitate, seem frightened, or spend too much time arranging your material, you are likely to make a less than positive first impression. Your best strategy is to have your materials ready, move swiftly to the speaking area, then pause to arrange your materials and survey your listeners to see if they are ready for you to start.

While giving your presentation, don't make random movements of your body. Don't pace back and forth or move your body in a repetitive manner. This distracts from the primary message. For instance, if you have an idea with two main points, then deliver one point from the right side of the podium and the other from the left.

If you are explaining why you disagree with or don't like some concept, then step back; if you agree with or like the concept, then step or lean forward.

Remember, don't be afraid to move if you have the room and if the movement seems to reinforce the primary message. If you don't have the room (e.g., if you are standing in front of your chair at a table) and if the movement does not seem to fit the spoken message, then you should concentrate on using gestures to give bodily reinforcement.

Gestures are a form of body movement that involve the hands and arms. We all use them in our normal conversation. However, beginning speakers think hands and arms are as large as a chair and weigh 20 pounds each. The solution is to approach the speaking situation as if it were an extended form of conversation. Except for large audiences, the gestures you normally use are appropriate for public speaking situations. Make sure your gestures can be seen and are clearly made.

Some speakers will practice using several gestures to determine which is most appropriate. Also, speakers can plan to use gestures at specific points in the message. If there are three reasons given to support an idea, then one, two, or three fingers could be used to signify each reason. Gestures often spring spontaneously from a speaker's enthusiasm for the subject. Often these are the best because they seem coordinated with the primary message.

Posture The way you stand communicates a secondary message to your audience. An erect or militarylike stance could tell the audience that you are a ready, no-nonsense person. Slumping or slouching, on the other hand, could communicate lack of interest in your listeners and your subject.

In general, the speaker should stand in a way that is physically comfortable and have a stance that communicates a sense of mental alertness and control of the situation. Audiences have a tendency to imitate the physical set of the speaker. If you come across as not caring about your speaking situation, the audience could reply in the same manner. Keep your feet fairly close together and try to avoid shifting your weight from one foot to the other. If you have room, stand one or two steps back from the speaker's podium. This will allow you room to move and to alter your posture if the primary message requires it.

USES OF PUBLIC SPEAKING

You have spent a considerable amount of time reading about the techniques useful in the researching, organization, and delivery of a speech. Now it is time for you to be introduced to the forms public speaking takes and to the occasions when it is used in an organization. All speeches need to be researched, organized, and practiced before being presented. However, a speech prepared for one occasion may not be appropriate for another. The circumstances surrounding a speech will influence the type of topic you select, the content you develop, and how you use your voice and body in delivering it.

To help in preparing your speech, this section will (1) identify speaking situations common to many organizations and (2) explain the most frequently used form of public speaking.

Speaking Situations Common to Organizations

The number of occasions on which a speech would be delivered will depend upon the size and complexity of the organization. While realizing that no two organizations are exactly alike. Goldhaber has identified the speaking situations frequently found in organizations. He divides them into *internal speaking activities* (when your audience is made up of fellow organization members) and *external speaking activities* (when you speak to people outside the organization *about* the organization).[5]

Internal speaking situations
1 Briefing and information session
2 Orientation session
3 Training programs
4 Oral technical reports
5 Social functions

External speaking situations
1 Convention or conference presentation
2 Commercial or advertising speech
3 Civic or social club presentations
4 Speakers bureaus
5 Goodwill speech

In each of these situations, we would expect the speaker to have ample time to prepare for the presentation. The topic would have been limited and researched, the audience identified and analyzed in regard to the selecting and phrasing of ideas, and, finally, the speaker would have pulled all the parts of the speech together. You will notice that most of the internal speaking activities are informative; that is, these speaking activities are used as a means of sharing knowledge about the organization with other members. Frequently, internal public speaking is used as a vehicle for disseminating information from one department to all other departments, from management to employees, from old members to new members, and so forth. The two forms of informative speaking we discuss later will be examples of this knowledge sharing as it occurs within an organization.

The external speaking situations could be classified as persuasive/stimulative. They seek to change the attitude or behavior of the audience. The "We need to raise the electricity rates" commercial speech of a utility company representative to the state utility rate commission would be an example of the organization seeking to influence the behavior of an external audience. Of course, not all external speaking situations involve company profits. The speakers bureau of Richdales department store could provide speakers for such topics as "Better Use of Your Clothing Budget" or "Interior

---

[5] Gerald M. Goldhaber, *Organizational Communication*, Brown, Dubuque, Io., 1974, p. 249.

Decoration for the New House." The goal of these speeches is to present alternatives and to shape attitudes. Often the external speaking situation involves selling a public audience on the idea that what is good for the organization is good for the public. The goodwill speech is an example of this type of presentation.

Forms of Public Speaking

From this point on we shall deal with three specific forms of public speaking found in organizations. To explain each form we will briefly discuss two examples. These examples will be examined in terms of the appropriate topic, the quality and quantity of the content, and the style of delivery of the speech.

Information Speaking   In this form of public speaking the speaker attempts to share knowledge, attitudes, experience, beliefs, etc., with the listeners. To be successful the speaker must know the audience's level of awareness of, and interest in, the topic. This is important in order to avoid speaking down to an audience, which could result in resentment or a lack of interest on the part of the audience toward the content of the speech. In addition, avoid speaking above the audience, which could result in its members not listening because they can't properly decode your message.

The Report or Briefing   This informative speech is most frequently used to inform the audience about ideas and developments on a specific topic. It can be used to introduce new information or to update old information. The audience is usually one that has prior experience with the topic and/or a high level of interest in it. The oral presentation is usually accompanied by visual or audio-visual aids. These could include graphs, drawings, slides, video tapes, and so forth.

The content of the report should center around one major topic. It should be an indepth analysis of the topic and make frequent use of factual examples, illustrations, and statistics. When the credit department manager briefs the retail department store heads on the use of a new credit card, he or she needs to explain the main points clearly by showing how the card will appear, when and where it can be used, procedures for daily reports, and methods for identification of bogus cards. The organization of a report speech should be simple and easy to follow. Emphasis should be placed on making clear transition between main points in order to enhance the listener's ability to follow the message development.

The rate of delivery of the report speech should be slow to moderate; it should be fast enough to maintain the listeners' attention, but not so fast that the audience will be overwhelmed by an avalanche of information. If the audience becomes restless, you can always speed up the pace. Moderate-to-heavy use of gestures and physical movement will be necessary to handle the visual aids and to help hold audience attention.

In his survey of eighteen organizations that use oral briefings, Hollingworth asked the organizations to list reasons for the occurrence of poor briefings. They reported that the use of technical jargon, lack of examples or analogies, overuse of time, poor delivery, and unclear organization were the major reasons for the lack of success when using oral briefings.[6]

---

[6] J. E. Hollingworth, "Oral Briefing," *Management Review*, 57:2–10, August 1968.

The Orientation Speech Many new employees experience their first internal speaking situation when they are the recipients of an orientation speech. The goal of this speech is to orient or acquaint people with the whole organization or a part of it. In some business and government agencies, new employees will be exposed to several days of orientation speeches. Of course, orientation speeches are used among experienced employees to acquaint them with new buildings, new organization structures, or new procedures and methods of carrying out their jobs. The orientation presentation is frequently a *how to* speech. Instructions on how to carry out a job task is a frequent topic. New police officers are trained in the techniques of written reports through the use of an orientation speech. Orientation speeches are also used to train experienced police officers about changes in the state criminal code of justice.

As with the briefing, the content of the orientation speech should be organized in a direct, simple manner with attention paid to clear transition between main points. In fact, all that was said about the content of the briefing is applicable to the content of the orientation speech, with one notable exception. The orientation speech is used to train people, that is, to equip them with the knowledge and experience to carry out a specific task or in some way to operate smoothly within the organization. This requires that the content of the orientation speech consistently refer to the current situation. It must accurately reflect the reality that will exist when the listener moves into his or her specific task within the organization.

Persuasive/Stimulative Speaking This form of public speaking deals with change. It seeks to change an opinion or to stimulate action. While this form of speaking can be employed on the occasion when you speak to other members of the organization (such as an appeal to fellow workers to give generously to the United Way), it is more frequently used on occasions when the listeners are not members of the organization. It is important to note that when you speak *about the organization* to outside audiences, you speak not as yourself, but rather as a member of the organization. You represent the organization. What you say is viewed as the thinking of the whole organization. If you wish to speak as a person and not as an organization member, you should so inform the audience.

To increase his ability to change attitudes or invoke behavior, a speaker needs to consider why an audience would want to follow his advice. The three factors that most influence people's attitudes and behavior are the speaker's credibility, the logic of his ideas, and the feelings he expresses for these ideas. In developing your speech, you should include material that tells the audience why you should be trusted and what type of experience you have with the topic. Present your ideas in a sound, well-supported manner. Use all the forms of support you can to help explain and prove your point of view. Finally, let the members of the audience know why the attitude or action is important. Explain the reasons for your strong feelings and ask them to share these feelings with you. You, your ideas, and your feelings make up three major variables that are involved in the listener's decision-making process.

Sales Presentation In this speaking situation, you are attempting to elicit an overt response from the audience. Many of the same strategies a salesperson would use in a one-to-one situation would work in a one-to-many presentation. Such strategies as relating product or service to the needs of the audience, clearly explaining the cost and time factor for buying, comparing your product or service to products or services offered by others—these and other strategies should be considered appropriate for sales presentations.

However, when speaking to large groups, one additional factor must be considered. The decision-making power may be in the hands of the group or of a second party. An example would be an audience made up of managers of sporting goods departments that listens to the sales presentation of a baseball glove firm salesman. The salesman cannot adjust his presentation to fit the needs and desires of each manager, since the decision will be made by the group. With groups of this type, the speaker should concentrate on informing the audience rather than on closing a sale. This can be done by making a product or service clear, attractive, and suited to the needs of the listeners. With group presentations, low-pressure selling is more successful than high-pressure selling. To be effective, high-pressure selling requires immediate decision making, which may be impossible with listeners who must reach a group decision or recommend a decision to a second party.

The delivery of the sales speech should be dynamic. Variety of vocal delivery is important. Rate, volume, and pitch should be varied to suit the size of the audience and to express the emotions the speaker wishes to exhibit. In addition, the verbal and nonverbal cues should be geared to presenting a person who is informed on the subject and wishes to openly share information with the audience.

Finally, use visual aids such as graphs, charts, pictures, slides, or audio-visuals. What you use is not as important as how you integrate them into the presentation. Your ideas and visual aids should appear completely compatible. One accentuates the other. If a visual aid does not directly relate to the content, it is better to omit it.

Goodwill Speech In recent years many organizations have developed speakers bureaus in which they train employees for public speaking. The goal of these speakers bureaus is to create a good impression about the organization in the mind of interested public. In most states the Bell Telephone system has a speakers organization. This is also true of the military branches, which work primarily out of their military bases. Universities and colleges will provide speakers for many occasions. These and other types of organizations are striving to generate public support (goodwill) through the use of public speaking.

Topics for the goodwill speech can vary. A topic may be directly related to the organization (how a power and light company computes the cost of your utilities), indirectly related (a company president who delivers a commencement speech on the prospect for jobs in the near future), or not related to the organization (the police officer who speaks about the need for a stronger moral code among today's youth). The speaker should refer to his or her organization in an unobtrusive manner. That is, don't sell the organization, but rather use it in some examples, stories, or factual quotes that picture it in a positive manner. Also, try to relate the organization to the lives of the listeners. In this way you are creating awareness and building attitudes favorable to the organization.

One additional note about the content. Present novel, interesting information. Give the members of the audience insights about matters on which they have little information. Make use of humor through stories, examples, and by poking fun at yourself or the organization. This will help hold your listeners' interest and show them that you are not selling your organization, but rather sharing some information with them.

Special Occasion Speaking   This third form of public speaking is often referred to as *ceremonial speaking*. That is, it is used on formal occasions when a person is expected to deliver an address. It may be a short opening speech such as the introduction of a principal speaker, a welcome to a group, or a presentation to an award recipient. Other forms of ceremonial speaking require more substantial speeches. Included among these would be a speech to pay tribute to someone's accomplishments, a speech to nominate a candidate at a convention, a speech to dedicate a building or memorial in honor of a person or cause.

With special occasion addresses, the speaker is concerned with touching the audience emotionally. To do this requires an attention to language and imagery. You can uplift the listeners' spirits or thoughts with words and phrases that are directed at their feelings of admiration, love, respect, and sympathy. By invoking images in the listeners' minds that relate favorably to the topic of the address, a speaker can move audiences to laughter or sorrow. The language and imagery used must suit the audience and the specific occasion. A humorous approach would be appropriate for a speech of introduction, but out of place for a dedication address.

Audience analysis is another key to the success of the special occasion speech. To relate your topic to the audience, consider the values of the listeners. How are your ideas related to the listeners' sense of self-esteem, honor, and worth? If courage is important to them, mention the person's courage. If you feel the audience considers service to humanity worthwhile, then try to develop a sense of the person's humanness with your topic. The same is true of your listeners' aspirations. Relate the subject to their hopes and ambitions. The ability to successfully adapt the aim of your speech to the needs of your listeners requires an understanding of your audience and your subject. The two must be joined together in order for your speech to be effective.

Introduction   The goal of this type of speech is to prepare the way for the main speaker. The topic is always the speaker who will follow. You want to arouse the audience's desire to hear the speaker. The task is similar to Ed McMahon's job of warming up the audience for Johnny Carson, or to that of the lesser-known rock groups that play before the big-name group appears. The length of the speech should range between 2 and 4 minutes. If you run any longer than that your speech will rival that of the main speaker's, and you will also use time the main speaker could use for his or her own speech.

The content of the message should center around the following:

1   Show why the speaker is a credible source of information. Detail his education, his job-related experience, or his other qualifications that would present him as a knowledgeable person. However, don't overpraise the speaker. It may embarrass him and, if for some reason his speech is less than great, you have lessened his impact on the audience.

2   Point out the importance of the speaker's topic. Note its value to the audience. In fact, if you can, connect the speech directly to the members of the audience. This will give them information about the topic and should heighten their interest. A word of caution is in order here—don't steal the speaker's thunder. That is, don't give the audience the same information the speaker will present.

Try to end the speech by mentioning the person and his topic. If titles or degrees are appropriate, then use them.

Your style of delivery should be simple and direct. It should reflect your personal enthusiasm. If you feel excited by and interested in what the speaker will say, then this will be sensed by the audience. If the main speaker's topic is a weighty one, then your words and actions should reflect this approach. If it is in a lighter vain, then some attempt at humor would be appropriate. In other words, always be enthusiastic but let your message reflect the tone of the main speaker.

Tribute   Speeches of tribute are used as a means of praising the accomplishments of people. When a person retires from the organization, he or she is often given a farewell gift and a speech of tribute. This is also done when a person is given an award. When the tribute is about someone deceased, then the speech is called a *eulogy*.

The basic goal of a speech of tribute is to identify and share with the audience the traits or accomplishments that have made the person outstanding. In fact, the content of your speech should be organized around this information. If you feel it adds praise to the individual, then explain the condition surrounding the accomplishment. How much information to use depends on the level of knowledge of the audience. Try not to list a series of accomplishments or to repeat commonly known facts. If possible, know how this person's life has had impact on those around him or her. If you wish to emphasize traits, then describe them in detail and relate them to accomplishments of the person. Be sure to emphasize those traits most admired by the audience.

The style of delivery should be open and honest. If the tribute is for a memorial service, then a dignified and formal style is appropriate. If the person is living and the audience knows him or her, then the praise should be presented in a more lively manner. Try to avoid a bombastic style of delivery. Such pretentious language is not part of our contemporary lifestyle, and this style of speech making often comes across as insincere and exaggerated.

Finally, remember that everyone is human and therefore imperfect, even in death. When we overpraise a person, we are distorting the truth. Try your best to accentuate the positive and to speak in glowing terms, but do be objective.

SUMMARY

As a member of an organization you may be called upon to make presentations within the organization as well as to act as its representative to external groups. On these occasions knowing how to assemble speech material as well as how to practice delivering the presentation will be invaluable to you. Use this chapter as a resource guide and refer to it when you need those kinds of guidelines. Many people fear public presentations unnecessarily. The suggestions advanced in this chapter should help you approach public communication with more confidence.

Part Four

Case Studies

This section will introduce you to case study analysis. The purpose is to have you read and analyze the communication breakdowns that are contained in the four case studies. The four case studies are designed to draw on material from the preceding chapters and to provide you with an opportunity to demonstrate your ability to apply theory to real situations.

When the reader has completed this section, he or she should be able to:

1 Analyze the major communication principles of this text in terms of their application to simulated organizational interactions
2 List specific insights that can be gained from using the case study method to analyze organizations
3 Identify your level of intellectual awareness of the communication principles discussed in this text
4 Identify your ability to apply your intellectual awareness to the understanding of human interaction
5 Analyze the common communication barriers that occur in organizations
6 Discuss the ways this text can offer solutions to overcoming communications barriers that occur in organizations

Chapter 10

Case Studies:
Barriers to
Effective Communication

The organizations to which we belong, in social or work settings, are human organizations. What most of us do in our organizations is interact with other people. This book has examined the communications activities of people who are dealing with other people. Our approach to studying communication within the organization has been a multidimensional one. We have not discussed avenues of communication such as speaking or networks as isolated variables. Rather, we have examined communication as a process of interaction among many variables. Our focus has been on the interrelationships of key variables that impact on the communication that takes place among people.

In this last chapter we will ask you to use your knowledge of these variables in a practical way. You will be applying what you have learned about communication within the organization to real life situations. This may be a new experience for you. In the past you have been asked to respond to questions put to you by the class instructor or you have applied your knowledge of the course to answering questions on a multiple-choice test and to writing answers to subjective essay questions. Little was required of you except to feed back your knowledge of the course material.

In keeping with the theme of the book, an applied approach to communication, we have developed exercises that allow you to analyze the communication variables as they occur in an organizational setting. We are referring here to the use of case studies.

A case study is a short narrative story that gives an account of the events surrounding interpersonal communications and of the interaction itself. The data given will not have all the details, but will contain enough information for you to grasp the basic ingredients of the story. You are asked to accept the case study as a factual and honest account of what took place.

Through the use of a case study, you will have an opportunity to discover not only if your knowledge of the theories/concepts is sufficient, but also if you can take ideas out of the textbook setting and apply them to a simulated organizational setting. In discussing the problem of applying classroom knowledge to an organizational setting, William V. Haney wrote, "There is often a decided gap between one's intellectual acquaintance with a subject matter and his internalization of it."[1] The case studies allow you to know if you can go beyond an awareness of or acquaintance with the course material and move toward an understanding that allows you to apply the text material to the communication problems that occur.

Lee[2] has identified several specific skills that can be acquired through the use of the case study method. First, *you learn the art of applying the abstract to the concrete.* The usefulness of communication knowledge is often determined by how it enhances our understanding of human interaction. If you react to a theory by saying, "There is nothing useful there," then perhaps you have not applied the abstract to the concrete. The ability to move from the abstract to the concrete and back again can be a very useful skill. Second, *you can see the relevance of the situation to your own life.* What occurs in a case study represents a slice of life. As a person analyzes the case, she is often able to draw parallels to her own experiences. The barriers to communication you have set up or you have encountered in an organization could be the same as those you read about in a case study. Third, *you develop your ability to interpret and present your knowledge.* Self-discovery can take place. You can realize that your judgments are based on your knowledge and perception and, therefore, are not infallible. Also, you must consider how best to present your judgments. These considerations can lead to your developing more thoughtful and clever ways of sharing your interpretations with others.

ANALYZING THE CASE STUDY

The four case studies presented in this chapter contain communication problems that can occur in an organization. You are asked to analyze these problems by using the material from preceding chapters and your own good judgment. To carry out the analysis, we suggest that you take the following steps:

1 Read the case study over once. Identify the characters involved, the chronological development of events, and the overall mood of the narrative.
2 Next, imagine yourself as a communications consultant who has been called in

---

[1] William V. Haney, *Communication and Organizational Behavior*, Irwin, Homewood, Ill., 1973, p. 8.

[2] Kim Patton and Bobby Patton, *Basic Readings in Interpersonal Communication: Theory and Application,* 2d ed., Harper & Row, New York, 1976, pp. 253–272.

to help identify and resolve the problem. You have been asked to write a report on the events that took place and the impact each participant had on the interaction.

3 As the consultant, reread the case for the second time. Try to identify patterns of relationships between people and among incidents that occurred. Make notes on your observations.

4 Next, use the study guide questions as the format for developing your analysis. Apply the communication theory you have studied to the reality of the interaction. If necessary, reread all or parts of the case study.

5 If you are working with a group, identify any insights that are shared by a majority of the members. Next, note the insights that are not held in common. Finally, share your feelings with the group about any insights that are in conflict with one another.

CROWN FASTENER COMPANY[3]

During the summer between his junior and senior years at Dartmouth College, Edgar Hagan took a job as a student trainee with Crown Fastener Company, a medium-sized manufacturer and distributor of nuts and bolts. The training program Hagan was placed in consisted of 4 weeks in the company warehouse, 4 weeks in the company factory, and 2 weeks in the company offices. There were five students in the program, all of whom had the understanding that they would receive jobs as salesmen with the company after two summers in the program.

On the first day of work all five of the trainees met in the office of John Cusick, the superintendent of the warehouse. Cusick was a man in his middle thirties, a decorated Navy verteran, and a graduate of Dartmouth College. After outlining the work program for the next 4 weeks and assigning each of the trainees to a specific department for the first 2 weeks, he offered this advice to them, "Fellows, I would be very careful in my relationships with the employees here if I were you. The majority of the people here are a pretty crude bunch. Their work is pretty much physical and routine in nature, and, as a result, we can afford to hire men of generally low intelligence. They're all from the slums, and they're tough customers. So watch out for your valuables, and don't start any trouble with them."

For the first 2 weeks, Hagan was assigned to the sixth floor, hexagon nut department, under the supervision of Guildo Bovanni, a man who had been with the company since its inception 22 years before. Bovanni, a short but extremely powerful man, spoke in broken English and had a difficult time reading any material with which he was not previously familiar. When Cusick introduced Hagan to Bovanni he said, "Guildo, this is Edgar Hagan, a college trainee who'll be with us for the summer. I've decided to have him work here for the first 2 weeks and I'd like you to teach him all you know about nuts. Give him all the odd jobs you have so he'll get experience with as many different types of nuts as possible. Well, good luck, Hagan. We'll get together again soon."

After Cusick had left, Bovanni said to Hagan, "A college boy, eh! I'll learn ya about nuts, but I'll do it my way. I guess Cusick there thinks I can learn ya in 2 weeks what I've learned in 20 years. Christ! Don't pay no attention to him. We'll start ya helping the packers so ya can work with the nuts we ship most of. You'll be lucky if ya can learn them in 2 weeks. Then each day I'll try to learn ya a few of the nuts we don't see very often."

Hagan was amazed that each of the nine employees in the hexagon nut department quickly told him almost the same thing as soon as he was alone with them. Typical of their comments was this statement by Ted Grant, an elderly black packer, "If I were you, I'd stay on the good side of Guildo. He's one hell of a good foreman and really knows his stuff. He can teach you more about nuts and bolts than any guy in this place. Work hard for him and you'll get along swell here."

Hagan did his best to follow this advice and soon found that Bovanni was spending more and more time with him. He was very surprised when on Friday Bovanni said, "Grab your lunch and let's go eat across the street." Bovanni regularly ate his lunch in a little bar across from the warehouse with a group of about seven other foremen. The conversation ranged from the men's families to sports but soon settled on Cusick. Hagan was amazed at this because he, a newcomer, was there, and interpreted such openness to mean that Bovanni must have spoken to the men and told them that he was OK. It was quickly apparent that Bovanni was the leader in this group, and when he summed up the conversation in the following manner, everyone seemed in complete agreement with him. "Cusick tries hard. He's tried to improve things here but he hasn't had the experience. He must be able to handle old man Crown though; look at the money he's got us for the new equipment. But, Christ, then he screws up and buys the wrong stuff. He just don't know what to do and won't listen when we tell him."

On Friday of Hagan's first week, Cusick issued a bulletin stating that all forms used in the routing of materials in the warehouse would be changed to a slightly more complicated type on which material locations could be designated more concisely. The bulletin was handed out to all warehouse employees with their pay envelopes at the close of work on Friday. Included in the pay envelopes were several of the new forms. The bulletin simply stated that the change was to be made and requested that each man familiarize himself with the new forms over the week end so that he could use them correctly on Monday. The men just took the material and stuffed it into their pockets in their haste to catch their streetcars home.

On Monday morning everyone in the hexagon nut department quickly went to work distributing the backlog of materials that had been delivered on Saturday, at the same time making a note of each shipment's ultimate location. As was the practice in this department, all of the department personnel met at Bovanni's desk at 10:30 a.m. to give this information to Bovanni so that he could copy it on to the formal forms that went to the office for inventory control. Bovanni claimed he used this procedure so that all forms would be uniformly filled out and not mutilated by the men carrying them around as they worked. It was quite obvious, however, that his main purpose in insisting on this procedure was that he wanted to know where every shipment on his floor was located, so that when orders came through from the office, he could tell the men exactly where the material order was located, from memory. Hagan had been constantly amazed by Bovanni's ability to remember exactly where, within each tier and row, a certain shipment was located. Bovanni had built up this ability over a period of years, and was justifiably proud of it.

At the Monday morning meeting there was a considerable difference of opinion among the department personnel as to how the locations should be entered on the new forms. Bovanni insisted that it should be done in the same manner as before, where the aisle and tier of each shipment was recorded, while most of the other men protested that additional information as to the next location within each aisle and tier should be noted. Bovanni argued that this would create unnecessary details and would only confuse things. He was quite adamant about this, and the other men quickly acceded to his point of view.

The next morning Cusick came up to the sixth floor and walked directly to Bovanni's desk. He said in a loud voice, "Guildo, you're filling out the forms all wrong. Didn't you read the notice? You're still doing it the old way, and that's just what we're trying to get away from. Do you think we would go to all this trouble only to have things done in the same old way? Now you've really got the office all fouled up. We need new forms on all the materials you received yesterday. You'd better get at it right away so they can make orders out on some of that material."

Guildo was sitting at his desk, looking up a catalog number, while Cusick was talking to him. He was obviously getting madder and madder as Cusick spoke. Finally he broke in, "Look, Mr. Cusick, this department never had no trouble with its locations before. We've been getting along fine. Why do you have to foul us up by making us change everything? I've been running this department for one hell of a long time, and I guess to Christ I know as much about it as you do. Why don't you handle the top brass and let me handle my department? As long as I get the work done, what do you care how I do it? When those orders come through, I'll be able to find those kegs just like I always have."

"That's the trouble with you, Guildo, you only think of yourself. I've made this change in the entire warehouse. You're the only one bitching about it. From now on the office wants a complete record of exactly where everything is. Now, dammit, as long as I'm running this warehouse, we're going to do it my way!"

Bovanni was getting madder all the time. "Listen, Cusick, you may run this warehouse, but I run this floor. Nobody really needs to know those locations except me, and you know it. The way we're doing things here works fine, and you know it. Why pick on me? Why don't you go climb on the backs of some of the other boys that don't get their work done? Why come nosing around here telling me how to do my job?"

Cusick moved around next to Bovanni and put his hand on Bovanni's shoulder. "Calm down, Guildo, remember who's boss around here. I won't stand for your talking that way. Now just calm down and quit shouting."

"Wait a second. Who started the shouting? You come up here and broadcast to everybody that I don't know what I'm doing. I've run this floor for 10 years, and you can't tell me how to do my job. Don't tell me to calm down and take your damn hand off me!"

Cusick began to pat Bovanni's shoulder. "There's no sense in your getting all steamed up about this. You know damn well you're going to end up doing it my way."

"Get your hand off my shoulder!"

"Let's not argue about it, Guildo, you're wrong and you know it!"

"Take your hand off my shoulder before I slug you!"

Cusick leaned his hand on Bovanni's shoulder. "Listen, no one talks to me that way. I won't stand for any punk telling me what to do. You'd better learn your place around here!"

"You heard me: Get your hand off me!"

With his hand still on Bovanni's shoulder, Cusick warned, "Hold on, Mac . . . ."

Bovanni then whirled and hit Cusick squarely on the shoulder, knocking him back into a stack of kegs. Cusick recovered his balance and walked away, saying, "Okay, Buster, if that's the way you want it. . . ."

CROWN FASTENER COMPANY
Study Guide Questions

These questions are to be used as a guide to help you focus on the relationships found in the case study. Add to this list by applying your knowledge of communication to the case study.

1. What is the significant human relations/communication problem that exists in the case study?
2. What was John Cusick's style of leadership? How did his style influence the communication he had with Guildo Bovanni?
3. What role did trust, or the lack of it, play in the communication between John Cusick and his subordinates?
4. Compare the types of power used by Cusick with those used by Bovanni. How did these types of power enhance or block communication?
5. What role did environment and touching play in the discussion between Cusick and Bovanni?
6. How do the principles of conflict resolution help us understand the communication problem between Cusick and Bovanni?
7. What would you suggest be done to prevent a recurrence of the problems?

FINLEY PRINTING COMPANY

Finley Printing Company was a small, but productive business that printed advertisements, posters, and booklets for a large national corporation in the same city. Half of the building was taken up by the pressroom where the products were photographed on to metal image plates and run off on the printing presses. The other half of the building housed the bindery room where the press products were cut, folded, bound, and boxed for shipment.

Joe Finley was the young, enterprising owner of the business, which he had inherited from his father at the age of 25. Since taking over 10 years before, he had expanded the business considerably. The number of people working for him had increased from five to twenty-two.

He was well liked by all his employees and he treated every one of them with a great deal of generosity and respect. He especially got along with Howard Shaw, the head of the bindery and the only one of the original five still working for him. Howard was in his early fifties and stood 6 ft 5 in. He was slow moving and usually self-controlled, but he was too often oversensitive to the words and actions of those around him.

As he wished to further expand the printing capabilities of his business, Mr. Finley bought a huge, used double-cylinder offset press. He hired Jerry Winters, an experienced, professional pressman, to operate the press.

To get him, Finley had to offer him a salary that was higher than any he was paying at that time to anyone else, including Howard. He felt that the income that the new press would bring in would more than compensate for his pay, and once it was operating regularly, he could give Howard a healthy raise that he richly deserved.

When Howard heard from the secretary in the front office that Jerry was making more money than he, he was irked. In his jealousy and disappointment, he let it be known to a friend that he was going to quit to go to work for a rival company across town. He lied that he had been offered a job there at better pay and would take it if he didn't get a raise from Finley. Even though he had made most of it up in his anger, he felt justified in fabricating a story that he thought would make him look better in his fellow workers' eyes.

Finley heard through the grapevine what Howard had said and, believing it to be true, began to question the trust he had in the older employee.

Howard decided the best way to deal with the situation was just to forget it and continue to do his job as before. He began to grow uneasy, however, when he realized that Finley had stopped coming around to talk with him every day.

When he would walk to the lavatory in the back of the pressroom, Howard noticed that Finley was spending a lot of time with the new press and talking with Jerry. It bothered him somewhat to see his employer so open and receptive to Jerry's smiling face and nodding head. One day he was really hurt when, as he walked toward them on his way back to his job, Finley crossed his arms and turned his back to him. He continued listening to Jerry who was leaning toward the boss, gesturing widely, and speaking in a loud expressive voice. The young owner was nodding his head slowly with a relaxed, understanding smile on his face, and virtually ignoring Howard.

Sometimes, at the end of the day, Howard would see the two of them leaning against the layout table, facing each other and laughing aloud over old press stories and jokes that they had heard through the years. Finley often treated his employees on equal, friendly terms, but it made Howard feel very uneasy to see the two of them laughing and backslapping.

When his boss and old friend did notice him, it was usually just to say an unfeeling, "Hi, Howard," without really looking him in the eyes. The tall bindery operator started to become confused and resentful. He would become especially angry when Jerry, who was only 5 ft 6 in, but solidly built and always smiling, would call out his "How ya doin' Howard, baby?" and give him a friendly punch to the shoulder.

Usually Howard would pretend he didn't mind and say, "Fine, thanks, Jerry, how are you?" with little feeling. One day, however, he just stopped short, and looking over his left shoulder at Jerry's nervous, smiling face, he glared silently and slowly walked away. Jerry's greetings from that time on became more restrained. He wanted to make friends with everyone in the shop, but something told him that Howard didn't care for him. Jerry wrinkled his forehead in puzzlement and wondered why.

Finally, one day Howard decided he had had enough of this uncertainty and not knowing where he stood. He felt he had to confront Joe Finley and find out the truth once and for all.

Joe was standing in the large doorway that separated the bindery and pressroom chewing on his cigar and seemingly lost in thought as he stared at the rhythmic rotations of the press cylinders. Howard walked up to him with a slight hesitancy in his usual purposeful stride. His voice cracked as he said, "Uh, Mr. Finley?" and he cleared his throat uneasily.

"Yeah, Howard," Mr. Finley answered in an expressionless voice as he continued to stare at the press.

"I've heard some rumors lately that this new guy, Winters, is drawing a fatter paycheck than me, and I've been thinking that maybe it's about time that I got that raise that you mentioned once when we used to eat lunch together."

Joe looked at the floor, spit a piece of his cigar into the corner, and, without looking at Howard, said, "Yeah, well, Howard, how about coming by the office tonight after work and we'll talk about it, all right?" He turned his head just enough to squint up into the big man's eyes. Howard shifted uneasily, backed away, and said, "OK, Mr. Finley, thank you very much."

For the rest of the day Howard was nervous and kept making mistakes, ruining several piles of heavy paper posters because he had set the adjustments wrong.

At quitting time Howard walked uncertainly to the boss's door, cleared his throat, knocked, and said, "Mr. Finley, it's Howard Shaw."

Instead of the usual enthusiastic, "Come in, Howard," there was a disconcerting silence followed by a monotone voice saying quietly, "Come in." In the past when Howard would visit Joe in his office, they would sit in comfortable easy chairs that faced one another at an angle near the front door.

Today he was very aware of Joe's positioning himself behind his large, elevated, walnut-grained desk where he seemed to be intently studying some papers. Without looking up, Mr. Finley motioned to a straight-backed wooden chair in front of the desk, and said again without emotion, "Sit down, Howard."

As Howard sat down in the uncomfortable chair, Mr. Finley raised his head, leaned back, and looked down at him. He said, "So, you've come about a raise, is that it?"

Howard looked up at Mr. Finley's face and then down at his hands. As he began to talk, his face wrinkled in displeasure, and he rubbed his hands together nervously. "That's right, Mr. Finley, I've worked with you longer than anyone here, and you know I've always turned out very high-quality work. I deserve a raise and certainly more than some shrimp who has worked here for only 3 weeks."

Mr. Finley leaned further back in his chair, and clasped his hands behind his head as he slowly replied in a stern voice. "To begin with, at this point in time, I am in no position to give raises to anyone. The press, and the man to operate it—a damn good man with high recommendations—come at a high price. Until the press begins to pay for itself through its production, a raise is out of the question."

As Mr. Finley talked, Howard's lips pressed tightly together and he continued to stare at the floor. When he finished, he looked up at his young but tired-looking employer and blurted out in frustration, "Why the hell is he getting more money than me, can you tell me that? And how come all that matters is that damn press and the bindery can go to hell?"

Mr. Finley looked up at the ceiling, sighed forcefully, and rocked forward. He stared at some papers on his desk, his forehead creased in controlled anger and his teeth clenched. He sighed again and spoke slowly but in a tone of warning and impatience as he stared angrily at the spectacled, balding Howard, "It is none of your damn business what I pay to anyone but to yourself, and that 'damn press,' as you call it, is going to make this company a lot of money so that eventually raises will be possible. That press and the man running it are very important right now, and if you can't accept that, then go ahead, get the hell out of here and get another job if you want!"

Mr. Finley's last comment sent a small jolt through Howard and he wondered if he had caught wind of his story. He shifted uneasily, rubbed his hand over his mouth, and, still looking down at the floor, said, "I don't want another job."

Mr. Finley raised his eyebrows skeptically and said nothing.

Howard avoided his boss's eyes, got up, said a quick "Thanks, Mr. Finley," and strode for the door. As he came out of the office, he saw Jerry washing his hands at the sink next to his press. Howard stared at him hatefully for a moment until Jerry looked up suddenly and saw Howard's frowning face. Howard turned and tensely walked away.

The next day Howard was still on edge and confused. He had to be very careful to make up for all the mistakes he had made the day before. He found it difficult to keep his mind on the job. When Jerry came over with a load of advertisements just off his press to be cut and folded, Howard felt his anger growing.

Jerry pushed the load up next to Howard and said, "Is this where you want it, Howard?"

Howard turned and glared at the small pressman and then noticed where he was trying to shove the skid full of paper. "No, not there, Winters! How do you expect me to work at that machine if you put them there?"

Jerry smiled and moved them back. "I don't know, but considering how long you've been working here, I'm sure you'll find a way." He walked over next to Howard and leaned against the cutting machine. "How long exactly have you been working here?"

Howard hated to have anyone lean against his machines while he was working on them. It was a pet peeve of his and it only served to make him angrier. "Get off of there, Winters, you're in my way."

Jerry's usually smiling expression melted away. He squinted at Howard and said sarcastically, "You know, Howard, I really don't understand why you're so loving and friendly to me. I mean, just because I'm helping to bring a lot more money in to this company doesn't mean you have to be so grateful all the time." Jerry flashed his teeth at Howard in mock friendliness, but put on a straight face when he saw what tremendous animosity Howard had in his eyes.

Howard stared intensely at Jerry, his hands clenched tightly and his entire body tense and rigid. His breathing was shallow; he said threateningly, "Just shut up and get the hell out of here. You've got no business hanging around, little man."

Jerry opened his eyes wide and raised his eyebrows as he talked in a serious but even voice. "Well, I can't control my size, but I can control my temper, and I'm not going to lose my cool just because you're losing yours. I don't like to cause anyone any problems, and if I'm doing something wrong, I'd rather have you tell me about it than hate me for it."

Jerry's frank and honest tone calmed Howard down, but he didn't feel he had anything worth saying. A moment before he had been on the verge of hitting the new worker, but now he felt very small and foolish. "Forget it" he said as he turned his back to Jerry and grabbed a pile of posters that needed cutting. "I, uh, I'm just having a tough day and you're not helping it any."

Patting him on the arm as he turned to go, Jerry said in a sympathetic voice, "Don't let the job get you down. You are the most skilled worker in this shop. We need your work if the finished product is to be a quality one."

Jerry was almost out of hearing range when he heard Howard's earnest reply, "Thanks, Jerry."

FINLEY PRINTING COMPANY
Study Guide Questions

These questions are to be used as a guide to help you focus on the relationships found in the case study. You should add to this list by applying your knowledge of communication to the case study.

1. What is the significant human relations/communication problem that exists in the case study?

2. What concepts of personal space were involved in the meeting Mr. Finley held in his office with Howard? How did personal space influence the communication that took place? What environmental influences came into play in the conversation between Mr. Finley and Howard?

3. How did personal space impact upon the communication between Jerry and Howard?

4. Using Howard or Mr. Finley as an example, explain the process through which roles and attribution theory influence perception. How did this create a communication barrier?

5. How can the research on kinesics help us to understand the communication interaction that took place between Mr. Finley and Jerry and between Mr. Finley and Howard?

6. What would you suggest be done to prevent a recurrence of the problem?

STATION WDTN

Scott Kirsh turned the steering wheel of his Corvette hard and guided the car into the parking place marked with his name. How many times had he repeated this same maneuver in the 7 years he had worked at WDTN, he wondered. It must have been hundreds of thousands of times. He turned off the engine and ran the equation through his head. As chief engineer, he was used to thinking this kind of problem out easily; "1,785 times," he mumbled to himself. "It seems more like a million."

Scott closed the car door, making sure to check that he had locked it. As he walked slowly across the parking lot, he heard a car door slam. "Hey, why don't you wait a minute; I'll walk with you," a woman called. Scott stopped abruptly and turned around. Nancy Miller came jogging quickly up to his side. She was a fairly attractive woman with short blonde hair. Like Scott, she was in her mid-thirties. "What's the matter, you antisocial or something?" she asked. He turned his head and glanced piercingly at her. Oh, God, she thought, I must have struck a nerve.

They walked silently across the rest of the lot and climbed the stairs that led to the building's lobby. "Well, here goes another day at the salt mines," Scott said as he opened the large glass door. It was funny, Nancy thought, but she had never looked at her job as a burden. In fact, she rather enjoyed it. It had taken her years to attain her position as WDTN's sales manager. But now all those years of struggle had been worth it. With her salary plus commissions, she had managed to acquire all the luxuries she wanted. Besides, she really loved competing against men. It gave her a feeling of power when she beat them.

Once inside the lobby, Scott and Nancy were stopped by the receptionist. "Mr. Davies would like to see both of you in the conference room," she said.

Miles Davies sat at the head of a big oval table in the oak-paneled meeting room. He was a big man, both physically and socially. As WDTN's general manager, he made it a point to keep in favor with those he regarded as the right people. Davies envisioned himself as a man moving up the ladder of success; WDTN was just an instrument to his getting there. He hoped that the improvements he had made in the past, and more importantly, those he had planned for the future, would draw him a job offer from the national network.

Davies looked around the table. At his left sat Jim Sanford, the news director/ anchorman. Standing next to him drinking a cup of coffee was the producer, Ted

Nelson. Davies shuffled some papers and waited impatiently. The door to the conference room opened as Nancy Miller and Scott Kirsh walked in and sat down.

"Well, now that we're all here," began Davies, "You're probably wondering what this meeting is all about. So, I'll spare you the small talk and get right down to business. As you are all aware, WDTN is the area's leading television station. The board of directors is proud of this and would like to see the station maintain its ratings. Consequently, the board has asked us to form a committee. Our inputs and ideas will be used in developing next season's programing. The board feels that this group should generate ideas that are significantly different from those we have used in the past."

"What exactly do you mean by 'different'?" asked Nancy Miller. "I don't know, just different from the ideas we have come up with in the past," Davies said. "Anyone have any suggestions?" Davies looked around the table.

"I think that's a good idea," Ted Nelson said. "I'm in favor of anything that improves the quality of the programing at this station." Nelson spoke enthusiastically; he meant everything he had said. In his 17 years at the station, he had tried to do all he could to improve it. Over the years, he had watched with pride as it grew. And now, even though it was the best in the area, he felt that it could be better.

"What kind of ideas do you want? Ideas for new programs or what?" Nancy Miller asked.

"I suppose that new program ideas are as good a place to start as any," Davies said. "Can anybody think of any?" Davies looked around the silent room.

Scott Kirsh leaned forward in his chair, placed his hands on the table, and said, "There's a station out on the West Coast that's developed a new type of talk show. So far it's . . ." Davies interrupted him, saying, "I think the idea should be revolutionary. It should break away from the existing formats and take some new direction." I should have known better, thought Kirsh, they never listen to what I say at these meetings. I'm just here so they can find out if their brilliant ideas are feasible.

"Does anyone have any ideas like this? How about you, Jim? You haven't said anything at all yet," Davies said as he looked to his left.

Jim Sanford wiggled uncomfortably in his chair. He knew what Davies was getting at. Just the day before, Davies had called him into his office to discuss some new ideas he had. "It wouldn't look right if I just brought them out," Davies had told him. "It would look like I was railroading them through. But, if you were to do it, I'm sure they would be looked upon more favorably." That bastard, Jim had thought, what does he mean he's not railroading them? Not only is he railroading them, he's setting me up to take the fall if they don't work. And if there was one thing he didn't need to do, it was to take a fall. Jim, now almost 45, had already made several job relocations due to the failure of either his or someone else's ideas. It had been hard on his wife and daughters to just pick up and move. He didn't want them to go through it again. Well, here goes, thought Jim. "What we could do is to invent and film our own series. That way we wouldn't have to rent old network reruns. We could offer the advertisers something new, something that couldn't be seen anywhere else except on this station." There, Jim thought, I've said it. I just hope I don't get fired because of it.

Nancy Miller was the first to react to this suggestion. "What you're talking about would be next to impossible. First of all we don't have the production facilities to do anything like that. Second, we'd have to either think up or buy a script. Then we'd have to hire actors and personnel for it. Finally, the advertisers would never buy it. What you're talking about would take a lot of time and money. Frankly, I just don't think we could do it." she said.

Davies was quick to jump to his idea's defense. "I think that it's a very good idea. It's about time local stations started taking matters like these into their own hands. Someone has to lead the way; it might as well be us."

"But what about the cost? It would be phenomenal," Nancy Miller said.

"If you look at it on a long-range basis, it wouldn't be that expensive," Davies replied. "In fact, we could probably make money on it after we made the initial outlay. Once the series took off, we could syndicate it and sell it to other local stations, outside of this market of course. Then later we could sell the reruns. And, once we built the production facilities, we could use them to film other shows. You have to look at this idea's long-range implications."

"The only implications I can see are us out on the street looking for new jobs after this thing fails. We could loose the station a lot of money if this thing isn't a success," Nancy Miller said.

"You're not looking at it properly," said Davies.

"No, *you're* not looking at it properly. In your search to find a unique idea, you've overlooked all the financial considerations involved. I think that we should go with something that's already been tested and tried, something that's worked well somewhere else. What was your idea, Scott?"

Scott just about had enough time to get the words "Well, I . . ." out of his mouth before Davies cut him off. "Wait just a minute, what's wrong with trying something new? We wouldn't be where we are today if someone hadn't had new ideas and invented new things," Davies said.

"Look, Miles," Nancy said, "You're not the one who has to go out and hustle the accounts. Advertisers want something that's been proven to be successful. They're not willing to gamble."

"Well, I am," said Davies. He stared down the table at everyone. His voice was trembling with anger as he asked, "Is anyone else?"

"Hold on a second now," Ted Nelson said. He had felt the tension that was growing in the room earlier, but he hadn't said anything about it in the hope that it would dissipate. However, now he felt that he had to do something before the two went at each other's throats.

"I think we're blowing this thing out of proportion," said Ted, "Everyone just cool down. What we need to do is to put this whole thing into perspective. Now both of you have legitimate points. I think that we should discuss them further."

"I think we should discuss Scott's idea," Nancy said, "What was it again, Scott?"

"Whoa there, I thought that we just decided to discuss Jim's idea a little further," Davies said.

"No, Miles, I'm afraid that's where you're wrong. You and Ted may have decided to continue that discussion, but I don't feel that it's worth wasting any more time on."

Davies was mad now. He didn't enjoy being made to look like a fool, especially since the person who was making him look that way was a woman.

"I don't think you realize that I'm the general manager here, Ms. Miller," he said, vehemently.

"What I think you fail to realize, Miles, is that you're not the dictator of this station. After all, the board of directors is over you, isn't it? The board members might not be too pleased to find out how undemocratically this meeting is being run," Nancy said.

Ted Nelson jumped to his feel when he heard Nancy's challenge to Davies. "Look, we're all supposed to be working together here, not fighting with each other. The only way we're going to get anything done around here is if we all stop criticizing one another. Now, what I think we all should do is take out a pencil and a piece of paper and write down our ideas. Then, when everyone is finished, we'll hand them in to someone who will compile them on to one sheet. When everyone gets a copy of this, he or she must try to determine what the best points of each idea are and write them down. Once we have put these all together on a second list, we can each have a chance to say which ideas we think are best, without criticism from anyone else. Then, we each must rank the ideas from best to worst, write them down, and turn them in again. The one with the most votes will be the one we submit to the board of directors."

Ted looked around the room expectantly. "Well, what do you think? Do you want to try it and see how it works out?" Miles Davies leaned forward and picked up his pen. "Excuse me, Nancy, but do you have a piece of paper you can lend me?" he asked.

STATION WDTN
Study Guide Questions

1. What is the significant human relations/communication problem that exists in the case study?

2. How far did the group go in the problem-solving sequence? What roles did the group members play in enhancing decision making or in presenting blocks toward decision making?

3. Please analyze the interpersonal relationships that existed among the group members in terms of their individual needs. Discuss the task or maintenance roles of the members.

4. Relate Bormann's ideas (found in Chapter 8) on the types of meetings that take place to the meeting at station WDTN. How does the station meeting relate to the communication barriers that developed among the members?

5. What type of leadership roles were used or were not used by Miles Davies?

6. Through what developmental stages of group process did this group move? How well did the members of the group develop the interpersonal structure and task activity? Was there a hidden agenda?

7. What would you suggest be done to prevent a recurrence of the problems?

RICHDALES

Sue Hamlin had dropped out of college after 2 years unsure of what direction she wanted to take. Her parents were having marital difficulties when Sue decided it was time to get a job and an apartment for herself.

After applying at various department stores in the city in which she lived, she was hired by Richdales to work as assistant manager in the women's wear department. She was also to be responsible for arranging the display windows featuring women's wear, and for running the department in the manager's absence.

Richdales was one of a chain of fashionable stores that attracted well-to-do clientele. Sue looked upon this job as a great opportunity to meet and talk with people, gain some responsibility, and express what she felt were her dormant creative needs. In the back of her mind she also hoped that it might eventually lead to a better position in the store chain, possibly as a buyer.

She was very open, energetic, and optimistic when she came to work the first day and met the manager of the department, Mrs. Joan Griffin.

Mrs. Griffin was in her early fifties and had worked for Richdales for over 20 years. She was a very proud woman who had developed women's wear into a highly productive, efficient, and respected department within Richdales.

Her first impression of Sue was cautiously positive. She said, "We're glad to have you working for us, Sue, and as long as you can follow directions and perform to your highest capabilities, we won't have any problems."

Mrs. Griffin then went on to outline what would be expected of her and revealed her reservations concerning the maturity and dependability of girls Sue's age. She said, "I had to let go all of my fulltime workers last week. It seems you can't get people to work anymore, especially the young girls. I had to watch them every minute, and they still goofed off. I'm depending on you, as assistant manager, to keep the others in line. You're going to have to be tough, and don't be afraid to discipline them if you have to. Sales are the most important thing. On Saturday when it's time to change the display windows, I want you to watch how I do it. In a couple of weeks, you will be responsible for that area yourself."

Sue's first 2 weeks on the job went well. Mrs. Griffin told her what needed to be done and she did it, although the manager seldom explained her reasoning, and Sue was often confused as to why she was doing certain things. When she asked Mrs. Griffin why she had to count the amount of a certain clothing item in stock, for instance, she was told, "Never mind the reason why, just do it."

Sue tried not to let this bother her, and looked forward to being able to arrange the display windows and to make some responsible, self-initiated decisions on her own.

When that day came, Mrs. Griffin said, "All right, Sue, you know basically how it's done. Now you can take over. I will continue to supervise, however, and make sure that it's done correctly."

Sue stayed an hour overtime without pay that night designing the layout for the windows, arranging and dressing the mannequins, and placing the appropriate props in what she felt were the ideal positions. She drove home that evening feeling extremely pleased and fulfilled for the first time in quite a while.

On Monday morning when Sue came to work, however, she was met by the perplexing sight of Mrs. Griffin busily rearranging the mannequins and props on which she had worked so hard. The owner and president of the huge store chain was making a rare surprise appearance at the store that day, and Mrs. Griffin wanted to do all she could to impress him.

Sue, not knowing this, and noticeably upset at seeing all her hard work and energy wasted, said somewhat harshly, "Mrs. Griffin, you said I would be free to design the windows in my own way, but you've completely rearranged them."

Mrs. Griffin, in a hurry to get the job done, didn't take time to explain. Instead, she replied, "Young lady, I am the manager of this department, and if I see fit to change some things that I feel aren't tasteful or proper, I will, and it certainly isn't your place to question my actions. Now I don't want to discuss the matter any further."

Sue felt she had been unjustly treated and wanted to express her discontent and confusion. Mrs. Griffin, however, rarely spoke with Sue or any of the other employees except to hand out directives or to criticize their work. When Sue attempted to approach Mrs. Griffin about the matter, she was met with a curt, "Not now Sue, I have to go call to make sure our new shipment of blouses are on schedule. You just do your job and everything will be fine."

In the following weeks, Sue continued to arrange the windows, but not without the regular criticism of Mrs. Griffin who always knew a better way to accomplish a certain effect. Sue felt frustrated and inhibited, more so because she couldn't discuss it with the person who was most responsible for her negative feelings, Mrs. Griffin.

Sue began to develop an attitude of resentment that became apparent through her actions, especially when Mrs. Griffin was around. Mrs. Griffin, sensing this, became defensive and prodded Sue to improve her working habits.

Sue had been working for nearly 2 months when she had the idea that the casual slacks would sell better facing the main aisle where more customers would see them, than they would placed back against the wall where they were then located. When Sue hesitantly suggested the change to Mrs. Griffin, however, she was met with an adamant rejection of her idea. Mrs. Griffin's husband was quite ill at the time, and that, combined with the pressure of an upcoming Richdales conference for department managers, had succeeded in placing her under a great deal of stress.

She said, "I have been managing women's wear for 13 years, Miss Hamlin, and during that time it has become one of the most efficiently run and profitable departments in the store. All you have to do is sell clothes, ensure customer satisfaction, and keep the department neatly organized and the other girls busy. Don't concern yourself with areas in which you have no business, is that understood?" She then turned and walked briskly away, not waiting for an answer.

When Mrs. Griffin departed for the week-long conference, Sue was left in charge. Sue got along well with the other two employees, Laura and Ellen, and the first day that Mrs. Griffin was gone they had a meeting to discuss their personal opinions concerning the department's needs and goals. Sue listened to Laura and Ellen air their complaints against Mrs. Griffin, and Sue shared some of her own frustrations with them.

She said, "Mrs. Griffin means well, but as manager she's under a lot of pressure to make women's wear profitable. You know it would be really great if we could find a way to increase our sales, don't you think? I think that would please Mrs. Griffin, and perhaps she'd respect us more and not assume we're always trying to avoid responsibility."

Laura and Ellen thought it was a good idea, and Sue told them her suggestion about switching the casual slacks with the dress slacks. They discussed the pros and cons and decided they had nothing to lose. If it didn't work, they would switch things back before the manager returned.

They all felt good about the decision because they had all participated in it, and they felt even better when the plan worked. In just a week's time, sales of casual slacks increased 50 percent over the sale of dress slacks, and almost 100 percent over what they had sold in the back of the store. Meanwhile, the dress slacks now in the back of the department continued to sell as well as they had before.

Sue was elated. She knew how important profits and efficiency were to her employer, and she felt quite confident that the sharp increase of sales would place her in a more favorable light in the manager's eyes.

When Mrs. Griffin returned, however, Sue painfully realized that she didn't know her boss as well as she had thought. The conference had not gone well, and Mrs. Griffin was not in a pleasant mood. When she noticed the rearrangement of the clothes, she didn't wait for an explanation.

In exasperation she lit into Sue in front of several customers and Laura and Ellen. She said, "I thought I made this clear to you before I left. I've had a feeling from the start that you were just like all the rest, though I had hopes that you would prove me wrong. If our spring clearance sale wasn't coming up, I'd fire you now, but I'm going to give you another chance. Either you shape up and cooperate, or start looking for another job. That is all I have to say."

"But, Mrs. Griffin, I was only trying . . ."

"I don't want to hear it. You have disobeyed me enough. I am the manager here and don't you forget it!"

The next day Sue gave notice and within a week had set up an interview with S. J. Harts Company, the up-and-coming new department store in town.

RICHDALES
Study Guide Questions

These questions are to be used as a guide to help you focus on the relationships found in the case study. Add to this list by applying your knowledge of communication to the case study.

1. What is the significant human relationship/communication problem that exists in this case study?

2. What was Mrs. Griffin's style of leadership? How did this leadership style influence communication with her subordinates? Also, what types of power were used by Mrs. Griffin?

3. What was Sue Hamlin's style of leadership and how did this influence her communication with the other girls?

4. How do Redding's conclusions about communication and effective leadership relate to Mrs. Griffin?

5. What role did trust, or the lack of it, play in the communication between Sue and Mrs. Griffin?

6. What types of feedback did Mrs. Griffin use in communicating with Sue?

7. What would you suggest be done to prevent a recurrence of the problems?

Part Five

Laboratory Manual

INTRODUCTION

This laboratory manual and the accompanying text were developed with the thought in mind that people learn by experiencing the consequences of their own actions. This text will provide you with information about some major theoretical and conceptual issues in organizational communication as well as with a variety of methods for you to use in applying those theories and concepts.

We believe that it is important for you, the student, to experience how you and how others communicate. The classroom is a relatively safe place for that to happen. An inappropriate response in a laboratory setting is far less damaging to you than an inappropriate response on the job. In the laboratory setting you are free to try out new communication behaviors, if you so desire, or to refine behaviors that you feel will be successful in an organizational environment. In addition, you will have an opportunity to discuss a variety of ways of approaching important problems and thereby to develop a broader repertoire of possible responses. You will have the opportunity to examine the *possible* impact an organization can have on you and how you communicate. You will also have the opportunity to examine how your value system will be affected and how that will affect you.

CLASS ACTIVITIES AND EXERCISES

Activities and exercises are organized according to the subject matter of the text. In some cases the arrangement of the exercises is arbitrary since some exercises demonstrate several different principles of communication. The collection of activities and exercises offered in the following pages may be from time to time augmented by the instructor with other projects or class exercises.

ASSIGNMENTS AND PROJECTS

In addition to the classroom activities you will participate in, you will have other opportunities to experience and explore organizational communication. Each chapter contains at least one homework contract. You and the instructor will have an opportunity to negotiate, much like you would in a business setting, such issues as your degree of involvement in the course and/or the grade that you should receive for your effort. Tests and other assignments that do not appear in the text will be added by your instructor to assist both of you in evaluating your understanding of the concepts, theories, behaviors, and skills studied.

PERSONAL DATA SHEET

The process of communication is easier when you know something about the other person. Your instructor would like to get to know you and the information you provide on this page will help him or her begin to know you.

Name _____

Nickname _____

Campus address _____ Campus phone _____

Home address _____ Home phone _____

Major _____ Is this course required for you? _____

Have you ever taken a speech/communication course(s) before? If so, briefly describe the course(s).

What are your hobbies and/or college activities?

What kind of a job (career) would you like upon graduation?

Do you work and, if so, parttime or fulltime? If you are employed, where do you work and what does your job entail?

Do you work during the summer? Parttime or fulltime? If so, where, describe what you do, and how long you've had the job.

Are you married, divorced, engaged, going steady?

Do you have children? If so, what are their names and ages?

How will the ability to communicate effectively in an organizational setting help you achieve your future goals?

What three *specific* things would you like to accomplish in this class?

1.

2.

3.

Do you have any special condition or situation that your instructor should know about? (Are you hard of hearing, especially anxious when meeting people, under a doctor's care for some illness, will you miss a number of classes due to some activity, etc.?)

What additional information can you provide your instructor that will help him or her relate better to you?

Communication and the Organization: An Overview

Exercise 1
WHAT ARE MY EXPECTATIONS?

Objective: To examine your expectations of this course.
To communicate those expectations to your instructor.

Procedure: What follows are a series of Likert-type scales. (By the way, this type of scale is frequently used in organizations for data collection.) Circle the number of each scale that most closely represents your feelings. Don't forget to fill in your name. This form is to be turned in to your instructor.

Name _____

By the end of this course, I would like to . . .

Gain new knowledge of organizational communication

1	2	3	4
unimportant to me	mildly important to me	moderately important to me	extremely important to me

Have a basis for assessing my future occupational objectives

1	2	3	4
unimportant to me	mildly important to me	moderately important to me	extremely important to me

Be able to improve my interviewing effectiveness in different organizational situations, i.e., employment, informative, persuasive

1	2	3	4
unimportant to me	mildly important to me	moderately important to me	extremely important to me

Have an understanding of how an organization communicates

1	2	3	4
unimportant to me	mildly important to me	moderately important to me	extremely important to me

Understand the importance of nonverbal communication in the organization

1	2	3	4
unimportant to me	mildly important to me	moderately important to me	extremely important to me

Improve my ability to take part in discussions

1	2	3	4
unimportant to me	mildly important to me	moderately important to me	extremely important to me

Improve my ability to perform effectively in public speaking situations within the organization

1	2	3	4
unimportant to me	mildly important to me	moderately important to me	extremely important to me

Gain a better understanding of myself as a communicator

1	2	3	4
unimportant to me	mildly important to me	moderately important to me	extremely important to me

Obtain a good grade for the course

1	2	3	4
unimportant to me	mildly important to me	moderately important to me	extremely important to me

Exercise 2
GETTING TO KNOW AN ORGANIZATION

Objective: To help you apply some of the major concepts that you learned in Chapter 1.

Procedure: Select an organization. If you are currently working or have recently worked in a business or industrial environment, it would be best if you chose that organization. If not, choose the educational institution you are now attending or some smaller organization at that institution. After you have responded to the following questions, the instructor will group you according to the type of organization you selected for this exercise. Your task will be to discuss each question and identify gross similarities and differences among the organizations. These will be reported to the class.

1. What is the overall objective of the organization?

2. What is the specific objective of the department or smaller unit you worked in?

3. In a way similar to the example of the TV station presented in Chapter 1, describe how you might study your organization from the following four perspectives or levels—intrapersonal, interpersonal, group, cultural. In other words, what *methods* might you use and what questions would you be seeking to answer?

Intrapersonal

Interpersonal

Group

Cultural

Using the same organization, give an example of formal and informal communication.

Formal communication

Informal communication

Exercise 3
THREE PRINCIPLES OF COMMUNICATION

Objective: To demonstrate your understanding of the three principles of communication and to introduce you to the case study method of analysis.

Procedure: Take a few minutes and read the following case study on Patrolman Ed Bolton. Next analyze what happened in the case study in terms of the three principles of communication. These principles are (1) meaning is in people, not in words; (2) communication is imperfect; and (3) communication is an irreversible and unrepeatable process. You will be placed in groups of four. Quickly select a secretary/spokesperson and discuss your individual case analysis. Create from these individual case analyses a group analysis. You will be allowed 20 to 25 minutes for this activity. When your instructor so indicates, each secretary/spokesperson will relate his or her group analysis to the class as a whole.

Patrolman Ed Bolton Communication Case

Patrolman Ed Bolton had been associated with the police force for 5 years. He was a dedicated officer—one who constantly strove to improve his communication effectiveness. Ed was well respected in the community as a hard-nosed cop. He was respected but not liked by most of the young people. Although Ed had never been overly physically aggressive with any of them (he rather liked young people), he had a reputation of being punishing with adult offenders. On this particular day he was patrolling an area near Fifth and Dayton streets. A group of youngsters was loitering on the corner. Patrolman Bolton, having a real interest in teen-agers, thought he would stop and inquire what the boys were doing. He stopped the car, got out, and walked over to the boys. As he approached the group he said softly but pleasantly, "Hi guys." Not being able to put his hand in his right pocket (his gun prevented him from using the it), he naturally rested his hand on the gun butt. Before he opened up his mouth one of the boys shouted, "Hey pig, you going to waste us?" With that the boys scattered in different directions. Patrolman Bolton figured the boys were guilty of something so he called for a back-up unit and conducted a search of the area. Actually, the boys were guilty of nothing but were scared by Patrolman Bolton's seemingly threatening gesture of putting his hand on the gun butt. Patrolman Bolton had no intention at all of going for his gun—he only wanted a place to rest his hand.

Case Analysis

Meaning is in people, not in words.

Communication is imperfect.

Communication is an irreversible and unrepeatable process.

Exercise 4
COMMUNICATION LOG

Objective: To increase your awareness of the types and frequency of communication you enter into while functioning within an organization.

Procedure: This exercise is designed to help you evaluate how much of your time is taken up with some form of communication activity within the organization. You may select a business organization where you now work or analyze the organization you are now a part of—the educational organization.

Select any one day and keep a careful accounting of your communication activities. A time frame from 8 a.m. to 5 p.m. is provided. (We realize that the time frame may not be adequate for your specific needs, so select the time periods that apply—add time periods or delete time periods.) Your instructor may request that you monitor other communication activities. Space has been provided for you to write in the appropriate heading(s).

After each hour fill in under the appropriate activity the approximate time spent. After you have completed the chart, answer the questions found below. Your instructor will provide time for you to discuss the exercise during your next class.

Organization: _____

Time period	Communication activity				
	Writing (A)	Speaking (B)	Listening (C)	Other (D)	Total (60 min.)
8:00–9:00	___ min.	___ min.	___ min.	___ min.	
9:00–10:00	___ min.	___ min.	___ min.	___ min.	
10:00–11:00	___ min.	___ min.	___ min.	___ min.	
11:00–12:00	___ min.	___ min.	___ min.	___ min.	
12:00–1:00	___ min.	___ min.	___ min.	___ min.	
1:00–2:00	___ min.	___ min.	___ min.	___ min.	
2:00–3:00	___ min.	___ min.	___ min.	___ min.	
3:00–4:00	___ min.	___ min.	___ min.	___ min.	
4:00–5:00	___ min.	___ min.	___ min.	___ min.	
Total time per activity					

1. Total time analyzed _____ (Add "total time per activity" for columns A, B, C, & D)

2. Total hours of communication activity _____ (Add totals for columns A, B, & C)

3. Percentage of time spent in some form of communication activity _____ _____ (Divide answer in 2 by answer in 1 and multiply by 100)

4. Percentage of time spent in written communication _____ (Divide total for column A by answer to 1 and multiply by 100)

5. Percentage of time spent in speaking _____ (Divide total for column B by answer to 1 and multiply by 100)

6. Percentage of time spent listening _____ (Divide total for column C by answer to 1 and multiply by 100)

7. Do the percentages of time spent in each communication activity reflect their importance to the total communication process? Why?

8. To become a more effective communicator how might you change the percentage of time you spend in each communication activity?

Organizational Theory

Exercise 1
DEFINING AN ORGANIZATION

Objective: To help you identify those characteristics basic to the definition of all organizations.

Procedure: Your instructor will ask you to list four characteristics for each of the following groups that define each one as an organization. The class will then be divided into five groups to discuss the results. You will be completing Parts A, B, and C on the following form.

Part A
  A social fraternity or sorority

    1.

    2.

    3.

    4.

Part B
A department store

1.

2.

3.

4.

Part C
A television station

1.

2.

3.

4.

Exercise 2
FAYOL'S PRINCIPLES

Objective: To introduce you to principles of management in action.

Procedure: Your instructor will ask you to divide into groups of four or five. Each group is to visit a police or fire department or a military organization. You are to talk with both management and employee representatives in an attempt to determine how many of Fayol's principles of management they follow. Draw up a list of those principles and be prepared to discuss your list with the class.

Observations on the Exercise

Principle 1

Principle 2

Principle 3

Principle 4

Principle 5

Principle 6

Principle 7

Principle 8

Principle 9

Principle 10

Principle 11

Principle 12

Principle 13

Principle 14

Exercise 3
ORGANIZATIONAL CHARTING

Objective: To provide you with an opportunity to explore the structural relationships of an organization.

To chart an organization.

Procedure: Your instructor will divide the class into pairs. You will then be asked to research two companies (one large and one small) and to draw an organizational chart for each. Upon completion of each chart you are to answer the following questions:

1. What is the typical span of control in each organization?
2. How many layers does each organization have?
3. What is the scalar chain in each organization?
4. What are the basic similarities and differences between a big and a small organization?

Please use the forms provided for each aspect of this exercise.

During the next class session the class will be divided into five groups and each pair will share their feelings with the entire group.

Organizational Chart   Big Company

Organizational Chart   Small Company

1. What is the typical span of control in each organization?

2. How many layers does each organization have?

3. What is the scalar chain in each organization?

4. What are the basic similarities and differences between a big and a small organization?

Observations on the Exercise

Exercise 4
MESSAGE TRANSMISSION

Objective: To chart an organization in terms of message flow.

Procedure: You are to plant a message in an organization you currently belong to. After waiting 2 days, you are to interview eight to ten members of the organization. Ask each person if he or she heard any portion of the message and, if so, when, where, and how he or she heard it. Using this information, you are to attempt to chart, on accompanying Forms A and B, both the formal and informal organizational contacts for those eight to ten people. This assignment will be discussed during class.

Form A   Formal organization

Form B   Informal organization

Assignment Contract: Industrial Humanism

Name _____ Date _____

Directions: You have just spent some time learning about the industrial humanism school. As is true of any learning process, transfer from a theoretical perspective to the environment is necessary if optional learning is to take place. (*Transfer* is a process whereby what is learned in the classroom is applied in a job setting or at least in the school.) Understanding will diminish if what has been learned is not practiced. Therefore, in order to enhance your understanding of the subject, you will gather examples of the use of the industrial humanism school of thought in organizations. You may achieve this through personal observation. Select an individual and department you entered to observe in Section I. Hand a copy of this section into your instructor, thereby agreeing to "contract" for this assignment. Have a discussion with the individual you have observed to check the accuracy of your observations and then complete Section II.

SECTION I   Assignment Preparation

Individual and department or time and place: _____

_____

Name of organization (group): _____

Planned date of observation: _____

_____

SECTION II   Assignment Review

Actual date of observation: _____

Points observed: Yes   No

1. Identify supervisory attitudes that reflect an acceptance
of industrial humanism principles   _____   _____

Examples:_____

_____

_____

2. Identify supervisory behaviors that reflect the use of
industrial humanism principles   _____   _____

Examples: _____

_____

_____

3. Specific programs designed to accommodate the human
potential of the subordinate   _____   _____

Examples: _____

_____

_____

What was supervisor's overall reaction to your observations? _____

_____

_____

How did you feel after the discussion? How accurate were your observations?

_____

_____

If you could have the discussion again, would you do anything differently? _____

_____

_____

Assignment Contract: Social System

Name _____ Date _____

Directions: You have just spent some time learning about the social systems school. As is true of any learning process, transfer from a theoretical perspective to the environment is necessary if optimal learning is to take place. (*Transfer* is a process whereby what is learned in the classroom is applied in a job setting or at least in the school.) Understanding will diminish if what has been learned is not practiced. Therefore, in order to enhance your understanding of the subject, you will gather examples of the use of the social systems school of thought in organization. You may achieve this through personal observation. Select an individual and department you entered to observe in Section I. Hand a copy of this section into your instructor, thereby agreeing to "contract" for this assignment. Have a discussion with the individual you have observed to check the accuracy of your observations, then complete Section II.

_____

SECTION I   Assignment Preparation

Individual and department or time and place: _____

_____

Name of organization (group): _____

Planned date of observation: _____

_____

SECTION II   Assignment Review

Actual date of observation: _____

Points observed: Yes   No

   1. Identify energy imports   _____   _____

   Examples: _____

_____

_____

   2. Change   _____   _____

   Describe: _____

_____

_____

   3. Negative feedback   _____   _____

   Examples: _____

_____

_____

   4. Equifinality as applied to a specific department   _____   _____

   Identify department _____

   Explain _____

_____

_____

What was supervisor's overall reaction to your observation? _____

_____

_____

How did you feel after the discussion? How accurate were your observations?

_____

_____

If you could have the discussion again, would you do anything differently? _____

_____

_____

_____

Communication Networks in Organizations

Exercise 1
ORGANIZATIONAL POSITION[1]

Objective: To allow you to analyze how your communication behavior differs with people of varying roles and status. (For the purpose of this exercise we are equating roles and status with organizational position.)

Procedure: You will be asked to complete Form A individually. This form will ask you to identify specific communication behaviors that might change from situation to situation. When you have completed this form, your instructor will ask you to break up into groups of three and discuss the information on your form. Next discuss the implications of that information.

Form A

How does the role you play, as dictated by your organizational position, in each of the following situations affect how you relate to others in the same environment?

---

[1] Adapted from "Roles I Play," by Lynn Phelps and Sue DeWine, *The Interpersonal Communication Journal*, West Publications, St. Paul, Minn., 1976.

Communication Behavior

Communication Context	Language used (cite examples)	Dress and general appearance	Nonverbal communication (posture, facial expression)	Amount of self-disclosure (scale of 1 to 10 with 10 being most open)
1. With friends at a party				
2. In a dormitory with classmates				
3. With a teacher in his or her office				
4. On the job with the boss				
5. With a younger brother, sister, cousin, etc.				
6. While baby-sitting with a child.				

1. Which roles produced similar communication behaviors? Why?

2. What communication behavior remains the same throughout all situations? Why?

3. Rank order the situations in the order in which you felt most comfortable giving orders. 1 will be most comfortable; 6 will be least comfortable.

Exercise 2
NETWORKS

Objective: To increase your awareness of the effect different communication networks can have on problem-solution results.

Procedure: Your instructor is going to ask you to solve a problem for him or her. After explaining the problem, he or she will divide the class into five groups. Each group will be assigned a group number from 1 to 5. Find your group number below. The diagram below your group number will indicate which communication network your group *must* use in finding a solution to the problem. You must solve the problem as quickly as possible, and you must produce a *group* solution that *everyone* in the group is in agreement with. Oh, one last point. The group that produces the best solution in the shortest time, as judged by the supervisor (instructor), will get a bonus in its pay envelope. The group that produces the poorest solution and takes the longest time will receive a pink slip in its pay envelope. Now, before you start discussing the problem, move into your groups and wait for your instructor to give you the signal to start. At the end of this exercise, you will be asked to discuss the problem-solution results.

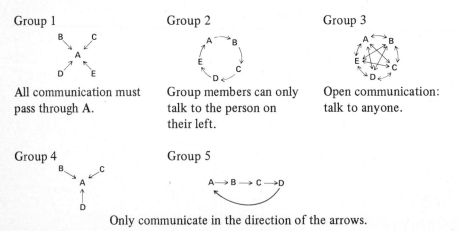

Group 1	Group 2	Group 3
All communication must pass through A.	Group members can only talk to the person on their left.	Open communication: talk to anyone.

Group 4   Group 5

Only communicate in the direction of the arrows.

1. Did the network help or hinder the problem-solution exercise?

2. Did the network affect the time it took to come to a decision? Why?

3. What effect did the pressure of the supervisor's decision have on your performance?

4. Which network produced the fastest/slowest results?

5. Which network produced the highest quality/lowest quality solution?

6. If you were in the group that was fired, how could you possibly avoid this outcome in the business world by utilizing the information you have learned as a result of this exercise?

7. Additional questions supplied by your instructor and your own comments or reactions.

Observations on the Exercise

Exercise 3
MESSAGE TRANSMISSION

Objective: To demonstrate how organizational hierarchy can affect the transmission of messages.

Procedure: Your instructor will select four students to leave the room and remain isolated until they are called back in one at a time. When these students return to the classroom, they will be asked to participate in a message transmission exercise. Use the appropriate space below to take notes on the message as it is passed from person to person.

Message 1 (the original message sent by the instructor)

Message 2

Sender's initials ⎯⎯⎯⎯

Message 3

Sender's initials ⎯⎯⎯⎯

Message 4

Sender's initials ⎯⎯⎯⎯

Message 5

Sender's initials ⎯⎯⎯⎯

Exercise 4[2]
ONE- AND TWO-WAY COMMUNICATION

Objectives: To provide you with an opportunity to compare different forms of communication.

To introduce you to the concept of *process*.

[2]Reprinted from J. William Pfeiffer and John E. Jones (eds.), *A Handbook of Structural Experiences for Human Relations Training,* vol. 1 (rev.), University Associates, La Jolla, Calif., 1974, pp. 13–18. Used with permission.

Procedure: In the space provided below, draw the figure described by your class-mate. Do not ask any questions or give any type of reaction (do not laugh, moan, etc.) during the exercise unless your instructor asks you to do so.

When you have finished drawing the figure, estimate on page 266 how many of its five parts you have drawn correctly.

During the second part of the exercise, you will again be asked to draw a figure, but this time you may ask questions of the person providing the description. If something is not clear, you may ask the sender to repeat his or her description. If a term used by the sender is not clear, you may want to offer an alternative suggestion. When you have finished drawing the second figure, again estimate your accuracy using the table on page 266.

Observations on the Exercise

Figure 1

Figure 2

Place a checkmark in the box under estimated accuracy according to your perceived
level of accuracy for each of the parts of the figure. For instance, if you perceive that
you have drawn four parts correctly, place your checkmark by the number 4 under
estimated accuracy.

One-way communication   Two-way communication

Time _____   Time _____

Figure 1   Figure 2

Estimated accuracy	Actual accuracy	Estimated accuracy	Actual accuracy
5			
4			
3			
2			
1			
0			

Draw five conclusions based on the one- and two-way exercises. Attempt to make your conclusions analytical rather than descriptive. For instance, to say that one-way communication took only half as long as two-way communication would be descriptive, but to say that two-way communication took longer than one-way communication, because of feedback, would be analytical.

1. _____

_____

_____

_____

2. _____

_____

_____

_____

3. _____

_____

_____

_____

4. _____

_____

_____

_____

5. _____

_____

_____

_____

Assignment Contract: Upward Communication

Name_____   Date _____

Directions: You have just spent some time learning about formal systems for upward communication. As is true of any learning process, transfer from a theoretical perspective to the environment is necessary if optimal learning is to take place. (*Transfer* is a process whereby what is learned in the classroom is applied in a job setting or at least in the school.) Understanding will diminish if what has been learned is not practiced. Therefore, in order to enhance your understanding of the subject, you will gather examples of the use of formal systems for upward communication. You may achieve this through personal observation. Select an individual and department you intend to observe in Section I. Hand a copy of this section in to your instructor, thereby agreeing to "contract" for this assignment. Have a discussion with the individual you have observed to check the accuracy of your observations and then complete Section II.

SECTION I Assignment Preparation

Individual and department or time and place: _____

_____

Name of organization (group): _____

Planned date of observation: _____

_____

SECTION II Assignment Review

Actual date of observation: _____

Points observed: Yes   No

1. The organization's grievance procedure   _____   _____

Examples: _____

_____

_____

2. The organization's formal counseling process (not to be confused with performance reviews)   _____   _____

Examples: _____

_____

_____

3. Policy regarding exit interview and where the information goes   _____   _____

Examples: _____

_____

_____

4. Does the organization have a suggestion box or other
systems?   ———— ————

Examples: ———————————————————————

———————————————————————

———————————————————————

What was supervisor's overall reaction to your observations? ———————

———————————————————————————

———————————————————————————

How did you feel after the discussion? How accurate were your observations?

———————————————————————————

———————————————————————————

If you could have the discussion again, would you do anything differently? ————

———————————————————————————

———————————————————————————

Assignment Contract: Horizontal Communication

Name ————————————————— Date ——————

Directions: You have just spent some time learning about horizontal communication. As is true of any learning process, transfer from a theoretical perspective to the environment is necessary if optimal learning is to take place. (*Transfer* is a process whereby what is learned in the classroom is applied in a job setting or at least in the school.) Understanding will diminish what has been learned is not practiced. Therefore, in order to enhance your understanding of the subject, you will gather examples of the use of formal systems for horizontal communication. You may achieve this through personal observation. Select an individual and department you intend to observe in Section I. Hand a copy of this section in to your instructor, thereby agreeing to "contract" for this assignment. Have a discussion with the individual you have observed to check the accuracy of your observations and then complete Section II.

SECTION I   Assignment Preparation

Individual and department or time and place: _____

_____

Name of organization (group): _____

Planned date of observation: _____

_____

SECTION II   Assignment Review

Actual date of observation: _____

Points observed: Yes   No

1. Fayol's gangplank   _____   _____

Examples: _____

_____

_____

2. How information moves horizontally through the
organization   _____   _____

Examples: _____

_____

_____

3. In which departments could increased horizontal communication facilitate conflict resolution?   _____   _____

Examples: _____

_____

_____

What was supervisor's overall reaction to your observations? _____

_____

_____

How did you feel after the discussion? How accurate were your observations?

_____

_____

If you could have the discussion again, would you do anything differently?   _____

_____

_____

Leadership and the Management of Human Resources

Exercise 1
LEADERSHIP BEHAVIOR

Objective: To have you evaluate the group members you have just interacted with.

Procedure: You just participated in an exercise with your classmates. How did you perceive the leadership styles of your classmates? How do you think they perceived you? The following exercise will give you an opportunity to give your classmates some honest feedback about your perceptions of them. They in return will do the same for you. The feedback will provide you with some insight about your leadership style.

On the scale beside each question, mark the number which best describes the way you see this person's participation in the group discussion. Use 1 to mean positive and 5 to mean negative.

Group members' initials

1. How well does this person
understand him- or herself in relation to this group?
2. In your opinion does this
person have an autocratic leadership style?
3. How effective do you think this
person would be in controlling the
group?
4. How effective do you think this
person would be in planning group
activities?
5. How effective do you think this
person would be in organizing the
group?
6. To what extent do you feel that
this person really understands your
ideas and feelings?

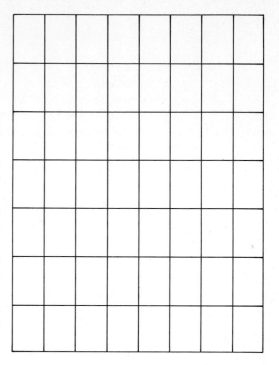

Exercise 2
DELEGATING RESPONSIBILITY

If a supervisor is to be a success, he or she must be able to successfully delegate responsibility. By delegating work the supervisor frees time formerly spent on the
simpler aspects of his or her job and creates time for dealing with the more difficult
tasks. By effectively delegating responsibility, the supervisor not only becomes a
more effective manager, but he or she also provides the employees with an opportunity to grow.

Objectives: To have you delegate responsibility to a subordinate.

Procedure: Let's assume for a moment that you have graduated from college and
are currently employed in a supervisory capacity for a company. A situation has
presented itself in which you *must* delegate responsibility to a subordinate. How
do you do it? What do you say? The following exercise will help prepare you for this
leadership situation. Pair off with a classmate. One of you will be the supervisor and
the other the employee. Think of a situation (preferably a real one) in which you
might have to delegate responsibility. Following the instructional steps on page 275,
role play the scene.

Instructional steps

1. Indicate what the new responsibility is you want the employee to handle and why.
2. In detail, describe the new responsibility and outline the specific task.
3. Describe the performance standard.
4. Ask for the employee's feelings and questions.
5. After responding to the employee's concerns, ask for his or her commitment and make it clear your assistance is readily available.
6. Thank the employee for his or her help and express your confidence in his or her ability to handle the new responsibility.

Now complete the following scale. Compare your answers to those of the employee.

Supervisor

1. What was the employee's overall reaction to the discussion?	very favorable	favor-able	unfavor-able	very un-favorable
2. How did the employee feel after the discussion?	very confident	confi-dent	unconfi-dent	very un-confident
3. How did you feel after the discussion?	very pleased	pleased	not pleased	upset

4. If you could have the discussion again, would you do anything differently?

Employee

1. What was the supervisor's overall reaction to the discussion?	very favorable	favor-able	unfavor-able	very un-favorable
2. How did the supervisor feel after the discussion?	very confident	confi-dent	unconfi-dent	very un-confident
3. How did you feel after the discussion?	very pleased	pleased	not pleased	upset

4. If you could have the discussion again, what do you think the supervisor could do differently?

Exercise 3
PERCEIVED LEADERSHIP STYLE

Objective: To allow you to examine how your classmates view your leadership style.

Procedure: You will work in a group with three classmates. Each person in the group is applying for a job. You have asked the others in your group to give you a reference regarding your leadership abilities. Each of you wants to help the others get the jobs they are applying for. Write a brief reference for each member in your group including yourself. You will be Reference 4.

Reference 1 Name _____	
Reference 2 Name _____	
Reference 3 Name _____	
Reference 4 Name _____	

Each person in turn gives his or her references for the other three people in the group. He should state his observations about each person *without giving names*. When he is finished, the others attempt to match each reference with the right person.

1. List below the similarities and differences among the references that have been given for each person.

(discuss with your group)

2. When every member of the group has had his or her turn, finish the following sentences: "I learned that I . . ."; "I was surprised to learn . . ."; "I was disappointed to find out . . ."

(need not be discussed)

Exercise 4
A LEADERSHIP SELF-ANALYSIS

Objectives: To allow you to discover leadership information about yourself through a self-analysis inventory.

To allow you an opportunity for introspection and growth.

Procedure: Write brief answers to each of the following questions. Your answers will be used in a class discussion. After the exercise is over, you may wish to go back over your answers and expand them.

1. How effective are you as a leader?

2. List your leadership strengths.

3. List your leadership weaknesses.

4. List specific steps you could take to overcome your weaknesses.

5. Describe situations in which you have the most trouble leading.

6. Describe why the situations in question 5 cause you difficulty in leading.

Assignment Contract: The Need for Leadership

Name _____ Date _____

Direction: You have just spent some time learning about the need for leadership. As is true of any learning process, transfer from a theoretical perspective to the environment is necessary if optimal learning is to take place. (*Transfer* is a process whereby what is learned in the classroom is applied in a job setting or at least in the school.) Understanding will diminish if what has been learned is not practiced. Therefore, in order to enhance your understanding of the subject, you will gather examples of each of the areas discussed in the section on the need for leadership. Select an individual and department you intend to observe in Section I. Hand a copy of this section in to your instructor, thereby agreeing to "contract" for this assignment. Have a discussion with the individual you have observed to check the accuracy of your observations and then complete Section II.

SECTION I Assignment Preparation

Individual or department name: _____

Name of organization: _____

Planned date of observation: _____

SECTION II Assignment Review

Actual date of observation: _____

Points observed: Yes   No

   1. Imperfection of the organization   _____   _____

   Examples: _____

   _____

   _____

   2. Changing external environmental conditions   _____   _____

   Examples: _____

   _____

   _____

   3. Changing internal dynamics   _____   _____

   Examples: _____

   _____

   _____

   4. Human beings in organizations   _____   _____

   Examples: _____

   _____

   _____

What was the supervisor's overall reaction to your observations? _____

_____

_____

How did you feel after the discussion? How accurate were your observations?

_____

_____

If you could have the discussion again, would you do anything differently? _____

_____

_____

Assignment Contract: Types of Power

Name _____ Date _____

Directions: You have just spent some time learning about types of power. As is true of any learning process, transfer from a theoretical perspective to the environment is necessary if optimal learning is to take place. (*Transfer* is a process whereby what is learned in the classroom is applied in a job setting or at least in the school.) Understanding will diminish if what has been learned is not practiced. Therefore, in order to enhance your understanding of the subject, you will gather examples illustrating the use of each type of power. You may achieve this through personal observations. Select an individual and department you intend to observe in Section I. Hand a copy of this section in to your instructor, thereby agreeing to "contract" for this assignment. Have a discussion with the individual you have observed to check the accuracy of your observations and then complete Section II.

SECTION I   Assignment Preparation

Individual and department or time and place: _____

_____

Name of organization (group): _____

Planned date of observation: _____

_____

SECTION II   Assignment Review

Actual date of observation: _____

Points observed: Yes   No

1. Legitimate power   _____   _____

   Examples: _____

   _____

   _____

2. Reward power   _____   _____

   Examples: _____

   _____

   _____

3. Coercive power   _____   _____

   Examples: _____

   _____

   _____

4. Referent power   _____   _____

   Examples: _____

   _____

   _____

5. Expert power   _____   _____

   Examples: _____

   _____

   _____

Were there always clear distinctions among the types of power being used or dis-

cussed? _____

_____

_____

Was it easy for you to identify the various types of power? _____

_____

_____

Which type of power appears to be the one most often used? _____

_____

_____ Why? _____

_____

_____

Interpersonal Interactions

Exercise 1
HOW DO WE PERCEIVE EACH OTHER?

Our view of the other person will influence how we communicate with that person. This perceptual image will be influenced by our own insights, self-knowledge, and previous experiences with this person. We may make inaccurate judgments of others due to various behaviors on our part including imposition of structure, halo effect, and leniency effect. This exercise is designed to help you analyze your own ability to perceive others as well as to provide you with some feedback about how others see you in a particular communication context. You may want to complete this exercise with another student in your class or with a stranger outside of class. You will be asked to draw conclusions about someone based on knowledge that gives you little basis for drawing such conclusions. Talk with the other person for about 10 to 15 minutes before completing the form. Do not attempt to talk about any of the issues on this form but talk generally about yourself and about issues that concern you.

After your conversation, complete the following questionnaire:

This person: 1 = yes   2 = probably yes   3 = undecided   4 = probably no   5 = no

1. Enjoys a romantic candlelight dinner	1	2	3	4	5
2. Sits in the front of most classrooms	1	2	3	4	5
3. Likes rowdy parties rather than a dinner with close friends	1	2	3	4	5
4. Has a parttime job	1	2	3	4	5
5. Has a large circle of friends	1	2	3	4	5
6. Would prefer to have a few very close friends	1	2	3	4	5

7. Is self-confident and outgoing   1   2   3   4   5

8. Enjoys most sports   1   2   3   4   5

9. Would rather read a good book than go to 1   2   3   4   5
   a movie

10. Is a conservative   1   2   3   4   5

What specific cues, either verbal or nonverbal, led you to make the preceding conclusions?

Exchange forms with your partner and give each other the correct answers.

Were you using any of the behaviors that cause misjudgments? (imposition of structure, halo effect, and leniency effect)

How did you feel about your partner's perception of you? How accurate was he or she? What aspects of yourself would you like to change?

Exercise 2
ORGANIZATIONAL ROLES

Developing an understanding of the various roles we play within the organizational setting will lead to a fuller appreciation of their effect on our communication behaviors. In the interpersonal relationship, it would be helpful for both individuals to understand not only their own role behavior but also that of their partner as well. Identify an organization of which you are currently a member. Select another individual from that organization and ask him or her to participate in your analysis of role behavior within your organization. Separately complete the following analysis of role behavior for yourself, and then compare each other's results.

Organizational   Communication Behavior
    context

	Amount of self-disclosure	Language used (cite examples)	Appearance	Nonverbals
A conversation with the boss				
Giving instructions to subordinates				
Informal meeting with colleagues				
Helping your partner solve a problem				

How did your roles vary from situation to situation?

How did your enactment of various roles differ from your partner's?

Are there differences between the ways in which you play your roles that could lead to barriers in your communications with each other? In what ways?

Exercise 3
THE O.K. MANAGER

Transactional analysis suggests that there are four positions that you may hold in regard to yourself and to others: I'm not O.K., you're O.K.; I'm not O.K., you're not O.K.; I'm O.K., you're not O.K.; and I'm O.K., you're O.K. Each of these positions can demonstrate the interrelatedness of our perception of our self and of others. Each time we communicate with others we communicate a part of ourselves and, indirectly, indicate which of these positions we currently hold. It is important to determine the effect of each of these positions on interpersonal relationships in the organization. Identify instances where you, as well as others in your organization, have held each of these positions.

Examples of my Own and Others' Life Positions

	My behavior			Others' behavior		
	Non-verbal cues	Verbal messages sent	Feeling level	Non-verbal cues	Verbal messages sent	Feeling level
I'm not O.K., you're O.K.						
I'm not O.K., you're not O.K.						
I'm O.K., you're not O.K.						
I'm O.K., you're O.K.						

Identify the effects on the organization as a whole when each of these positions has been enacted in the past:

I'm O.K., you're not O.K.

I'm not O.K., you're not O.K.

I'm O.K., you're not O.K.

I'm O.K., you're O.K.

What have been the effects on you personally?

Exercise 4
SAY WHAT YOU MEAN

The *pseudo question* sets up a unique barrier to interpersonal communication that can lead to misunderstandings. In this case, the person is asking a question only to disguise a statement. Framing the statement in the form of a question lowers the risk that the statement will be rejected outright. This is an indirect form of communicating. Experiencing the effect of such questions on the mood and tone of an interaction may lead to your own increased ability to control their use. In this exercise you are asked to try out some behaviors in order to test their influence on conversations. During the next 2 weeks, attempt to introduce each one of the eight types of questions into a conversation and note with care the response you receive. Be especially aware of the direction the conversation takes following your question. How did the question change or affect the interaction?

	Situation in which question was used	*Reaction to question*
1. Cooptive question		
2. Punitive question		
3. Hypothetical question		
4. Imperative question		
5. Screened question		
6. Set-up question		
7. Rhetorical question		
8. Got-cha question		

Behavior Contract: Using Feedback Effectively

Name _____ Date _____

Directions: You have just spent some time learning about interpersonal communication. As is true of any learning process, transfer from a theoretical perspective to the
environment is necessary if optimal learning is to take place. (*Transfer* is a process in
which classroom training is encouraged to be practiced in the job setting or at least on
the campus.) Understanding will diminish if the learned concept is not used. Therefore, you are being asked to practice the use of feedback in a real life setting. Select a
situation in which you would like to be able to give more effective feedback to ano-
there individual. In this case we are not asking that *you* observe the effect of your behavior on the situation but that you also ask for the observations of the person to
whom you have given feedback. There is a portion of the contract to be filled out by
yourself, and a portion to be filled out by your communication "partner." After completing Section I of this form, hand a copy in to your instructor, thereby agreeing to
"contract" for this assignment. Complete Section II immediately following the interaction and complete Section III after the classroom discussion of this experience.

SECTION I

My name _____

Name of person with whom I wish to change my behavior _____

Planned setting for attempting to give feedback _____

SECTION II

Filled out by you:

Type of feedback attempted (descriptive, evaluative, or interpretive):

Effect of each type of feedback:

Filled out by communication partner:

This was my reaction to _____'s feedback to me:

signed _____

SECTION III

1. Which type of feedback seemed most effective? Why?

2. Think of five people to whom you would like to give some negative feedback. Phrase what you would like to say to them in the form of descriptive feedback.

    a.

    b.

    c.

    d.

    e.

Nonverbal Communication

Exercise 1
CONDUCTING A FIELD STUDY

People watching can be one of the most interesting as well as one of the most informative pastimes. By observing posture, facial expressions, gestures, use of personal as well as environmental space, the influence of environmental factors, and tactile communication, one can often determine how two or more individuals are relating to one another as they communicate. In this exercise you are asked to observe the nonverbal cues of others. Select a location where people often interact and where you can observe their interactions unobtrusively. Position yourself so that you can watch others' nonverbal cues but so that you cannot hear the verbal content of their messages. Suggested locations include the following: the interior of a shopping mall (locate yourself on a bench and watch individuals sitting on corresponding benches), school library, dorm lounge or dining hall, restaurant, business office, etc. The observation period should be about 1 hour in length. During that time try to focus on one interaction at a time and base your analysis of the interactions on the principles presented in this chapter. To assist you in your field study, you might note examples of any of the following nonverbal cues:

Cue	*Emphasis or impact on conversation*

Gestures—types
    illustrators, affect displays, regulators,
    adaptors

Gestures—functions
    repeating, contradicting, substituting
    complementing, relating, and regulating

| *Cue* | *Emphasis or impact on conversation* |

Distance and posture
    affect on attitudes demonstrated,
    status, moods, approval-seeking,
    inclusiveness, interaction markers

    personal, intimate, social, and public
    distances

Environment
    feature-fixed space

    semifixed-feature space

Exercise 2
PERSONAL SPACE IN THE ORGANIZATION

Each person's identification of his or her own personal space as well as the use made of the environment in which that individual is located influences one's ability to send and receive messages effectively. The preceding chapter discussed four different types of personal space: personal, intimate, social, and public distances. Each are used in different settings and with a variety of topics and individuals. Select an organization with which you are very familiar. The organization need not be large but must have a formal structure as opposed to that of an informal small group. Try to observe this organization as much as possible so that your examples are specific and not general or vague. Analyze the use made of nonverbal cues in that organization in the areas indicated.

Areas indicated:

Name of the organization observed _____

Cite examples of the following:

What message do these cues
send in this particular
organization?

Intimate distance ————————————→
Examples:

Personal distance ————————————→
Examples:

Social distance ————————————————→
Examples:

Public distance ————————————————→
Examples:

Cite any examples when use was made of the inappropriate distance in a conversation in this organization. What were the effects on the conversation or relationship?

What topics are normally discussed at each of these distances within this particular setting?

Exercise 3
SEMIFIXED-FEATURE SPACE—HOW DO I USE IT?

Semifixed-feature space includes the arrangement of movable objects such as tables and chairs. In many organizations the environmental space is divided by chairs and desks. This unspoken division sometimes speaks loudly in terms of status and control of communication processes. In the following examples try to imagine yourself as a member of an organization and identify in what locations within that context you would be most comfortable.

A. Imagine that this is a picture of seating arrangements in your boss's office. You and two other employees have been sent for, since you are consistently late for work. Which seating arrangements would you prefer (A indicates you)?

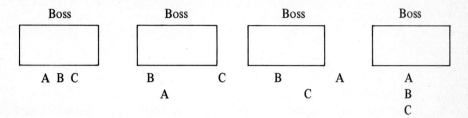

1. Where would you most likely be singled out?

2. Where would you least likely be singled out? Why?

3. Explain why you are more comfortable in certain locations than in others.

4. If you were the boss, which seating arrangement would you prefer? Why?

B. Imagine that you are being interviewed for a job. Which seating arrangement would you prefer (A is you, B is the interviewer)?

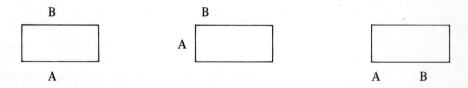

1. What are your reasons for selecting the position above?

2. Describe how each of these patterns of seating might influence the interviewing process.

3. What does the seating arrangement say about status and power in a conversation?

C. If you were the manager of a fairly large organization and conducted much of your work in your office, how would you arrange your office in order to facilitate conversations with subordinates? Superiors? In the space below, indicate where you would place your desk and chair and where you would place others in the room. How would the rest of the environment enhance your goal in communications?

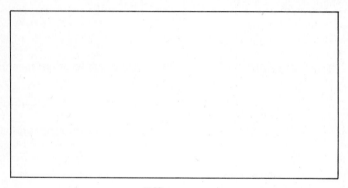

Office space

Exercise 4
GUESS MY ATTITUDE

We have indicated that nonverbal cues can clearly state attitudes, likes and dislikes, status, and level of comfort. In the next exercise you are asked to test how clearly attitudes can be established through nonverbal cues. This will require that you role play certain attitudes in a conversation outside of the classroom (or in the classroom if your instructor suggests that as a procedure). As well as testing the theory you will also be able to obtain feedback from others about how clearly you send messages. During a conversation with a friend (either in class or out of class), choose one of the following situations to role play. Following the conversation ask your friend if he or she clearly understood how you felt about what was being said in the conversation. Check the accuracy of your friend's interpretation of your nonverbal cues. Analyze what you did or might have done to enhance this communication situation through nonverbal messages. You might want to try out each of the role plays with different people.

Role play situations	Feedback from friend	Analysis
1. Indicate through nonverbal cues that you feel your friend has a higher status than yourself. You are submissive. After the conversation, ask your friend if he or she thought you were dominant in the conversation.		
2. Indicate through specific nonverbal cues that you are uncomfortable and nervous. Following the conversation, ask your friend how relaxed he or she thought you were.		
3. Indicate through nonverbal cues that you like your friend and enjoy his or her company. Following the conversation, ask your friend what he thinks your feelings are for him and what he bases this conclusion on.		

4. What emotions do you have the most difficulty expressing nonverbally? Which emotions are easier for you to express nonverbally than verbally?

Assignment Contract: The Organizational Golden Rules

Name _____ Date _____

Directions: You have now spent some time learning about the effect of nonverbal communication on messages sent and received. As is true of any learning process, transfer from a theoretical perspective to the environment is necessary if optimal learning is to take place. (*Transfer* is a process whereby what is learned in the classroom is applied in a job setting or at least in the school.) Understanding will diminish if what has been learned is not practiced. Therefore, in order to enhance your understanding of the subject, you will gather examples illustrating each of the golden rules of nonverbal communication in the organization. After completing Section I of this form, hand a copy in to your instructor. Complete Section II after your observations.

SECTION I Assignment Preparation

Name of individual(s) observed: _____

Name of organization: _____

Planned date of observation: _____

SECTION II Assignment Review

Actual date of observation: _____

Points observed:

1. Examples of "The higher up one is within an organization, the more and better space he or she will have."

2. Examples of "The higher up one is within an organization, the better protected his or her territory is."

3. Examples of "The higher up one is within an organization, the easier it is to invade the territory of lower-status personnel."

4. How do these three principles act as barriers to the communication process in this organization?

5. How do these principles act as gateways to communication in this organization?

Interviewing: Functions and Skills

Exercise 1
DEVELOPING A RESUME

Using the material from the text, develop your own basic resume. Be sure to include all past and present personal information that could help people realize your talents and abilities. A variation of this exercise is to identify several specific jobs and modify your resume to fit the needs of these jobs. For instance, how would you present yourself for a retailing job in which you meet the public as compared to a job in a personnel office where you work primarily with forms and files?

All-purpose resume
    Personal data
    Educational background
    Work experience
    Extracurricular activities
    Professional goals
    References

Changes in resume for job 1

Changes in resume for job 2

Exercise 2
USE OF QUESTIONS

Select a partner and conduct a 5- to 10-minute interview with him on his feelings and beliefs about (1) pollution, (2) energy shortages, or (3) popular music. Develop a moderately scheduled interview with examples of *open, closed,* and *follow-up* questions. Ask a third person to observe the interview and to keep a list of the questions she felt you used. On this form list and compare your questions to the third person's observations:

Questions asked	*Questions observed*
1.	1.
2.	2.
3.	3.
4.	4.
5.	5.
6.	6.
7.	7.
8.	8.
9.	9.
10.	10.

Exercise 3
EVALUATING THE INTERVIEWER

Directions: The evaluation form presented below can be used by the student or instructor as an instrument for providing feedback to the interviewer in an information interview. The list of items can be changed or the scale may be altered by either expanding or contracting it.

Information Interview Performance Scale

Date _____ Interviewer _____ Interviewee _____

Criteria	Rating 1 to 5	Comments
A. Structure		
1. Opening		
2. Closing		
B. Body		
1. Style of questioning		
2. Language		
3. Use of questions		
C. Communication skills		
1. Vocal delivery		
2. Enthusiasm		

Scale: 5–Excellent, 4–Above-average, 3–Average, 2–Fair, 1–Poor

Exercise 4
ANSWERING QUESTIONS

For this exercise you need to identify a controversial subject on which you feel strongly. Select a partner, and tell him or her on which side of the controversy you stand. Ask him or her to prepare a 10- to 15-minute moderately scheduled interview that asks you to explain your beliefs and feelings. Tape record the interview. Next, listen to the interview and analyze your style of answering the questions. Include the material in the chapter on how to answer questions: (1) answer the question the way it was asked; (2) when answering follow-up questions, did you attempt to determine what the interviewer was seeking?; (3) how did you handle confidential topics in your responses?; and (4) if you resisted answering a question, how did you handle it?

Subject area covered	*Style of answer*
1.	1.
2.	2.
3.	3.
4.	4.
5.	5.
6.	6.
7.	7.

Assignment Contract: Information Interviewing

Name _____ Date _____

Directions: You have just spent some time learning about the process of interviewing. As is true of any learning process, transfer from a theoretical perspective to the environment is necessary if optimal learning is to take place. (*Transfer* is a process whereby what is learned in the classroom is applied in a job setting or at least in the school.) Understanding will diminish if what has been learned is not practiced. Therefore, in order to enhance your understanding of the subject, you will gather examples illustrating the principal concepts presented in the chapter on interviewing. You are asked to decide where and how you can use the principal concepts of information-getting interviewing as presented in the preceding chapter. After completing Section I, make a copy and give it to your instructor. Keep the original copy and use it to prepare for your interview. Complete Section II after your interview.

SECTION I Assignment Preparation

Individual and department name: _____

Name of organization: _____

Planned date of interview: _____

SECTION II Assignment Review

Actual date of interview: _____

Concepts discussed:

1. How did the interviewee handle the opening of the interview? _____

_____

2. What style of questioning did you use?   _____

_____

3. How much use did you make of open versus closed questions? _____

_____

4. What role did nonverbal cues play in your perception of the interviewee?

_____

What was the interviewee's overall reaction to the interview? _____

_____

How did you feel after the interview? _____

_____

If you could have the interview again, would you do anything differently? _____

_____

Assignment Contract: Employment Interview

Name _____ Date _____

Directions: You have just spent some time learning about the process of interviewing. As is true of any learning process, transfer from a theoretical perspective to the environment is necessary if optimal learning is to take place. (*Transfer* is a process whereby what is learned in the classroom is applied in a job setting or at least in the school.) Understanding will diminish if what has been learned is not practiced. Therefore, in order to enhance your understanding of the subject, you will gather examples illustrating the principal concepts presented in the chapter on interviewing. After completing Section I of this form, make a copy and give it to your instructor. Keep the original copy and use it to prepare for your interview. Complete Section II after your interview.

SECTION I Assignment Preparation

Name of the organization offering job: _____

Name of the interviewer: _____

Planned date of interview: _____

SECTION II Assignment Review

Actual date of interview: _____

Concepts discussed:

1. How did the interviewer (employer) open the interview? _____

_____

2. What use did the interviewer make of your resume? _____

_____

3. What use did the interviewer make of follow-up questions after you answered

a question? _____

_____

4. How did the interviewer explore your experience in the particular job area?

_____

_____

What was the interviewer's overall reaction to the interview?   _____

_____

How did you feel after the interview?   _____

_____

If you could have the interview again, would you do anything differently?   _____

_____

Small Group Behavior

Exercise 1
IDENTIFYING GROUP DEVELOPMENT STAGES

It is important to be able to monitor and influence the developmental stages of organizational groups. Group members and organizational leaders both need a high level of awareness of the stages of growth that any group may experience. Determining the stages of development increases behavioral options for everyone involved in, or influenced by, the group. Select a group to observe. Choose one of which you are not a member and therefore one of which you can be an objective observer. Observe the members of the group during one meeting, preferably when they are making some major decisions about their group or organization. Note examples of each of the group phases described in this chapter and respond to the questions that follow the observation chart. Be prepared to discuss what you found out during class.

	Group identity	Goals of group
Stages	Interpersonal structure	Task activity
1. Polite	Testing and dependence *examples:*	Orientation to task *examples:*
2. Goal orientation	Trial behavior *examples:*	Information sharing *examples:*

3. Bid for power	Intragroup conflict *examples:*	Emotional reaction to task demands *examples:*
4. Constructive	Development of group cohesion *examples:*	Open exchange of relevant interpretations *examples:*
5. Synergistic collaboration	Interdependence and group commitment *examples:*	Emergence of solutions and action steps *examples:*

Analysis questions

1. How did the phases of group development differ for the group you observed as compared to the model in your text?

2. Did the group get stuck on any one of the phases, and become unable to move on? What behaviors on the part of group members might have caused this to happen?

3. If you were asked to make suggestions to the members of the group to improve their problem-solving ability, what suggestions would you make to them?

4. Which part of the development model seemed the most difficult for this group to complete: interpersonal structure or task activity? Why?

Exercise 2
CONDUCTING YOUR OWN FORCE FIELD ANALYSIS

Lewin's force field analysis is a way of analyzing the positive and negative forces affecting a problem. The theory states that there are restraining forces that keep individuals from moving in a particular direction and motivating forces that help support that movement. This combination of forces is known as a *force field*. If restraining forces can be reduced or eliminated, a lower degree of tension will result. Identify a personal problem about which you must soon make a decision. Complete each step of the following force field analysis using this decision you must make as a model. Be sure that the problem you select has *not* already been solved.

Force Field Analysis Procedure

Step 1
Clearly identify the problem.

Step 2
List all possible driving and restraining forces affecting the solution to this problem. These forces may be issues, relationship structures, individuals, groups of people, or yourself.

Driving forces   *Restraining forces*

a._____   a._____

b._____   b._____

c._____   c._____

d._____   d._____

e._____   e._____

Step 3
Evaluate the strength of each of these forces. In others words, which driving force is most important or is strongest? Which restraining force is strongest (or causes the most difficulty)? Rank order each of the forces in terms of their relative strength and place them on the following diagram. The length of the arrow from the name of the force to the middle line will indicate its strength. For example, the restraining force that is the strongest should be indicated with the longest arrow.

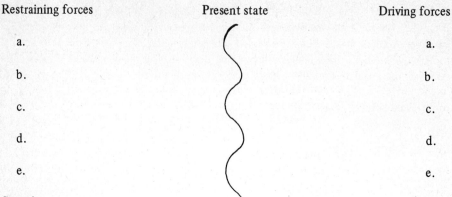

Restraining forces	Present state	Driving forces
a.		a.
b.		b.
c.		c.
d.		d.
e.		e.

Step 4
Identify which driving forces you could add to and strengthen.

Identify which restraining forces you could remove or at least make less strong.

Step 5
Identify specific action steps that you could take to remove or diminish at least one of the restraining forces.

Action to be taken	Who will take the action	Setting and occasion

Step 6
Evaluate the outcome of your action.

Exercise 3
MEMBER ROLE FEEDBACK

One of the most productive observations that one can make about a group is to distinguish between the task and maintenance behaviors of its members. Members who exhibit *task* behavior tend to facilitate and coordinate the collective effort to get the group task accomplished. Members who exhibit *maintenance* behavior are oriented toward the functioning of the group as a group, focusing on the building of interpersonal relationships in the group setting. Most groups need both kinds of behavior and it is best to work out a balance of task and maintenance activities. The following feedback form is provided so that information about this process can take place. There are several ways this form might be used. First, there could be a group discussion in your own classroom with half of the students acting as group participants and the other half acting as observers. Once the discussion is finished, the observers would identify which roles they observed various individuals playing during the discussion. You could also use the form to observe an ongoing group. Attend a meeting of a group that is part of a larger organization, for example, a faculty committee meeting, a local chamber of commerce committee meeting, or any public meeting to which you have access. As you listen to the group members discuss various issues, identify what roles are helping and what roles are hindering the progress of the group. Cite examples of comments made that indicated to you that the speaker was playing a certain role.

After you have concluded your observations, answer the following questions.

1. Which roles were absent from this discussion? Was their absence a hindrance to the group? Why or why not?

2. What roles were present most of the time? How did these roles affect the success of the group?

3. Did any members consistently play one role or another? How did this influence this individual's success within the group?

4. Were all these roles necessary in this group? Explain.

Group Member Roles

Task roles

Initiating	Seeking information	Giving information	Clarifying	Summarizing	Consensus testing

Maintenance roles

Harmonizing	Gate keeping	Encouraging	Compromising	Standard setting

Exercise 4
BEING A CONSULTANT

One of the best ways to learn about group behavior is to act as a consultant to someone else. In this exercise you are asked to observe the activities and behaviors of one
other individual and act as a private consultant to that person. As a consultant your
task is to help a group member become aware of his or her behavior and its effect
on the group process. The following are guidelines for improving your success as a
consultant.

1. *Don't preach* It is very easy to fall into the trap of telling someone else how
   easy it would be for him to influence the group if only he would act in a certain
   way. If the consultant comes off as a know-it-all he or she will be quickly tuned
   out.
2. *Don't analyze* Often we feel we know how someone is feeling and why without being told. Without any specific training to do so, we constantly try to
   figure the other person out.
3. *Do give descriptive feedback* We are able, as observers, to simply describe what
   we see happening without judging or criticizing. This allows the other person to
   make a choice about how she will use the information.
4. *Do give specific examples* We can't expect to help another become aware of
   his or her group behavior unless we watch and listen closely enough so that we
   are able to give very definite examples of types of behavior. This takes a great
   deal of involvement on the part of the observer in the other person.

As you observe your client, make note of the following behaviors.

	Examples of member behaviors	Effect of behaviors on group
Verbal		
Nonverbal		

Assignment Contract: My Style

Name _____ Date _____

Directions: You have just spent some time learning about group communication patterns. As is true of any learning process, transfer from a theoretical perspective to the environment is necessary if optimal learning is to take place. (*Transfer* is a process whereby what is learned in the classroom is applied in a job setting or at least in the school.) Understanding will diminish if what has been learned is not practiced. Therefore, in order to enhance your understanding of the subject, you will choose a situation in which you would like to have your own communication behavior observed. Select a group of which you are a leader or ask your instructor if you could have an opportunity to lead a group discussion in class. Ask someone to be a *process observer* for you (in other words, he or she will observe the process you use as a leader rather than focus on the content of your words). Ask him or her to complete the following form and return it to you for feedback. After completing Section I, hand in a copy to your instructor. Complete Section III after your discussion.

SECTION I Assignment Preparation

My name: _____

Name and purpose of the group of which I will act as leader: _____

_____

Name of process observer: _____

Planned date of discussion: _____

SECTION II (to be filled out by process observer)

1. List all task and/or maintenance roles used by this individual during this group interaction and note their influence on the group.

2. Refer to the chapter on group communication and identify which of the following leadership roles this individual used.

Structurer   Examples:

Energizer   Examples:

Nonleader/observer   Examples:

Modeler   Examples

Resourcer   Examples:

Empathizer   Examples:

3. What suggestions would you make to this individual that would improve his or her leadership effectiveness?

SECTION III   Assignment Review

Actual date of observation: _____

Points observed:

1. What behaviors were identified for you that you were unaware of prior to this process observation activity?

_____

2. Were there any behaviors displayed by your classmates that you think you might engage in as well? List these behaviors.

_____

_____

3. Which of the behaviors that the observer noticed would you like to eliminate? Why?

_____

4. Which of the behaviors that the observer noticed would you like to retain and improve upon? Why?

_____

5. Based on this classroom discussion, what behaviors seemed to lead to the most successful leadership? Least effective leadership?

_____

_____

Public Communication

Exercise 1
DEVELOPING AND ARRANGING MAIN POINTS

For each of the key ideas listed below, you are asked to create three to five main points. After you have developed the main points, you should arrange them in one of the four patterns identified in the chapter.

Key idea	Main points	Type of arrangement
Making candles is fun and can be accomplished in four easy steps.	1. 2. 3. 4.	

Key idea	Main points	Type of arrangement
The Birthright organization provides a number of services to pregnant women.	1. 2. 3. 4. 5.	
Over the past 25 years Bill Miller has made four major contributions to our company.	1. 2. 3. 4.	

Exercise 2
GATHERING SUPPORTING INFORMATION

This exercise is designed to help you search for and identify the types of information used as subpoints in your speech. There are two parallel outlines listed below. You are to research each topic using the *Reader's Guide to Periodical Literature Index*. Read the articles listed, searching for examples of the four types of information described in this chapter, and then use them as subpoints in the outline. Identify the sources here and on a separate sheet of paper present the supporting information.

Key idea: The energy crisis has affected the American economy.
    Main point   A.   Shortages of natural gas have curtailed business.
       Subpoint   1.
       Subpoint   2.
    Main point   B.   The cost of all types of fossil fuels has risen.
       Subpoint   1.
       Subpoint   2.

Key idea: Our planet is approaching a food crisis.
    Main point   A.   The number of people is increasing faster than the food supply.
       Subpoint   1.
       Subpoint   2.
    Main point   B.   There is a significant difference in the quality and quantity of food consumed among countries.
       Subpoint   1.
       Subpoint   2.

Exercise 3
VOCAL AND PHYSICAL DELIVERY

You can analyze your own delivery. When you are practicing your speech, make a tape recording of it. Come as close to actual performance standards as possible. Listen to the tape and use this sheet to identify your strengths and weaknesses. After you have finished, turn this sheet into your instructor.

Name _____ Date _____

Variable	Strength	Weakness
Comments on volume		
Comments on rate and pause		
Comments on pitch		
Overall comments on vocal variety		

Ask a friend to be your audience. Give him this form and ask him to record his comments concerning your physical delivery.

Variable	Strength	Weakness
Comments on facial expression		
Comments on body movement including gestures		
Comments on eye contact		

Exercise 4
DEVELOPMENT OF INTRODUCTIONS

One major purpose of the introduction is to attract the audience's attention. The text listed and described four techniques that could be used to achieve this end. This exercise asks you to select one of these techniques and use it to develop a short introduction for each of the following key idea statements.

Key idea	Attention-getting technique used	Development of the technique
A. There are many benefits derived from the space program.		
B. Taking a music appreciation course can be a useful experience.		
C. A manager's communication style will influence the work of his or her subordinates.		

Key idea	Attention-getting technique used	Development of the technique
D. There are four main styles to follow in using the new computer-ized inventory system.		

Assignment Contract: Public Speaking

Name _____ Date _____

Directions: You have just spent some time learning about the role of public speaking in the organization. As is true of any learning process, transfer from a theoretical perspective to the environment is necessary if optimal learning is to take place. (*Transfer* is a process whereby what is learned in the classroom is applied in a job setting or at least in the school.) Understanding will diminish if what has been learned is not practiced. Therefore, in order to enhance your understanding of the subject, you will gather examples illustrating the principal concepts of public speaking. After completing Section I of this form, make a copy and give it to your instructor. Keep the original copy and use it to prepare for your discussion. Complete Section II after the discussion.

SECTION I Assignment Preparation

Individual and department name: _____

Name of the organization: _____

Planned date of discussion: _____

SECTION II Assignment Review

Actual date of discussion:

Concepts discussed:

   1. What are the goals of public speaking in this organization?_____

_____

2. What facilities are available for researching the speech topic?_____

_____

3. How important is delivery to the success of a speech?_____

_____

4. What forms of public speaking are most frequently used? Why?_____

_____

What was the person's overall reaction to the discussion?   _____

_____

How did you feel after the discussion?   _____

_____

If you could have the discussion again, would you do anything differently?   _____

_____

Assignment Contract: Observing a Public Communication Event

Name _____ Date _____

Directions: You have just spent some time learning about the role of public speaking in the organization. As is true of any learning process, transfer from a theoretical perspective to the environment is necessary if optimal learning is to take place. (*Transfer* is a process whereby what is learned in the classroom is applied in a job setting or at least in the school.) Understanding will diminish if what has been learned is not practiced. Therefore, in order to enhance your understanding of the subject, you will gather examples illustrating the principal concepts of public speaking. After completing Section I of this form, make a copy and give it to your instructor. Complete Section II after the observation.

SECTION I   Assignment Preparation

Speaker and audience: _____

Planned date of speech: _____

Occasion for the speech: _____

SECTION II   Assignment Review

Actual date of speech: _____

What did the speaker do in the introduction to gain the attention of the audience?

_____

_____

Cite several examples of the speaker's use of supporting material (illustrations, com-

parisons, statistics, etc.) _____

_____

What organizational patterns did the speaker use in developing the main points of the

speech? _____

_____

How did the speaker conclude his or her speech? Identify and evaluate the method

used. _____

_____

_____

What was your overall reaction to the speech? _____

_____

If the speaker were to ask you for advice, what would you tell him or her to do the

next time he or she gives the speech? _____

_____

_____

Name Index

Anatol, Karl W. E., 188*n*
Applbaum, Ronald L., 188*n*
Argyris, Chris, 43, 67, 76*n*
Austin, David, 163

Bales, R. F., 177
Barnard, Chester, 5, 24*n*, 37, 57
Barrett, Dermot, 49–50
Bassett, Glenn A., 182
Bateson, Gregory, 15
Bavelas, Alex, 49–50
Beavin, Janet Hemlick, 91
Benne, K. D., 194
Bennis, Warren, 44, 177
Berlo, David, 51
Bertalanffy, Ludwig von, 38
Bick, Ross, 125*n*
Bodaken, Edward M., 188*n*
Bormann, Ernest G., 172
Bowditch, James, 26*n*
Bradford, L. P., 193
Brammer, Lawrence M., 111
Braunstein, Daniel N., 90*n*
Burgoon, Judee K., 127
Byrnes, Anne, 98

Cannell, Charles F., 155*n*
Carkhuff, Robert, 111
Cash, William B., 144, 145*n*, 149, 150, 157,
   158*n*, 163*n*
Caul, William, 125*n*
Chemers, Martin, 72*n*

Dahle, Thomas L., 104
Davies, Ivor K., 180
Davis, Keith, 57, 59*n*, 60, 71–72
Davitz, Joel R., 135*n*
Davitz, Lois Jean, 135*n*
Delahanty, David, 116, 132, 136
Deutsch, Karl W., 50*n*
DeWine, Mike, 178–180
DeWine, Sue, 103, 108, 189*n*, 190*n*
Dohrenwend, Barbara S., 152*n*
Douglas, John, 169
Drucker, Peter, 87, 182

Egan, Gerald, 111
Ekman, Paul, 120, 123
Ellsworth, P., 126*n*

Fayol, Henry, 25–26, 57
Fiedler, Fred E., 72–73, 85
Filley, Alan, 72, 107, 132–133, 170*n*
Fleishmann, E. A., 63–64
Flippo, E., 80*n*
Ford, Daniel L., 188*n*
French, John R., 64–65
Friesen, Wallace, 120, 123

Gantt, Henry, 25
Garth, H. H., 27*n*
Giffin, Kim, 7*n*, 189*n*
Gilbert, Shirley J., 99
Gilbreth, Frank, 25
Gilbreth, Lillian, 25
Goffman, E., 122
Goldhaber, Gerald M., 5*n*, 34*n*, 58, 129–130,
   136*n*
Gordon, Thomas, 106
Goyer, Robert S., 141*n*, 142*n*, 146*n*
Graicunas, A. V., 31
Greene, James, 186
Guest, R. H., 80*n*

Hall, Edward T., 127, 131–133
Hall, Jay, 108
Hamilton, General Ian, 31
Haney, William V., 224
Harris, Thomas, 98–99
Harrison, Randall P., 115
Hastorf, Albert H., 93*n*
Hatfield, John D., 105*n*
Hayakawa, S. I., 102
Hayes, Merwyn A., 129
Henley, Nancy M., 126, 136
Herzberg, Frederick, 42
Heston, Judee, 132*n*
Hollingworth, J. E., 216
Holm, James N., 148, 153*n*
House, Robert, 72
Howell, William S., 172*n*
Huber, G., 56
Hull, Raymond, 94*n*
Huse, Edgar, 26*n*
Huseman, Richard C., 105*n*, 171*n*

Irvine, Alec, 97*n*, 101
Irwin, Theodore, 123*n*

Subject Index

Affection, 97–98
Agenda, 83–84, 193
Analogic communication, 92
Appraisal interview, 154
Attribution theory, 95
Authoritarian leadership, 74–75
Authority, 26, 28
  bureaucratic, 26
  charismatic, 26
  traditional, 26
  (*See also* Domination)

Baiting, 181
Bank Wiring Room study, 35–36
Body movement, 118–123, 213–214
  (*See also* Kinesics; Nonverbal communication)
Brainstorming, 109, 187–188
Bureaucracy, 26–27
Bureaucratic authority, 26

Case studies, 223–238
  Crown Fastener Company, 225–228
  Finley Printing Company, 228–232
  Richdales, 235–238
  WDTN, 232–235
Centralization, 31–32
Chain of command, 28, 30
  (*See also* Scalar and functional processes)
Change, 39–41, 44, 47
Channels, 11
  (*See also* Formal channels; Informal channels; Networks)
Charismatic authority, 26
Classical school of organization theory, 24–33, 45–46
  division of labor, 27–28, 45
  scalar and functional processes, 28–31
  span of control, 31–32, 45
    centralized, 31–32
    decentralized, 31–32
    flat, 32, 45–46
    tall, 32, 45–46
  structure, 28–31
    line, 29–30
    staff, 29–30
Client-centered therapy, 40
Cliques, 181
Coercive power, 65–67
Communication:
  cultural, 15, 19
  definition of, 9, 10, 16

Communication:
  group, 15, 19
  interpersonal, 15, 19, 90–112
    definition of, 90
  intrapersonal, 15, 19
  nonverbal, 11, 113–139, 164–165
    definition of, 115
    functions of, 115–116
  principles of, 13
  process, 9, 10
  (*See also* Interpersonal communication; Nonverbal communication)
Complementary relationships, 92
Conclusions to speeches:
  appeals, 206–207
  personal references, 207
  quotations, 206
  summaries, 206
Conflict management, 106–110
Connotative meaning, 11, 102
Consensus, 168, 181
Control, 50, 97
Counseling:
  directive, 110
  nondirective, 110
Crown Fastener Company, 225–228
Cultural communication, 15, 19

Decentralization, 31–32
Decision making (*see* Group decision making; Problem solving)
Definitions:
  connotative, 11
  denotative, 11
Delivery, 209–214
  body movement, 209–214
  facial expression, 213
  pitch, 211
  posture, 214
  rate, 211
  volume, 210
Democratic leadership, 75–76
Denotative meaning, 11, 102
Departmentalization, 28, 31
Digital communication, 92
Directive counseling, 110
Directive leadership, 82
Distance:
  intimate, 131–132
  personal, 132
  public, 132
  social, 133